GREAT RESORTS OF
NORTH AMERICA

GREAT RESORTS

OF

NORTH AMERICA

ANDREW HEPBURN

DOUBLEDAY & COMPANY, INC., GARDEN CITY,

NEW YORK, 1965

CONTENTS

INTRODUCTION   ix

1. GREEN HILLS AND HOT SPRINGS   1
      Resorts of the Virginia and West Virginia mountains:
      THE HOMESTEAD . . . GREENBRIER

2. NEW ENGLAND'S ROCK-BOUND SHORE   17
      Resorts of the coast of New England: WENTWORTH-
      BY-THE-SEA . . . MARSHALL HOUSE

3. MOUNTAINS OF NEW ENGLAND   28
      Resorts of the Green Mountains of Vermont, White
      Mountains of New Hampshire, and the Wilderness
      lake and mountains region of Maine: MOUNTAIN
      VIEW HOUSE . . . WAUMBEK . . . MOUNTAIN TOP INN
      . . . LODGE AT SMUGGLERS' NOTCH . . . MOUNT
      KINEO HOTEL . . . SEVERANCE LODGE

4. PINELANDS AND SAND HILLS   53
      Resorts of the Piedmont region of North and South
      Carolina: PINEHURST, HOTEL CAROLINA . . . HOLLY
      INN . . . MID-PINES CLUB AND GOLFOTEL . . . PINE
      NEEDLES LODGE AND COUNTRY CLUB

5. TIDELANDS AND GOLDEN ISLES   64
    Resorts of the tideland region of Virginia and the off-
    shore islands of Georgia: SEA ISLAND, CLOISTER . . .
    ST. SIMONS ISLAND, EPWORTH-BY-THE-SEA . . .
    JEKYLL ISLAND . . . THE TIDES INN

6. GOLD COAST AND GULF SHORE   83
    Resorts of Florida's Atlantic and Gulf coasts, and the
    Gulf coast of Alabama: BOCA RATON HOTEL . . .
    PONTE VEDRA INN AND CLUB . . . BREAKERS . . .
    BELLEVIEW-BILTMORE . . . GRAND HOTEL

7. MIDDLE LAKES AND MOUNTAINS   106
    Resorts of the Adirondacks, central New York, and
    eastern Pennsylvania: WHITEFACE INN . . . OTESAGA
    HOTEL . . . INN AT BUCK HILL FALLS . . . HOTEL
    HERSHEY

8. HIGH MOUNTAINS OF THE WEST   128
    Resorts of the Canadian and Colorado Rockies, the
    Sawtooth Mountains of Idaho, the California High
    Sierras, and New Mexico's Sangre de Cristo Moun-
    tains: CHATEAU LAKE LOUISE . . . BANFF SPRINGS
    HOTEL . . . SUN VALLEY LODGE . . . CHALLENGE INN
    . . . BROADMOOR . . . FEATHER RIVER INN . . . BISH-
    OP'S LODGE

9. THE GREAT VALLEY AND THE GREAT LAKES   157
    Resorts of Lake Michigan and the Ohio Valley:
    GRAND HOTEL . . . FRENCH LICK SPRINGS HOTEL

10. THE WESTERN SHORE   171
    Resorts of the Pacific Coast, British Columbia, and
    California: THE HARRISON HOTEL . . . DEL MONTE
    LODGE . . . HOTEL DEL CORONADO

11. DESERT OASES   186
          Resorts and resort communities of the Southwest des-
          ert: SAN MARCOS HOTEL AND COUNTRY CLUB . . .
          CAMELBACK INN . . . PARADISE INN . . . ARIZONA
          INN

12. CANADA'S GREAT RIVER AND ATLANTIC   203
    SHORE
          Resorts of the St. Lawrence River and the Maritime
          Provinces of Canada: MANOIR RICHELIEU . . . AL-
          GONQUIN HOTEL

13. MEXICO: TROPICAL SHORES, MOUNTAIN   211
    RAVINES, TROPICAL FLOWERS
          Resorts of Mexico: ACAPULCO, LAS BRISAS, PIERRE
          MARQUES, HOTEL RUIZ GALINDO, SAN JOSÉ PURUA

INDEX   223

INTRODUCTION

Perhaps the first resort was on the banks of the Euphrates River in the ancient kingdom of Babylonia, whose rulers built *ziggurats,* structures for religious ceremonies and for pleasure. The Babylonian royal gathering place for its priests and nobles closely fits the classic definition of a resort, which the Oxford Universal Dictionary gives as: "A place to which people repair, as for holiday making, health . . ."

From the days of Babylon resorts were established and flourished in every region and in every age where a combination of four economic and social elements existed. The four elements were, and still are, wealth, leisure, suitable setting, and accessibility. Wherever a substantial number of people of a region had more money than they needed for ordinary living, and enough leisure time to get away from it all, where there was a climatically and scenically desirable spot (usually in the mountains, at the seashore, or on an island) and the pleasant place was readily accessible, the creation of a resort was almost automatic. The development of resorts throughout history may be said to follow a nearly infallible social and economic law—perhaps suitably called the Sybaritic Law. It operated in Babylonia four thousand years ago, and it operates today in North America.

The court of the Pharaohs in ancient Egypt had resorts set in oases on the banks of the Nile, on islands in the Nile, and at Aswan and at Luxor (ancient Thebes and Karnak), reached by slave-drawn barges on the Nile, as vast ruins testify. The sea-roving Phoenicians, made rich from trade in tin and timber, silk and dyes, relaxed from far journeys at resorts on slopes of Mount Lebanon, among groves of beautiful cedars. (There are resorts there now, including ski resorts, the most popular around the Mediterranean.) Among the Himalayan ranges the high and beautiful Vale of Kashmir, fertile, lush, and cool, has been a resort for more than a thousand years, favorite pleasure spot among the Mogul emperors of the East. It is interesting that the imaginary Himalayan paradise Shangri-La was a kind of place favored for resorts the world over, a high, pleasant mountain valley.

The Romans, when they ran most of the world, were great resort builders, partly because they were also great road builders and were able to open up regions favorable for resort development. They introduced mineral baths, hot and cold, and mineral water drunk for reasons of health. Vichy, in the South of France, now a luxurious resort famed for bottled water and a cold potato soup, began as a favorite Roman watering place, because of alkaline springs good for the liver and stomach. The Romans called it Aquae Calidae. Warm sulphur springs in what is now West Germany made Aachen (Aix la Chapelle) another favorite pleasure place for Roman colonists. They called it Aquisgranum. Some luxury-loving Roman emperors established resort centers for their courts even closer to home. Augustus and Tiberius both had resort palaces on the rugged little island of Capri, in the Bay of Naples. A nearby island, Ischia, which had warm mineral springs as well as pleasant scenery, became a Roman resort after first winning popularity among Greek settlers of the coastal region.

Even in bleak and distant Britain the Roman legionaires established and used a resort. In the first century A.D. they discovered warm springs in southeastern Britain and built elaborate baths to use them. They called the place Aquae Solis. In the eighteenth century the Roman bath site became famous as a fashionable resort of the English court, called Bath, one of the most celebrated places of its kind in England. It gave its name to places in the New World then being settled. One, Bath County in Virginia, where there is a whole chain of mineral springs, hot, warm, and intermediate, was the setting for the first resorts developed by English settlers in the New World. Two great and luxurious hotels, the Homestead and the Greenbrier, near each other in the mountains, are there today, direct heirs to the British resort of Bath.

During Roman, medieval, and Renaissance days, Germany became studded with mineral spring resorts. Dozens of them sprang up, usually christened Bad or Baden (meaning Bath or Bathe). But the Belgians gave to a resort a name that has become an almost universal label for a smart and fashionable watering place. The discovery of mineral springs there led, in the sixteenth century, to the establishment of a health resort at the city of Spa, in eastern Belgium. It became so famous and so popular over the years that its name became a common noun and a resort of any pretension which offered mineral springs as a basis for therapy was thereafter called a "spa."

Starting in the eighteenth century and multiplying more rapidly in the nineteenth century as transportation improved, spas, or resorts, were created in every country. Visiting a resort was the thing to do if you could afford it. At spas you met and mingled with the right people, the elite of the world. Drinking or bathing in the resort waters (always, of course, under the close supervision of a trained staff of doctors, or alleged doctors) was a standard part of a spa holiday. Vacationing at watering places in Europe took on the aspects of cult worship. A whole library of watering-place literature evolved, including special guidebooks that told where the resorts were, what they offered in accommodation and social opportunity, the chemical analysis of the various resort waters, and a documented list of ills that the waters would cure. A fat volume published in London about 1900, the *Twentieth Century Health and Pleasure Resort Guide*, briefly describes seven hundred fifty resorts in twenty-six countries in and near Europe. In 1903 Bradshaw's *Dictionary of Mineral Waters, Climatic Health Resorts, Sea Baths and Hydropathic Establishments* describes ten types of mineral waters used for resort bathing or for drinking, tells what each would cure, "improve or ameliorate." A long alphabetical list of afflictions, diseases, and ailments, with the mineral water best suited to make each fade or disappear, includes such wildly different problems as albuminuria, tuberculosis, stuttering, children's delicacy, gout, and old age.

So, with almost everyone in Europe aware of resorts, particularly spas and watering places, and eager, if their means permitted, to visit one and "take the cure," it is not surprising that in time resorts began to appear in the New World, where settlements were slowly spreading west from the coastal cities.

The first resorts to be established in North America, north of Mexico, that is, conformed precisely to the Sybaritic Law—wealth, leisure, setting, and accessibility. Among the colonists, wealth and leisure first came together for a considerable number of people in the tidewater regions of Virginia, Maryland, North Carolina, and South Carolina. The plantation owners were becoming rich by growing tobacco and rice and by producing indigo. But plantation life in the tidewater in summer was humid and uncomfortable, despite the spacious and elegant manor houses the planters had built for themselves, so toward the middle of the eighteenth century, word got around that in the beautiful mountains that lifted like a blue cloud against the western sky (soon called the Blue Ridge) there were pleasant, accessible mountain valleys always cool in summer—and these valleys had mineral springs that Indians and trappers claimed would cure anything. A good horse to ride or a horse and carriage would get you there in a few days over rough but passable roads.

So, the health springs of Bath County, Virginia, became, toward the end of the eighteenth century, America's first resorts. One of them, Warm Springs, has been in continuous use for about two hundred years, and another, not far away, called White Sulphur Springs, has been famed for effective therapy almost as long.

But it was a long time after the Virginia resorts were established before other resorts were built in any number, mainly for lack of transportation. Except up and down the coast, there were few roads, and travel over the rough roads that did exist was distinctly uncomfortable. It was easier for rich colonists to go to Europe or the West Indies, and that is where most of them went until the railways began to open up the country.

There were two exceptions before the middle of the nineteenth century, resorts that offered special climatic advantage and could be reached by boat. Both served plantation owners made wealthy from the booming sale of cotton in the lower Mississippi Valley. One was Point Clear, on the east shore of Mobile Bay. The other was Mackinac Island, at the north end of Lake Michigan, reached by boat from Chicago or Detroit. Both are great resorts today. Though at Point Clear, you can now drive your car through the gates of the Grand Hotel, you still reach Mackinac Island by boat.

A third resort that could be reached only by boat, one that developed after the railroads had helped scatter resorts across the continent, was a millionaires' club, on Jekyll Island, off the coast of Georgia. Its curious story is told later in this book as a part of the story of Sea Island's resort which grew up on an island made accessible by another mode of transportation, the automobile.

The rapid proliferation of resorts in North America, a special, spectacular phenomenon of growth, resulted from almost simultaneous growth of the railways spanning the United States and Canada, and from the widespread building of personal fortunes. In a period of about forty years, starting just after the Civil War and extending well into the first decade of this century, more resorts were established than at any other time in the history of the continent. They were built in every part of the country, along the ocean shore and in the mountains, on islands and inland lakes. Railroad operators were directly responsible for many of them, first selecting the resort sites, running spur tracks to them when necessary, then building and operating the great hotels. And, since quick, comfortable transportation was the first necessity for any resort, the railroads were at least indirectly responsible for all of them.

As the Chesapeake & Ohio sliced through the mountains of Virginia, it took over the pioneer resorts at Hot Springs and White Sulphur Springs and rebuilt the hotels. The historic Homestead was long associated with C. & O. management, and the big and elegant Greenbrier is now wholly owned and operated by the C. & O. As the Canadian Pacific Railway spread out over Canada, two spectacularly scenic sites in the high Rockies of southwestern Canada were selected for resorts. On them were built two great luxury hotels, Chateau Lake Louise and the Banff Springs Hotel, both owned and operated by the Canadian Pacific. When the Western Pacific completed the trestles, fills, and cuts that thread the Feather River Canyon, of California, dramatic possibilities were seen for a hotel built in the heart of the canyon, where the Feather River Inn stands today.

The influence of railroads on hotel and resort building was most remarkable in Florida. Two men, Henry Flagler and Henry Plant, building rival railway systems there, flanked their tracks with magnificent resort facilities. In addition to hotels they built entire resort cities, such as St. Augustine, Palm Beach, and Miami, on the east coast, and St. Petersburg and Clearwater, on the west coast. Among the sumptuous hotels they built in the early years, still going strong, are the Breakers, at Palm Beach, and the Belleview-Biltmore, at Clearwater. Finally, Sun Valley, in Idaho, the finest and most celebrated ski and winter sports resort in North America, was planned, built, and until quite recently was operated by the Union Pacific Railroad.

The buildings erected during this extraordinary boom often tended to resemble each other in aspect and facility, no matter where they were built. The larger ones, backed by unlimited corporate funds, were huge, rambling wooden buildings, crowned with cupolas and towers, generously decorated with porches (equipped with inviting rows of wooden rockers), and trimmed with "gingerbread" ornamentation. The product of an era renowned for atrocious taste in building design and décor, they were remarkably homely. The few that survive as important resorts, stripped of their scroll-saw excesses and modernized, are usually described as having "Victorian charm." But in those expansive, elegant days they were the last word in luxury, equipped with the very latest in modern conveniences—even hydraulic elevators. (One resort in the Adirondacks was built with money made from the invention of the passenger elevator by Elisha Graves Otis.) They also boasted electric lights and the ultimate luxury of private baths.

Because many of the big Victorian hotels were wooden, fires were numerous. Many buildings burned to the ground, often in spectacular fires during the off season. Some resorts burned several times, as though fires were tradition. A few of the great wooden hotels survive today, fireproofed and greatly modified.

Resort life during the last part of the nineteenth century and the first decade of this one was extremely social, leisurely, and luxurious, but it didn't much resemble life at the great resorts today. There was, for one thing, no golf; it was only beginning to be played here and there. A small resort in the sand hills and piny woods of North Carolina was experimenting with the sport, and it would become in time the greatest golfing resort in the world: Pinehurst. A few resorts had tennis courts. Nearly all provided facilities for croquet, which was quite the rage. So was bicycling. Guests peddled everywhere, or got about on horses and in carriages. There were no swimming pools, but beaches were popular, graced by hotel guests in elaborate and overwhelming beach attire. Dining was formal, many-coursed, balanced among the resorts that boasted mineral springs by firm schedules of water drinking. Social occasions were many and frequent. There were much dancing and card playing, gambling and conversation, which usually flowed in waves along the big porches. (The Grand Hotel, at Mackinac Island, still has a front porch eight hundred feet long and several hundred rocking chairs to go with it.)

The specific origins of many of the famous resorts that grew up during the last years of the nineteenth century and the early years of the twentieth are delightful facets of the country's surging growth. Many resorts of distinction grew from small and curious beginnings. One of the most popular mountain resorts in the country (it is also the highest in altitude, about 7500 feet), near Santa Fe, New Mexico, began as the chapel and retreat of the Archbishop of New Mexico, Bishop Lamy. One of the nation's most ornate hotels, a palatial Spanish structure in Florida, began as the elegant core of a golden dream by an architectural genius. The dream faded, but the beginning of it became the opulent Boca Raton. Several resorts developed from the ambitions of very rich men. The chocolate fortune of Milton Hershey resulted in the Hotel Hershey, at Hershey, Pennsylvania. Tom Taggart turned a mineral spring at French Lick, Southern Indiana, into a bottled laxative called Pluto Water, and used some of his profits to build the vast French Lick Springs Hotel. A fortune made from soda fountains by New Englander James W. Tufts was responsible for Pinehurst, in North Carolina. And in Colorado millions made by Spencer Penrose from mining gold and silver went into the building of one of the most lavish resorts in the world, the Broadmoor, at Colorado Springs. A barn with a spectacular view in the mountains of Vermont evolved into a small but distinguished resort called Mountain Top Inn. And a highway accident in New England started a hospitable farm owner on the way to developing the famous Mountain View House. The desperate needs of a Mexican woman attempting to homestead a patch of Arizona desert were responsible for the building of Paradise Inn, near Phoenix. A fishing camp that burned down on the shore of a Maine lake triggered the development of one of the most luxurious resorts in the north woods, Severance Lodge. In New Hampshire a gruesome murder gave a big boost in patronage to the great seaside resort of Wentworth-by-the-Sea. And an automobile dealer's love of boating led to one of the most unusual boating resorts in the country, The Tides Inn, in the tidewater region of Virginia.

Though the European concept of a resort spa or watering place was directly translated to the colonies with the establishment of the first resorts in the mountains of Virginia, the spa tradition developed in different ways in the New World, occasionally with odd and amusing results. The early Virginia springs were primitive and bore little resemblance to the sophisticated spas of Europe, but as great resorts developed from them, the springs and their use became minor. Mineral water therapy was translated into complex systems of relaxation and treatment called "hydrotherapy," involving programs of baths and massage calculated to make participants "feel like a million dollars," but promising to cure nothing. The Greenbrier, where the original White Sulphur Spring is now enshrined in a temple-like building, has carried the concept to an ultimate of sophistication with the establishment of one of the finest diagnostic clinics in the world, having little or nothing to do with mineral water and its magical properties.

When the resort hotel boom was at its peak in the early years of this century, the great resort districts from Bar Harbor to Palm Beach, and from Newport to Monterey, were the anointed gathering places for the rich and the elect. The places one had to be seen, they were a pointed demonstration of the Sybaritic Law. But though few portents suggested it, these oasis-like islands of luxurious ease were doomed by the economic and social revolutions soon to come. The best story of that gilded era and of the rich and elite of business and society who kept it alive, who paid the bills at resorts, has been told by Cleveland Amory in a delightful and witty book called *The Last Resorts*. The implication of Mr. Amory's title was both right and wrong. He was right in his assumption that there would be no more great society resorts, but he was wrong in suggesting that there would be no more great resort hotels. But then, Mr. Amory is a social historian and not a prophet.

The first rays of the dawn of the new resort era after World War II gave little promise of the bright noontime that we know today. It took a number of years, a lot of money, and a great deal of careful planning and imagination, but the result is that today there are more fine resorts on the North American Continent than ever before, and most of them enjoy increased prosperity.

There are differences between the fine resorts we have now and the same or comparable resorts of fifty or sixty years ago. The patronage is different. It no longer derives solely from the rich, the social arbiters, and their coteries. The rich still go, and so do the socially prominent, but they are lost in the new army of resort patrons. Resort life is different too. It is likely to be more luxurious; it is almost always more comfortable. It is also more active, or perhaps a better word is strenuous.

Five basic general factors have brought this about:

(1) Widespread family affluence
(2) Quick, cheap transportation
(3) Golf—an important national pastime
(4) Skiing—another important national pastime
(5) Conventions and business meetings

Most students of the economy agree that there are probably several million American families that can afford the time and money regularly to visit the best resorts in the country even though resort life is relatively expensive. There are additional millions that make occasional resort visits. And they take the children.

The increasing presence of children at the larger resorts has worked a revolution in resort dining habits and menus. Many resorts have separate dining rooms for children, where they eat earlier, under supervision, and from special menus. The resort social calendar provides a full range of junior activities. And resort rates (mostly American plan, covering both room and board) make special concessions for children.

Another difference from former days, when many guests came prepared to spend the whole summer (or winter), is the shorter average stay. It is seldom longer than a month and is more likely to be two or three weeks.

The development of a national network of high-speed roads and their use by tens of millions of automobile-owning families are responsible for several notable resorts that could not have been built during the days of rail travel alone. At least two, beautiful and sophisticated Sea Island, on an offshore Georgia island, and The Tides Inn, in Virginia, developed only after new highways made their sites accessible. In the old days most resorts had private sidings where chartered Pullmans or private cars could be shunted onto the resort grounds. At such resorts as The Homestead, the French Lick Springs Hotel, and the Belleview-Biltmore Hotel it was not unusual to see a half-dozen private cars lined up on the sidings. Now the sidings are gone, replaced by huge parking lots.

Only by considering the recent history of golf as a national pastime is it possible to understand how important it has become as a resort activity. At the turn of the century many fine resorts had no golf course at all, and those that did considered a nine-hole course quite adequate. Now no major resort lacks at least one eighteen-hole "championship" course, many offer their guests two courses, some even have three. Pinehurst, the great golfing resort of the East, has five eighteen-hole courses, all true championship courses in the best sense of the word. On the West Coast, the famous Del Monte Lodge overlooking Monterey Bay, offers its patrons their choice of six excellent courses.

To a lesser degree the tremendous popularity of skiing has changed resort facilities and contributed strongly to the present boom. Where climate and terrain permit, many resorts have added ski slopes and tows and classes in skiing instruction. In New England some mountain resorts now stay open the year round, offering skiing facilities of their own or serving as accommodation and social centers for ski districts. All-year resorts in Southern areas, such as The Homestead, in the mountains of Virginia, have gained brisk prosperity during a once dull winter season by adding skiing—making snow mechanically, if necessary.

Conventions and executive meetings also have become a boon to resorts. Though their contribution to resort prosperity varies greatly with the location and type of resort, the total amount of business generated by such gatherings is tremendous, often making the difference between profit and loss. Some of the older, more sedate hotels are a little coy about suggesting that they seek and welcome company or industry meetings; they shy away from the word "convention," preferring the euphemism "executive conference." But nearly all the larger resorts actively solicit business groups and provide for their use all sorts of special facilities and equipment.

Many resorts try to limit their use by convention or business groups to the period just before or just after the so-called normal "social season," and in those periods provide special menus and special convention rates. But some resorts frankly take conventions at any time of the year.

For many companies, associations, or business groups, the setting of the self-contained resort estate is ideal, providing a nice balance of controlled attendance at meetings with superb service and restful surroundings. The resort hotel generally is so located that wandering away from carefully planned programs is either difficult or impossible. Usually there is no place to wander.

Throughout the mainland areas of the United States and Canada there now are several hundred vacation establishments that call themselves resorts and that by the generally accepted definition are resorts. Of the total number, perhaps a hundred can be called luxury resorts. They are in all parts of the land, in the mountains and along the ocean shores, on offshore islands and on the shores of lakes and islands of lakes. They are in the desert Southwest, they rim the Gulf of Mexico, and some are within great resort communities such as Palm Beach, Miami Beach, Palm Springs, and Las Vegas.

This work describes a selection of the finest, most unusual, most distinctive, and most interesting resorts of the United States, Canada, and Mexico. The selection is limited by the title of the book; the qualifying factors are "great" and "North America." The geographical limit is an arbitrary one, so there are no resorts described in such island areas as Bermuda, the Caribbean, or the Hawaiian Islands.

In the sense in which the word "great" is used here, it has explicit connotation. It means, first of all, a self-contained resort estate where all or nearly all the facilities and opportunities available to guests are controlled by the resort itself. The book therefore does not include some very fine and luxurious hotels whose guests must go beyond the hotel property for diversion.

The word "great" does not necessarily mean a resort with a long and colorful history, though a number of the resorts described do have vigorous and fascinating life stories going back a hundred years or more, and at least two have an unbroken heritage of operation reaching back almost two hundred years. But several of our resorts were opened not more than thirty years ago.

"Great" does not imply uniform facilities, either, though there are certain common denominators usually found at every fine resort—a good golf course (or several courses), swimming pool and patio, excellent dining room, and a whole galaxy of fringe diversions and activities. The type of facility varies with and is generally dictated by setting and climate. Desert resorts make a big thing of horseback riding and chuckwagon picnics, while many Eastern resorts emphasize fishing and boating.

But the resorts selected for description have earned the accolade "great" from certain characteristics they all have: luxurious accommodations, superb cuisine, and warmth of service. These are the qualities that set them apart, that give to each of them the stamp of genuine distinction.

GREAT RESORTS OF
NORTH AMERICA

CHAPTER 1

GREEN HILLS AND
HOT SPRINGS

The first settlement of English colonists in the New World was in Virginia, at Jamestown, on the James River, in 1607. The colonization of Virginia continued steadily, and the settlers became steadily richer, chiefly through the raising of tobacco.

The nature of tobacco cultivation resulted in a unique type of social and economic life, built around the tidewater plantation, generally a large tract along a tidal river, with fertile fields stretching back from the river. The tobacco planters lived in some of the handsomest dwellings ever built in this country, great and graceful manor houses overlooking rivers such as the Potomac, the Rappahannock, the James, and the York. Tobacco was a commodity for which there was a steady demand, and it commanded high prices. And, because the pattern of the plantation life gave the owners and their families much free time, the magic combination of leisure and wealth that had been responsible for the development of resorts the world over appeared first in the New World among the planters of the Virginia tidewater and to some extent among those of Maryland to the north and South Carolina to the south.

The tidewater region had one failing. During the summer months the climate was oppressively hot and humid. Inevitably, the plantation owners and their families began to look for ways to escape summer heat. To the west, almost within sight of their plantation fields, loomed mountain ranges, usually shrouded in a delicate blue haze. Hunters and trappers had long before reported that the mountains were cool in summer. It was generally understood that the mountains of western Virginia (before long they were known as the Blue Ridge) were part of a greater Appalachian system that extended north and south along the whole eastern section of the country. In the north they became abrupt and inhospitable, but in Virginia and in what was much later to become West Virginia they were relatively low, seldom rising above four thousand feet. Between the mountain ridges were wide, pleasant valleys that were the homes of swift-flowing, clear rivers. The setting was one that was to become the site of the earliest known resorts on the North American Continent. It beckoned the plantation owners of the tidewater, lured them to a new land of cool and pleasant summer days and nights.

Within this wilderness Eden was a particular region of unique character, an area about seventy-five miles in diameter, extending into what is now West Virginia. The streams there were fed by the gushing flow of springs with special qualities. They were hot and had a high mineral content. Dozens of hot springs, some large enough to form great placid pools, were in the forest. They varied in temperature but were never too hot to make bathing intolerable.

Though there is no evidence that animals used the hot springs, there is much evidence that Indians did. From the tidewater they trudged into the mountains, bathed in the springs, and hunted the game that swarmed through the forest. It was tacitly agreed among the tribes of the region that the combination of magical pools and good hunting made the forest a sanctuary open to all tribes, and scalp-taking was forbidden. The early white trappers, penetrating the heart of the forest ranges, reported a network of Indian and animal trails leading into the valleys where the hot springs burbled from their rocky depths.

As the tidewater was settled, plantations were established, and their owners prospered, settlers who drifted into the mountains found the area of the springs actually two separate areas. One was a valley about twenty-five miles long at an altitude of about 2500 feet between fairly parallel ranges, with a chain of many springs. The other lay several mountain ridges away, forty miles to the southwest, where a mountain river now called Greenbrier channeled a broad valley between wooded ranges. It was natural that the more accessible valley, nearer the tidewater, would be settled first. In 1727 the governor of Virginia Colony received a petition for a grant of land along the little river that threaded the nearer valley. The river was called Cow Pasture, and it still is. A few years later, about 1750, a visitor wrote: "We visited the hot spring and found six invalids there. The spring is very clear and warmer than new milk."

In 1751 the first title of land in the valley was surveyed, an area of a hundred forty acres with springs called Warm Springs. Four years later Thomas Bullitt built a primitive hotel at Hot Springs, about five miles south of Warm Springs. It wasn't much of a hotel, but historically an important one, for out of it grew, more than a hundred fifty years later, the great luxury resort The Homestead. At the site of the Bullitt Hot Springs, which in the first years was called Little Warm Springs, there has been a resort of sorts ever since, which gives The Homestead the right to call itself the oldest resort hotel in the country.

In the meantime settlers had pushed west through the mountains, with the result that in 1778 Mrs. John Anderson, wife of a settler, discovered a spring of hot and smelly water that had, she said, pleasant and curative properties. The spring was called White Sulphur Springs. A town by that name is near it now, a shopping and community center for what is now another great resort, which took its name from the river of its valley, the Greenbrier.

By 1791 the area around Hot Springs and Warm Springs was so populous that it was made a separate county, with the village of Warm Springs its county seat. The county name was, appropriately, Bath County, suggesting that the springs had useful purposes. They did indeed. By 1800, Warm Springs had become a well-known and fashionable resort. Moneyed families from the tidewater traveled to the mountains to escape the miasma of lowland summers. Warm Springs was the place to go.

After the turn of the century, both spring areas began to develop rapidly. Close to White Sulphur Springs, in the Greenbrier Valley, Stephen Henderson, a sugar planter from New Orleans, built a house within sight of the sulphur spring. It was a pillared residence of elegance and style, and from his porch the Scotsman owner, "a sober-sided gentleman with a rebellious 60-year-old liver," could see all that happened at the spring, who came and went, and what they did. More and more came. The spring was famous. But so were rival springs in the valley to the northeast.

The Warm Springs Hotel had become a spa of renown. Its registers (now in the archives of The Homestead) are sprinkled with names of prominent Virginians. One was Thomas Jefferson. Then, when Warm Springs had outstripped adjacent Hot Springs in prestige and patronage, Thomas Goode, a physician, settled in the valley. By 1832 he owned Hot Springs and the shabby little hotel that stood there, and soon he began to develop a true spa with healing baths and treatments. In 1846 he built a new hotel, elegant and spacious. Goode was not only a doctor, but an adroit promoter with a flair for advertising. He printed pamphlets crowded with testimonials of guests who had benefited from his treatments. Among the ailments and afflictions cured or eased by Hot Springs baths, he claimed, were: "hepatitis, rheumatism, gout, dysentery, phthisis, dropsy, cholera, jaundice, deafness, loss of voice, dyspepsia." Dr. Goode's methods helped turn the tide of patronage. His resort, soon to be called The Homestead, attracted more and more visitors and quickly became the leading resort in the area.

But things had not been standing still in the Greenbrier district near White Sulphur Springs. In 1830 the increasingly famous and popular spring in view of Stephen Henderson's front porch was enclosed within a spring house, a white-columned circular building with a domed white roof, the familiar symbol of the Greenbrier Hotel today. In 1858 the Greenbrier area surged ahead of Hot Springs with the building of an opulent resort, the Old White Hotel, unlike anything seen before—big, elegant, and luxurious. Around it developed a resort and vacation community.

Then came the Civil War. Troops marched up and down Dr. Goode's valley. The Old White Hotel, near White Sulphur Springs, was occupied alternately by troops of both armies and was used as a hospital by both. Before the war was over, the area of the Greenbrier was no longer Virginia, one of the Confederate states, but had become West Virginia, a mountain state clearly allied with the North. In the years immediately following the Civil War, the hotel at Hot Springs, which had become known as The Homestead, forged ahead as a resort of fashion. So did the Old White, in the Greenbrier district.

An event that was to determine the growth and character of both The Homestead and the Greenbrier occurred in 1868, when Collis P. Huntington, who had made a fortune in the gold fields of California and pioneered development of Western railways, organized the Chesapeake & Ohio Railway. Two years later its tracks came through the region, linking both the Old White, at White Sulphur Springs, and The Homestead, at Hot Springs. From that time on, the C. & O. was to play a decisive part in the development of both resorts.

In 1890 a syndicate headed by M. E. Ingalls, then president of the C. & O., bought The Homestead and the springs, and a little later the C. & O. acquired the Old White property. Despite their mutual ties with the C. & O. Railway and their common interest in the area, from about 1900 on the two resorts developed separately, in a tradition of friendly rivalry.

THE HOMESTEAD

The Homestead, today a baronial resort estate spreading over 17,000 acres, with facilities as diverse as its own commercial airport and trout stream, operating farms and a newspaper, and employing almost everybody for miles around, grew to its present character as the result of a calamity.

Eleven years after Ingalls' syndicate acquired the Hot Springs property, while they were beginning to make extensive plans for its improvement and enlargement, a fire destroyed most of the buildings. With the curious impetus that fires sometimes generate, it gave Mr. Ingalls and his backers the excuse they needed to design and erect a modern resort hotel, a spa that would rival the best in Europe. The first unit of the new building was completed in about a year, but it took thirty years of growth and change to bring The Homestead to its present character. Throughout its development the architectural style chosen for the new building has been strictly adhered to, an adaptation of Georgian colonial which seems to suit perfectly the wooded mountain slopes that rise all around, and which eloquently states the colonial beginnings of the resort. The last major development at The Homestead was the construction of an impressive central tower that has become the hotel's trademark.

Over the years between the great fire of 1901 and the completion of the tower, The Homestead began to emerge as a truly national resort, drawing patronage from everywhere. Though it was still a favored sanctuary for old families of tidewater Virginia whose patronage spanned generations, names from almost every state and many foreign countries began to appear on the guest register. The names included leaders of business, diplomats, and governors of states, with now and then even a president of the United States.

Part of the growing prestige of The Homestead resulted from the steady expansion of its facilities, both in variety and dimension. One of these was the curious game of golf. Though the people across the mountains in the Greenbrier Valley claimed that golf had been played at their resort at an earlier date, The Homestead claimed to be a pioneer in golf with the establishment in 1889 of its first course, the Virginia Hot Springs Golf and Tennis Club. It was a modest six-hole course where the hazards were sometimes the stone walls dividing former pastures. But it was the forebear in direct ancestry of the three magnificent courses The Homestead now maintains.

Another Homestead development that visitors talked about was the service and character of its dining room. In the rebuilt hotel, the dining room itself was vast, decorated with colonial elegance. The staff, nearly all local residents, often living on Homestead property and as likely as not descendants of others who had worked there in earlier days, were trained to provide impeccable service rendered with courtly Old World grace. A renowned feature was a unique skill gained with long practice of carrying loaded trays on heads, particularly in room service. This led to an occasional demonstration called the Tray Dance, in which the most skillful tray carriers competed, to the delight of diners.

Gradually other facilities for the beguilement of guests were added. Horseback riding provided a means of exploring the hundreds of miles of forest trails on the property. More and more Homestead carriages drawn by spanking teams of fine horses were seen rolling over country roads, driven by uniformed coachmen and filled with happy pampered guests. The spa gradually added to its natural springs of hot mineral water all the facilities of the best European watering places. A theater presented nightly entertainment and in the great ballroom orchestras played for dancing. During the 1920's a final note of sporting elegance was added—fox hunting based on Homestead stables, maintained with all the panoply of pink coats and jumping horses, and called the Bath County Hounds.

Then came the Depression. Keeping The Homestead open and its standards up grew difficult. The effort to do so brought about a complete financial and corporate reorganization that eliminated the C. & O. Railway, leaving the hotel in the hands of a company headed by members of the Ingalls family. In the last years of the Depression they were beginning to look about for ways again to fill their resort. The problem was solved by an event that occurred about six thousand miles to the southwest in the Pacific Ocean, the beginning of World War II.

One day, early in the war, Fay Ingalls, whose father had organized the syndicate that bought the resort and who had been acting as a resident owner, received a telephone call from Washington asking The Homestead to house and feed several hundred Japanese internees, members of the diplomatic and consular forces, newspapermen, and businessmen. The internment was to be under the control of the State

Department and the FBI, and part of the agreement with the resort was that the internees were to have the same service and the same quality of food that had been standard for prewar guests. The theory was that the treatment of the Japanese nationals interned in the United States might determine how Americans interned in Japan would be treated. It all lasted about a year, during which the hotel guarded like Fort Knox, provided luxurious room and board for 363 Japanese.

With the war's end The Homestead and its valley returned to the old ways, but things would never be quite the same again. Most guests came now by automobile instead of by rail, and an increasing number came by airplane, a fact that soon required the hotel to build one of the first of its modern accessories, a fully equipped airstrip. The postwar years at the resort brought marked changes, too, in the kind of people who visited the resort. Many of the old-timers returned, but they were outnumbered by guests a full generation younger and by others who brought their families along. It wasn't long before a fully equipped children's playground and a special children's playroom were built. Bowling alleys were added, and a skeet and trap-shooting range was set up in the nearby hills. The resort's newest addition has been a complete winter sports facility.

South from the resort the valley road leads to the picturesque village of Healing Springs, once the home of a vigorous colonial character, Mad Ann Bailey, renowned for riding like a demon and swearing like a man. A small memorial in the village marks the site of her family hut. Just outside is a scenic oddity called Falling Springs, which Thomas Jefferson called "an extraordinary cascade," falling two hundred feet over the edge of a rock into the valley, from which it is channeled into Healing Springs' most notable institution, Cascades Inn. This is a delightful small resort now owned by The Homestead. In a pleasant colonial-type building, it offers meals and accommodations chiefly for those who come to play the celebrated Cascades Course, just outside the inn door, or to fish the Cascades Stream, maintained by The Homestead through its own hatchery.

The Homestead itself, with its 560 guest rooms and suites, stands like the proud castle of a feudal lord. From the balcony of one of the tower suites, a guest may look out in all directions over the grounds of the resort. Just to the west, within a beautifully landscaped tract of lawn and trees and flowers, framed with the spreading wings of the main hotel building, is a building that dates back to earlier days, called the Casino, but not now a casino in the usual sense. It exists as an informal dining center for golfers, tennis and lawn-bowling players, and others. Weather permitting, they can be served on the Casino's lawn. From one end of the west wing of the hotel, linked to it by a covered arcade, is the spa building, which houses the original spring. This controlled facility is one of the best-equipped hydrotherapeutic centers in the world. Within it is an indoor swimming pool and just beside it a huge outdoor pool with its own beach. Part of the building is a children's play center.

In a grove of trees to one side of the west wing is a double row of cottages, the favorite accommodation for family groups, flanking a pleasant cove beside a burbling brook.

The roster of participant sports and recreations provided by The Homestead sounds like the headings of a sporting-goods catalogue. Golf, the pre-eminent sport, is played on three courses. The oldest is the course of the Virginia Hot Springs Golf and Tennis Club, beside the hotel. The course is 6016 yards, par 71. All of its eighteen holes are a delight to play because of the perfection of greens and magnificent turf of the fairways. The Cascades Course, down the valley at Healing Springs and linked to the hotel by bus service, is a true championship layout, 6714 yards, par 71, and a frequent setting for major golf tournaments. The Cascades Stream winds through the fairways of this course in a succession of riffles and quiet pools. The stream is richly stocked with rainbow trout, and it is a constant lure and challenge to fly fishermen who find that trudging along a golf fairway or casting into a pool from a golf green is a delight. The third course was opened in 1963. It is called the Lower Cascades Course and is six miles from the hotel. Designed by Robert Trent Jones, it makes brilliant use of the valley lands and the mountain streams. Each course has its own clubhouse and professional, and club rentals.

Few resorts offer riding under conditions more rewarding than those of The Homestead. A mounting block below an ancient tree in front of the hotel is generally surrounded by a cluster of saddle horses awaiting guests to ride singly or in groups on stretches of several hundred miles of forest trails on the grounds. If you prefer a carriage ride, grooms with matched teams are available.

Tennis is becoming increasingly a family sport at the resort, with eight beautifully maintained courts near the hotel.

Two immaculate lawn-bowling greens are a favorite rendezvous for older guests, while eight new ten-pin alleys with automatic pin-setting equipment in a brand-new bowling building attract younger players.

Skeet and trapshooters have four fields about a mile from the main hotel, with guns to rent and a professional for instruction. The fields crown a mountain ridge surrounded by a great laurel grove laid out to championship standards for sixteen-yard traps.

During the trout season the Cascades Club is authorized to issue nonresident state licenses and provides tackle in case you don't bring your own.

The unique ski and skating facility, climbing the slope of Warm Springs Mountain, above the hotel, has given the resort a new season and a new type of patronage during the winter months. A trestle car lift carries skiers to a 3200-foot crest where a ski run with a drop of 500 feet begins, linked to one mile of subsidiary trails. At the base of the ski run is a lodge with a snack bar and restaurant, open fireplace, sunning decks, and a shop for buying and renting equipment. Next to the lodge is an Olympic-sized skating rink. The new ski facility is open from December 15, to March 15.

The Homestead is easy to reach. Most guests arrive in their own cars, but many others still use the train and an increasing number fly in. Motoring guests will arrive from either the north or south along the valley on U.S. 220, linking to the south with east-west U.S. 60 at Covington, and to the north at Warm Springs with Route 39. Distances by highway are: New York, 440 miles; Cincinnati, 350; Washington, 200; Cleveland, 370; Richmond, Virginia, 169.

The C. & O. Railway has daily train service from Washington, Baltimore, Philadelphia, and New York. Trains that do not have through service are met by car at Covington, eighteen miles to the south.

Recently, Ingalls Field, on a mountaintop a few minutes drive from The Homestead, has been made a commercial field served by Piedmont Airline.

Homestead rates are completely American plan, starting at $24 per day for single-room occupancy. Double-room rates begin at $45.50, and increase depending on the type and location of the room. For guests preferring a more modest accommodation, the Cascades Inn, which is under Homestead management at Healing Spring, has forty-eight guest rooms and five cottages, and provides single-accommodation American-plan rates starting at $16, with double-room rates starting at $32. Guests at Cascades have all Homestead privileges.

THE GREENBRIER

Before The Homestead began to outstrip its nearby rival at Warm Springs and assume the proportions of a modern spa, a watering place of regional renown had begun to develop forty miles southwest in the valley of the Greenbrier River near White Sulphur Springs, which had been discovered in 1778 by the wife of an English settler. Cottages had been built near the spring as early as 1800. The largest and most famous, called the President's Cottage, was built in 1816. In 1830 the spring, which had proved itself to many people as a source of healing and comfort, was roofed and enshrined by a circular white building.

As the fame of the spring spread and more people flocked to sip its waters, there was a good deal of talk about putting up a resort that would be a true spa, like those sophisticated visitors had seen in Europe. The spring was owned by James Calwell, whose tavern was a gathering place for visitors to the spring and for residents of the cottages, which overlooked the spa. Calwell was under constant pressure to build something better than a frontier tavern, and in 1835 he added a ballroom and kitchen. In 1851 he yielded to pressure by having a set of elaborate plans drawn for a magnificent new hotel, which he proposed to call the Grand Central. Before he could build his resort, he died at the age of seventy-eight, leaving his financial affairs completely tangled. Two years later a syndicate from Richmond, Virginia, bought the Calwell properties, including seven thousand acres of land and buildings, and began to construct a new hotel a few years later. It was opened in 1858 and was the wonder of the South—a gigantic four-story building, surrounded by arcades and porticoes and topped with a dome. The hotel building adjacent to the spring and surrounded by about a hundred cottages contained guest rooms and an assortment of public rooms that for size and elegance were unmatched anywhere. Its dining room was the largest in the country, and its public rooms were equally impressive.

News of the "Old White" got around rapidly. Fashionable and wealthy guests from all parts of the South flocked there. The South was enjoying prosperity at that time from tobacco and cotton.

Soon the Old White, by which the hotel was known instead of by its official name, the Grand Central, was a success. In those days of opulent leisure, it was customary for a lady to travel with at least two

1. The Homestead, set within twelve thousand mountain acres, is the oldest resort in the United States and is one of the most complete resort estates in the world.

2. Of the many diversions offered by The Homestead, horseback riding over several hundred miles of forest roads is one of the most popular.

3. At The Homestead roads that wind through a fine golf course offer guests an off-beat diversion in carriage-riding.

4. Golf and/or fly casting for trout are practiced with equal ease on The Homestead's fine Cascades Course, threaded with the pools and riffles of the resort's own well-stocked trout stream.

5. The elegant classic façade of the historic Greenbrier overlooks thousands of countryside acres at White Sulphur Springs, West Virginia.

6. Almost a trademark for the Greenbrier is the little domed temple that enshrines one of the most famous mineral springs in the country—White Sulphur.

7. Old White was the name of the remarkable resort hotel that preceded the present Greenbrier, shown here as it appeared at the height of its fame, about 1875.

personal servants—a maid and a "fetch and carry girl." Summer was the traditional season for the Old White, for the mountain valley was cool. The hotel became a center of fashion, a marriage mart of importance, and a gathering place for regional politicians.

However, the glamour and elegance ended abruptly with the beginning of the Civil War. During the conflict the resort was turned into a hospital and also was used as a military headquarters. The owners had lost their money during the war and had none for repairs and renovation of the great property. It was leased to another syndicate and reopened in 1866, but business was slow. In its heyday before the Civil War, nearly all the guests of the Old White were Southerners, but now they had no money and Northerners were not inclined to travel south of the Mason-Dixon line. To lure them and others who could afford to visit it, additional improvements were made, including a race course.

In 1867, after the renovated hotel had been reopened, its patronage was given a boost by General Robert E. Lee, who at that time was president of Washington College. One of his reasons for visiting White Sulphur Springs was that his wife suffered from rheumatism, and he hoped that the spring waters at Old White would help her. Another reason was political—he was concerned with the bitter feelings existing between North and South. Before the Civil War, when he was an officer in the Army of the United States and later the superintendent of West Point, he had made close friends in the North. They still regarded him as a friend, and it occurred to him that he might persuade some of them to visit White Sulphur, where they could meet his Southern friends and help heal the wounds of the terrible conflict.

In carrying out his plan, General Lee visited White Sulphur early in the summer of 1867, riding his horse Traveller and accompanied by friends. Mrs. Lee followed in a coach with a wheel chair strapped on top. The Lees took up residence in one of the cottages near the hotel, now called Baltimore G.

Lee's strategy at White Sulphur was a success. It brought business to the resort from far and near as Lee's friends flocked there to see him. It was a turning point, and with the Lee visit, repeated each summer until his death in 1870, the Old White began a new era of fame and prosperity.

The year 1870 was a decisive one for the resort. General Lee, who had done more than anyone else to bring prosperity and prestige to the hotel, died, and in that year the C. & O. Railway tracks came through the valley. Access to the valley by rail meant that the resort's horizons would soon stretch far beyond earlier limits. The Chesapeake & Ohio acquired the Old White in 1910. The first nine holes of golf were added to the resort property that year.

The year after buying the resort the railway added the bath wing, with an indoor swimming pool, and mineral baths. Two years later the first unit of the present Greenbrier building, with two hundred fifty rooms, was built, and that year the golf course was extended to eighteen holes. In 1922 the Old White building was torn down; in 1930 the former race track was converted to an airport, one of the first operated by a resort. In 1931 three more wings were added to the main building. The hotel's fame had become national. Patronage flowed in from all directions.

But it was a different kind of business from what the hotel had known. Families began to arrive in their own cars, and more and more companies and business organizations began to choose the Greenbrier as the setting for meetings.

Then came World War II. The resort became a host for a different type of guest. It was selected as an internment center for foreign diplomats and nationals, and between 1941 and 1942 about two thousand German and Japanese internees lived there. In 1943 the Government bought the hotel and its grounds and turned them over to the Army for use as a permanent hospital. Army engineers converted spacious rooms into cubicles for officers, clinics, supply rooms, and patients' quarters. Like other projects started in the haste and heat of war, it was an incredible waste. For obvious reasons the building was not easily adapted to hospital purposes. Soon the Government decided that Ashford General Hospital was not a practical project. In 1945 the C. & O. bought it back and began reconverting the hospital into a resort. The job took years, but the results were both dramatic and stunning. A grand reopening was held in 1948. That year a presidential suite, perhaps the largest and most luxurious private suite in any hotel in the country, was added. In the same year the Greenbrier opened its famous clinic for health checkups for businessmen. The resort has continued to grow: a gun club was added on a nearby mountaintop in 1953; a new wing with auditorium, meeting rooms, theater, post office, cafeterias, and business offices was added in 1954. In 1957 a tremendous outdoor swimming pool was opened and a unique alpine-type lodge was built at the crest of Kate's Mountain, just to the south. Bowling alleys have been built, and in 1962 the entire golf facility of the Greenbrier was revised and extended, giving the hotel three complete eighteen-hole courses. A separate West Virginia wing was completed to contain a group of luxurious guest rooms and suites, a huge exhibit hall, and completely new quarters for the Greenbrier clinic, which is equipped with the most modern technical and diagnostic medical equipment.

Now, long after Mrs. John Anderson, crippled with rheumatism, allowed herself to be immersed in the hot bubbling pool called White Sulphur Springs, the Greenbrier commands an estate of about 6500 wooded mountain acres. At the heart of this high, cool mountain valley stands a tract of twenty-five superbly landscaped acres that are the immediate grounds of the resort. They are dominated by the vast main building of the hotel, which is Georgian in design. The whole resort is a remarkable and fascinating blend of historic relic and ultramodern facility. Some of the buildings are more than a hundred fifty years old; others are brand new. On low, wooded ridges around the main hotel are the cottages, the first of which was built in 1800. The President's Cottage is one of the best examples of Federal architecture in the South. This house has accommodated more guests who were or had been presidents of the United States than any other resort building in the country. Today it is maintained as a museum furnished with souvenirs and records of early White Sulphur days. The spring, which started it all, is directly in front of the President's Cottage. It is still hot, it still bubbles, and it still has that distinctive odor. And it still stands under the canopy of a dome-shaped roof resembling a huge mushroom. Some of the old cottages, which extend in long rows on a tree-shaded drive, are available to guests and their families. Several near the President's Cottage have been converted into a remarkable creative arts colony, where the arts and crafts of colonial days have been revived. The only older building not standing today is the Old White, the original resort structure. It exists, however, in memory and in the records that are maintained and exhibited by the hotel, and its site is marked by a tablet standing near a formal garden. As one observer of the Greenbrier has said, the resort today is as old-fashioned as antimacassar and as modern as a thermostat.

Another relatively new addition to the hotel is called the Virginia Wing. It overlooks the main entrance and, like the main building, maintains the gleaming grace of Georgian design. It houses the Old White Club, the Greenbrier's answer to the West Virginia law prohibiting cocktail lounges and bars. The club overlooks one of the most delightful informal gardens imaginable, and on the upper floors of the wing is the Presidential Suite.

In its modern period, patronage at the Greenbrier consists of two types of guests: family groups, chiefly middle and upper middle class, who generally arrive in their own cars; and officials and employees of American business groups, for whom the resort now provides a unique range of meeting facilities.

The resort has six hundred fifty rooms and suites, from relatively modest accommodations to some of the most spacious imaginable. Guest recreation facilities reflect the changing character of patronage. For family groups the Greenbrier maintains two summer schools, one for children from three to six years of age, and a sports school for children from seven to fourteen. The sports school offers instruction and participation in shuffleboard, swimming, golf, fishing, riding, archery, bowling, and crafts. The housekeeping department has a full staff of baby-sitters, and there is a children's dining table with a counselor and chaperon in attendance, with special children's rates for meals.

For active adults the range of sports is broad. Most dominant and popular is golf, with the three eighteen-hole layouts varying in challenge and terrain and so designed that the first tee for each course is just outside the golf clubhouse. The three courses, called the Old White, the Greenbrier, and a new eighteen-hole Lakeside Course, are all par 70. Each is about 6500 yards in length, and there is challenge for every type of player. The entire golf program is under the direction of Sam Snead, West Virginia's most celebrated golfer.

For tennis fans there are five fast-drying, hard-surface courts.

Swimming is year-round. There is a heated outdoor pool with a clubhouse beside the golf and tennis club. An indoor pool in the mineral-baths wing of the main hotel is one of the largest in the country.

From the earliest days at White Sulphur Springs, horseback riding has been a popular activity. The resort maintains two hundred miles of bridle trails and a stable full of horses. For guests who prefer padded cushions to the saddle, there are carriages drawn by matched teams that tool smartly through the vast grounds of the estate in an off-beat rustic sight-seeing adventure.

Trap and skeet fans have four combination ranges on top of Kate's Mountain, to the south of the hotel, with free transportation, guns, shells, and instruction available.

For those who like the spice of variety in their exercise there is an almost endless array of other activity available, including shuffleboard, archery, horseshoes, practice putting and driving range, bowling lanes. The Greenbrier maintains a resident naturalist who conducts nature walks.

The mineral baths are the most venerable feature of the Greenbrier, going back to the primitive duckings in the magic fountain of the White Sulphur pool. Now modern mineral baths are located in a special bath wing. Although they are no longer considered a cure, they often reduce tensions and alleviate muscular aches and pains.

Guests find that the hotel is an unusually good base for sight-seeing. Many find driving through the nearby countryside over country lanes a pleasant adventure in discovery. There are a number of state parks in the area, with lovely scenery and picnic facilities. Seventy-three miles to the east is Virginia's Natural Bridge, a curiosity that has been attracting sight-seers ever since George Washington and Thomas Jefferson surveyed it. The Virginia Military Institute, whose shrines include the tombs of both General Robert E. Lee and General Stonewall Jackson, is in Lexington, Virginia. In the opposite direction is a remarkable coal mine called the Pocahontas, perhaps the only coal mine in the world into which you can drive your car. It is maintained as a demonstration of coal mining.

Antique shops are located in almost every town in the area.

The Greenbrier is not hard to reach: it is an approximate midway point on main transportation routes, both rail and highway. New York is 465 miles to the northeast; Washington 245 miles to the east; Cincinnati 315 miles to the west. The nearest cities are Roanoke, Virginia, 75 miles; Charleston, West Virginia, 100 miles; Richmond, Virginia, 195 miles. Traditionally the hotel is served by rail travel, since the resort is owned and maintained by the Chesapeake & Ohio Railway. The White Sulphur Springs station of the C. & O. is just outside the main gates of the resort, and though its extensive sidings are seldom lined with the private cars of rich guests, as was the case during the first years of the century, the station is a regular stop of all trains on the C. & O.

A recent resort innovation has been a series of winter-month house parties, when a special railway-excursion rate and reduced rates at the resort itself bring large groups of guests in on special cars from all the larger cities served by the C. & O.

The White Sulphur Springs airport is a mile from the hotel and is not served by scheduled flights of regular airlines. It is linked to communities where scheduled flights are maintained: Roanoke, Virginia, in the east, served by American, Eastern, and Piedmont airlines; and Charleston, West Virginia, to the west, served by United and Lake Central airlines. Charter service is maintained by the resort airport, which has runways of up to five thousand feet and is used increasingly by private aircraft of companies and individuals.

Most Greenbrier guests arrive by automobile. U.S. 60 cuts through the resort's property. Both east and west it connects with main highway routes that make the Greenbrier readily accessible by automobile from any point. It is approximately a six-hour drive to Washington, and Columbus and Cincinnati, to the west, are a comfortable day's drive away.

The Greenbrier is an American-plan resort in rate scale. The rate for a single room begins at $25 per day and includes all meals. Double-room rates start at $50 per day. The rate for suites are higher, depending on type and size. Accommodation for maids and chauffeurs in comfortable employee quarters is $10 per day for room and meals. Rates for sports facilities are: golf, $5 per day including locker; tennis, 50 cents per hour; riding, $5 per hour. Skeet shooting and trapshooting is $4.50 per round of twenty-five shots. A carriage drive is $4 per person. Rates for other facilities: mineral baths, a complete one-hour treatment with Swedish massage for $8; Swedish massage alone for $5. There are no seasonal variations in rates at the Greenbrier except that at certain times reduced hotel rates are combined with excursion rates on the railway.

CHAPTER 2

NEW ENGLAND'S

ROCK-BOUND SHORE

The shore of New England is one of the most picturesque places in the world. Since the coast of New England was settled very early in colonial times, it seems logical that resorts offering pleasant sanctuary to those with the time and money to take summer vacations would have developed at strategic shore points.

That this did *not* occur until the last half of the nineteenth century is a curious fact that sociologists will probably explain by saying that New Englanders who could afford summer holidays didn't need resort hotels. The cottages built along the shore grew into resort communities and regions, quite distinct from the self-contained resort estates. One of the very first resort communities in all the colonies was established by Captain Miles Standish east of Plymouth on high bluffs overlooking the ocean and Plymouth Bay. The village he started was, and is, called Duxbury. Miles Standish and his daughters are buried there, and a towering monument in a state park is a memorial to him. Duxbury is a resort community today that draws people from nearby Boston and other points in Massachusetts. Nearby Cape Cod is another kind of resort community that grew slowly over the years and in a quiet way attracted the same families from not distant cities year after year.

Other resort communities—some of them very opulent and exclusive indeed—were to develop later in New England. Bar Harbor, on Mount Desert Island off the coast of Maine, was one. It became a special summer refuge for the very wealthy and the elite. So did Newport, Rhode Island, the most prestigious and gilded of all New England resort communities, and the most famous and conspicuous of them.

But in none of these, Newport, Bar Harbor, Cape Cod, Duxbury, did the big, luxurious, self-contained resort estates develop. They did not begin to develop anywhere along the shore until the second half of the nineteenth century. Then, suddenly, they began to rise on granite peninsulas thrusting out from New England's coast. They grew so fast that within a period of about thirty years scarcely a promontory lacked its pretentious resort. They stood above the sea on every offshore island.

The boom in New England shore resorts between about 1870 and 1900 was probably the result of two factors: better transportation—a network of new rail lines along the shore offering quick and easy access to almost every point along the shore—and greatly improved economic conditions. Long-established, well-to-do families became richer and richer. Thousands of other families, having money for the first time and time to take summer holidays, helped to build these resorts.

Most of the shore resorts that developed from this growth of travel and prosperity were built and promoted by city groups who saw the way vacation moods were turning. Some were amateur financiers and planners, others were professionals, and still others owned real estate and thought the properties might make good resort sites.

Since nearly all of their resorts were built during the Victorian era, most of the shore hotels were big, barnlike, and relatively ugly. They usually had commanding settings overlooking the ocean or an ocean bay. Unlike some of the resorts in the New England mountains that grew from sturdy farmhouses or barns with fine views, the shore resorts were designed to be resorts from the beginning. They were patterned for family entertaining and family accommodation—big rooms, big closets, quarters for maids, and even kennels for pets.

Most of them were built of wood, and so, inevitably, most of them burned down sooner or later, often sooner. Some were replaced, and some were not. Among those that were rebuilt after fires and continued to operate for years, the change in times and customs forced many into bankruptcy and final abandonment. Most of them changed hands many times.

Though New England's shore is as popular as ever, with cottage colonies ranging from shabby and modest to elegant and exclusive, lining almost every cove, crowning headlands, and pre-empting islands, there are left only a very few great resort estates.

Two of these resorts have prospered, grown, and adapted themselves to the changing times and the changing moods of summer visitors. These two are almost within sight of each other in one of the most picturesque sections of the New England shore, where the Piscataqua

River comes down to the sea in a wide, deep, tidal estuary studded with islands. One resort—a few miles north of the mouth of the river is in Maine—at York Harbor. It is the handsome, medium-sized resort called Marshall House, uniquely set in the center of a big safe harbor. The other, one of the truly great resort estates of the country, is the remarkable Wentworth-by-the-Sea, just east of Portsmouth, New Hampshire, and set on a rocky ridge overlooking the bay, the ocean, and the river. Wentworth-by-the-Sea has, among several claims to fame, the unique distinction of never having had its buildings destroyed by fire.

WHERE LIBERTY BEGAN

Compared to the hundreds of miles of Atlantic shore claimed by both Maine and Massachusetts, the seacoast of New Hampshire, between Maine on the north and Massachusetts on the south, doesn't amount to much in length—less than twenty miles. Though it is short in length, New Hampshire's coast is long in historic association and scenic variety. It has picturesque salt marshes threaded by a maze of quiet channels, a half-dozen excellent sand beaches, and a great estuary where the Piscataqua River comes down to the ocean in a wide channel. This channel is filled with islands that have names like Snuff-box, Clam Pit, and Pest. A few miles inland from the sea on the south bank of the Piscataqua is New Hampshire's port city of Portsmouth, one of the handsomest, oldest, and most interesting cities in New England. Founded in 1623, it claims to be the birthplace of the United States Navy by reason of shipbuilding. A few miles east of Portsmouth is the Fort Point Lighthouse, erected in 1771 and one of the oldest lighthouses along the New England shore. It adjoins a tract that has been a military reservation for almost two hundred years, now called Fort Constitution, originally Fort William and Mary.

West of Fort Constitution and overlooking the shore of the river from the north is one of the most attractive small villages in New England, New Castle. Through the first three-quarters of the eighteenth century up to the Revolutionary War, New Castle was an important city in New Hampshire. Benning Wentworth, the royal governor, maintained a home there and often held meetings of his royal council.

Adjoining New Castle on the west, about midway between the mouth of the river and Portsmouth, is one of the largest, most unusual and celebrated resort hotels in New England, bearing the name of the royal governor of New Hampshire. It is called Wentworth-by-the-Sea. Though there is no direct association other than proximity between the luxury resort and the village of New Castle, the resort helped to make history, just as the village had a hundred years earlier.

Ninety-eight years after the citizens of New Castle overwhelmed the guard at Fort William and Mary and seized the garrison's powder kegs, a group of New England promoters and residents, including a prominent family of New Castle by the name of Campbell, conceived the idea that the banks of the Piscataqua River were an ideal place for a new summer resort hotel. They hoped to make it the most elegant and aristocratic along the entire New England shore. And they succeeded.

The period was one of booming resort development: summer hotels were being built in the lush climate of prosperity that followed the end of the Civil War on almost every headland that could be reached by new highways being built along the shore. Dozens of new hotels were erected. Out of the dozens built, only a few survive today. Wentworth-by-the-Sea opened its doors to the carriage trade of New England in 1874.

The site for the new hotel was the crest of a low ridge that ran down the center of a peninsula that had the shore of the river to the north and a bay from the ocean on the south. It was immediately west of New Castle and was situated on property owned by the Campbell family. The hotel was all that its promoters intended—luxurious and spacious for the day, in a day when everything was likely to be spacious. It had eighty-two rooms and was designed to accommodate whole families, mainly in four-room suites with enormous closets. Families arrived about June 1 and usually stayed until September 1. They consisted of father, mother, several children, a nurse, a coachman, and occasionally the family dog. In the beginning the guest register of the hotel showed families representing some of the most distinguished in New England, such as the Cabots of Boston and the Holmeses of Cambridge. As the Wentworth's reputation spread, it began to draw guests from Washington, New York, St. Louis, and Philadelphia. The present owners of the hotel say that descendants of the families who made up the guest register in the first few decades after the hotel opened still come back today as occasional guests.

From the beginning, Wentworth-by-the-Sea was involved in public occasions. No resort in the country has been associated with more of them. In 1905, President Theodore Roosevelt undertook to stage treaty negotiations as an end to the Russo-Japanese War, which Japan had just won. Portsmouth was selected as the site for the negotiations. Almost immediately Wentworth-by-the-Sea became involved in the treaty. Delegates had to have a place to stay, and the Wentworth was chosen. Delegates from Japan and Russia and distinguished newspapermen from all over the world were housed there during the negotiations. Photographs taken at the time show the Russian and Japanese delegates leaving the main entrance to the hotel on the way to sessions of the treaty conference—the Japanese in an extraordinary Pope-Toledo touring car provided by the United States Government, and the more cautious and sedate Russians in a horse-drawn carriage.

The treaty of Portsmouth negotiations were the first of many such meetings held in the hotel in succeeding years. The resort has become one of the most popular meeting places in New England for business meetings and conferences of all types.

From its inception, Wentworth-by-the-Sea became renowned throughout New England as a resort that offered its guests a wide range of cultural opportunities and recreation. Tennis courts were established in 1880 and within a few years were attracting leading players of the country for a succession of tournaments that the hotel sponsored and staged. Tennis has remained one of the most important sports there, and exhibition matches are played on its fine courts by nearly all the top stars in the country, professional and amateur.

The resort's unique setting in a complex association of land and water naturally made boating and fishing important and gave guests a choice of several bathing beaches and a full array of fishing opportunity, from the sheltered waters of the river and bay to deep sea fishing from the resort's own fishing cruisers. Golf came later, with a nine-hole course to the west of the resort proper on the mainland.

Through the years Wentworth-by-the-Sea remained open during every summer except for two seasons during World War II, when it was taken over by the military, blacked out, and put to secret use. Following World War II the big resort came under the control and management of new ownership, headed by James Barker Smith, an experienced resort manager with an imaginative flair for making the most of his superb setting, the resort's unusual facilities, and its long and colorful reputation as one of the truly great seaside resorts of the East. Under his management the whole property was remodeled, refurbished, and re-equipped. Old-fashioned family suites were cut down to single but spacious room units with huge closets and big bathrooms. Public rooms were entirely redecorated. The great main dining room, capable of seating the entire guest register or a banquet of a thousand or more, was made one of the most beautiful and colorful dining rooms in the East. Various special rooms were added, including a handsome new cocktail lounge overlooking the bay to the north. A number of pleasant cottages were built in the partially wooded grounds between the main hotel and the shore to the south, several set in superbly gardened grounds, and all of them available for group use.

Outside the hotel, Mr. Smith wisely retained the distinctive Victorian character of design but removed some more frivolous excesses. Narrow wooden porches where groups of delegates to the 1905 peace conference were photographed were converted to glass-walled arcades.

But the greatest changes have been made on the extensive grounds of the resort. A new boat dock and pier have been added as a base for fishing cruisers and other craft. At the shore end of the dock a tremendous, semicircular salt-water pool has been built, flanked by a sun terrace in front of a curious building somewhat resembling a ship with the facilities of a club. Its upper floors are dedicated to a resort program that is probably the only one of its kind in the country—the studio and gallery of a talented artist, Robert Chase, the resort's resident artist, who conducts art classes and arranges shows of his own and students' works.

Spreading over several acres of grounds immediately in front of the hotel is one of the most unusual pitch-and-putt golf courses in the country. Playing it involves pitching up and down steep slopes, playing around and through flower beds and other challenging situations that beguile even talented golfers. The resort's nine-hole golf course, recently redesigned, is about a quarter mile away to the west on the mainland, with a number of fairways flanking the shore. The course is 3004 yards in length, a par 35. Several holes are scenic; most have enough challenge to keep even the best golfers satisfied. The shortest hole is a par 3, 153 yards, with the green set on a point overlooking the ocean. The longest is a long 520 yards, par 5.

In a grove of pine trees overlooking a rocky beach, the resort has established roasting and steaming ovens and stages the most popular clambakes in New England, held every Friday during the summer season and almost daily during spring and fall convention periods. They are under the direction of a crusty but talented Yankee clambake specialist. The clambakes draw as many as a thousand guests and are sometimes given twice daily to take care of enthusiastic crowds. The clambake menus involve far more than clams: lobster, chicken, and corn cooked over hot rocks layered with seaweed and steamed several hours with salt water. The appetizer of a clambake is usually a bowl of steaming clam chowder. The traditional desert is ice-cold watermelon.

The resort's grounds have always been famous for flowers, with some of the most lavish and varied displays in New England. But the flower gardens, scattered all over the property, are also famous for a special reason. They are under the direction of Mrs. Alice Hackney, who in 1910, at the age of ten, began helping her aunt, who was then the head gardener at the resort, and has been busy in the garden ever since. She is probably the only woman resort gardener in the country, and certainly the only one whose predecessor was also a woman. Her floral arrangements for special occasions are celebrated. Photographs of her work have appeared in several gardening magazines.

The tradition of diversion and entertainment which began early at Wentworth-by-the-Sea has been greatly developed by the present management. It is scheduled in a bewildering succession of events including music, theatrical performances, dancing, lectures, fashion shows, variety shows, and motion pictures. A former stable near the hotel has been converted into a kind of theatrical warehouse full of every conceivable prop and scenic accessory, including historic vehicles used during the earliest days of the resort's operation. It is the contention of Mr. Smith and his associates that sooner or later all of the assorted props and decorative oddities in the big stable will be useful in helping make guests happy with special entertainment.

Dining at Wentworth is traditional New England in type, with a heavy emphasis on seafood and lobster. The resort probably uses more lobsters than any other hotel in the country, and serves them in many different ways. On the extensive menu other notable New England specialties appear from time to time, often based on recipes that have been popular at the resort for more than half a century.

Many guests soon discover that Wentworth, with its scenic setting, is also a fine base for exploring one of the most interesting sections of New England's shore. There are dozens of worth-while sights within short drives of the resort itself. A few minutes' walk to the east, along the promontory at the mouth of the Piscataqua River, brings one to New Castle, which, though it has a population of less than a thousand, is one of the most delightful to visit. One quickly learns that it is best seen by strolling along its quiet, narrow streets. The only suggestion of modern days is the telephone lines. The little town has dozens of charming old cottages, most of which are set in graceful gardens and grounds. On the edge of the town is a historic burying ground.

Portsmouth is a ten-minute drive from the resort. The town has notable streets lined with fine old houses, relics of its seagoing past. Several of them are open to visitors. The most famous is the John Paul Jones House, where the naval hero lived while his ship, the *Ranger,* was being fitted. It was built in 1758 and now is the home of the Portsmouth Historical Society. The United States Naval Base is of interest, though admission to it is gained only by special arrangement.

Wentworth guests visiting Portsmouth are also attracted by a remarkable section of the city called Strawberry Banke, which is part of the original community of Portsmouth, dating from 1630. About thirty houses, many of them beautiful examples of the colonial and Federal periods, scattered over a nine-acre area, are being handsomely and authentically restored. Dozens of other attractive and historic small cities of both southern Maine and New Hampshire are within a one- or two-hour drive from the resort.

Wentworth-by-the-Sea is easily accessible by highway, air, and rail. Some of the principal highways of New England pass through nearby Portsmouth. Boston is less than fifty miles to the south, linked to Portsmouth by Interstate 95 and U.S. 1. New England to the north is linked to Portsmouth by the extension of Interstate 95 as the Maine Turnpike in Maine and by the continuation of U.S. 1. A variety of main routes to western areas converge on Boston to the south and Portsmouth itself and provide fast and easy access to the coast by automobile. From Portsmouth the resort is reached by Route 1B.

Rail service into Portsmouth is provided by the Boston & Maine railroad, and air service is available to Boston. Both trains and planes are met in Boston by hotel cars on request. Bus service from Boston is available to Portsmouth, where special taxi service will take guests to the resort.

Wentworth-by-the-Sea has one of the longest summer seasons of any New England resort, opening in early May and extending until late October. The periods from May to July 1 and from Labor Day to the closing in October are generally regarded as both vacation and convention seasons, though the resort is open at that time to transient guests. The traditional social season begins in July and usually ends on Labor Day. The resort is operated on full American plan. Single rooms start at $18 per day, double rooms at $28. Lanai suites, each with a glass-enclosed porch, are among the most attractive room combinations in the hotel;

they begin at $36 for a double room. Cottages are available for groups or families, either with or without meals included in the rates; they vary in rates with size and conditions.

CLAMBAKES EVERY FRIDAY

York County, at the extreme southeast corner of the state, is the oldest county in Maine, settled within a few years after the landing of the Pilgrims in Massachusetts. There the small York River meets the sea in a picturesque harbor set with islands, its shores typical of Maine's rock-ribbed, rugged coast. The city of York, settled in 1624, is one of the most attractive and unspoiled small towns in the East, with shaded, winding streets and beautiful old houses. York was the first English city chartered in America. Adjoining it on the shore of the harbor is the village of York Harbor, which is actually a summer resort extension of the original village of York. It has a country club and golf course, and the fairways flank the York River. And dominating a harbor island is one of Maine's oldest resort estates—Marshall House.

For many years after its opening in 1871, Marshall House was a family enterprise. Built by Nathaniel G. Marshall, it was owned and operated by him and his sons for almost seventy-five years. Like all of the early resorts of New England, it was a wooden hotel. Its unique setting, almost in the center of the harbor, with the open ocean on one side and sheltered coves behind, quickly made it popular among New Englanders. Its fame and popularity grew, and so did the hotel building. Remodeled and extended several times, it became a historic, traditional New England resort. But like many such places of the period, it was to meet the fate that seemed destined for summer hotels. Marshall House was destroyed by fire of unknown origin in January 1916, while completely closed up and shuttered. The Marshall family promptly decided to rebuild, and within six months had completed the new, fireproof building—a massive L-shaped hotel of no particular architectural style. It had more than a hundred fifty guest rooms, spacious and pleasant public rooms, and offered guests, not only a modern hotel, but a breeze-cooled and secluded setting with a variety of recreational facilities, on the island itself and in York Harbor village, a few minutes away.

In 1958 the final transition of Marshall House occurred. Its ownership and management passed from the Marshall family to the control of another famous New England family. It was bought by Pinehurst,

Incorporated, operators of the world's most celebrated golfing resort at Pinehurst, North Carolina. Pinehurst is owned by the Tufts family, which had migrated from New England to found that resort about the time the first Marshall House began its operation on an island off the coast of Maine.

Pinehurst's management has given the hotel a new distinction and quality. Many of the staff members from the two hotels at Pinehurst—the famed Carolina Hotel and Holly Inn—move to the Marshall House in summer and there maintain the New England traditions of hospitality and service which have made Pinehurst one of the truly memorable resorts of the country.

They have also given to the Marshall House the trappings of a true resort estate. Within a few minutes' walk of the massive main hotel building is a tremendous heated salt-water pool, flanking a surf beach and the open ocean. Nearby are tennis courts, and two miles away, on the mainland, is the golf course of the York Golf and Tennis Club, where hotel guests have privileges. The York course, eighteen holes, 6205 yards, is pleasant to play and beautifully maintained. Most of the holes are medium in length and average in playing challenge. The hotel offers guests one unique opportunity—boating and fishing in the channels and offshore waters that surround it. Its harbor, notable as a sheltered haven during storms, is usually crowded with motored craft, many brought there by hotel guests.

The menus at Marshall House, prepared by dining-room and kitchen staffs from Pinehurst, feature old-fashioned New England cooking, with emphasis on seafood, particularly local Maine lobsters. A notable dining occasion is a clambake every Friday on the beach. Clams are cooked in typical Maine fashion in a huge flat boiler with seaweed.

The distinctive location of the resort offers guests an unusual bonus in sight-seeing. The rugged, often dramatic shore stretches in both directions, with winding roads cutting to and from the shore. York Village itself, less than five minutes away, has beautiful old houses and some historic buildings. Most notable is an old jail, which the New Englanders spell as "gaol," built in 1653, now a museum. It is said to be the oldest English public building in the United States that was used as a jail. Five miles away at York Beach is the Animal Forest Park. Historic New England cities are nearby, and the whole area is filled with charming small villages.

Marshall House is easy to reach by train, plane, or automobile. It is sixty miles north of Boston and is linked to that city by express highways, including Interstate 95 and U.S. 1, from which Alternate U.S. 1 leads to the resort. Guests arriving by train have frequent service from Portsmouth, New Hampshire, nine miles south, or Dover, New Hampshire, thirteen miles away. They are met on request by the hotel. Plane service is by Northeast Airlines to Manchester, New Hampshire, or to Portland, Maine, and by many lines into Logan Airport, Boston.

Open during the summer season only, Marshall House rates are American plan. Single-room rates begin at $18 per day, double-room rates at $32. Combinations of double and single rooms with bath between start at $51. Golfing fees are $5 per day on weekends, $3 on other days.

CHAPTER 3

MOUNTAINS OF
NEW ENGLAND

The mountains of New England are very old—among the oldest in the
world, geologists say. Long ago a mile-deep sheet of glacial ice began to
mold and round their peaks and carve sharp ravines that New Englanders call notches. In time slender valleys became lakes. Much later
these softened and ice-sculptured slopes and crests were clothed in superb forests. Though all part of a vast upland system, the mountains of
the three northern New England states—Vermont, New Hampshire,
and Maine—consist of two groups, the Green Mountains of Vermont and
the White Mountains, which have their highest crests in New Hampshire but spill over into tumbled ranges studded with innumerable lakes
in western and northern Maine.

Though the mountains of New England were relatively close to seaboard settlements that grew into important cities during the seventeenth
and eighteenth centuries, the mountains themselves were explored and
settled slowly. Finally, villages began to string out along the mountain
valleys. In forest clearings small farms were established, where, with
desperately hard work, farm families managed to wrest a meager living
from the land—often after clearing it of glacial boulders.

Toward the middle of the nineteenth century, regular stagecoach
lines (soon to be supplanted by railroads) began to link the mountain
settlements with seaboard cities and the centers to the west in New York
and the north in Canada.

Travelers through New England's mountains soon discovered that
the pleasant high valleys had special virtues that the seaboard lacked.
They were cool and delightful during the hot summer months, and
their lakes were clear and full of fish. Following the establishment of

railroads, the numerous resorts of New England's mountains began to develop. By the end of the nineteenth century there were dozens of resorts, at least one in every pleasant mountain valley, and some at the crests of mountain ridges. Some of these resorts grew casually from scenically set farms, evolving over the years from farmhouses to summer guesthouses, and finally into full-scale resorts. Others, particularly after railways permitted mass movements of summer visitors, started out as vast, rambling wooden hotels designed specifically as mountain resorts, built with the money of syndicates of promoters and advertised throughout the land by the distribution of brochures.

Many of the New England mountain resorts died of economic starvation induced by the hazards of a short summer season. Others burned down. But others, surviving depressions and fire, became truly distinctive resort estates. Six of them are described in the stories that follow. Each of the six has its own special charm of setting and facility. Two are in Vermont, two in New Hampshire, and two in Maine. Two, thanks to winter sports, are now open year round. Two stand high in the mountains and command superb views; two are set on the shores of beautiful lakes; and two nestle in mountain valleys with slopes and peaks rising all around.

Of these six fine resorts of New England's mountains today, one of the oldest, Mountain View House, began as a farm that commanded a superb view of the central Presidential Range of the White Mountains. A highway accident brought stagecoach passengers to it one summer, and visitors have been coming back ever since. Mountain View House, now grown into a sophisticated resort estate set in thousands of superbly maintained mountain acres, and one of the handsomest and most celebrated resorts of New England, has been managed and owned by the same family for almost a hundred years, from the time when it was a farm with a fine view a few miles north of Whitefield, New Hampshire.

Another New Hampshire resort with a view of the White Mountains is the Waumbek (which means White Hills in Indian dialect), near Jefferson. Situated in a high mountain valley, it is only a few miles northeast of the Mountain View House and, like that resort, has views of the Presidential Range, but from the valley instead of the ridge crest. The Waumbek was established as the result of a book being written by an itinerant minister who extolled the beauty of the White Mountains and particularly the valley near Jefferson. The minister recommended it as a site for a hotel. Soon a fine building was established there, taking maximum advantage of a notable setting. Today the Waumbek is now a complete resort, famed not only for its setting but for a notable golf course.

Vermont's two famous resort estates both started as mountain farms. One, the Mountain Top Inn, north of Chittenden, grew from a sturdy barn with a fine panoramic view of distant mountains and nearby lake. The farm was finally abandoned, but the barn, because of its view, was acquired as a guesthouse, and this in time grew to a full-scale resort—first a summer hotel, then, quite recently, because of good skiing in the area, a winter resort as well.

The second of Vermont's two fine resorts is near the village of Stowe in the middle of the most important skiing and winter-resort area of Vermont. The Lodge at Smugglers' Notch, is at the base of Mount Mansfield, just where a toll road snakes up the mountain and ski lifts converge. Beginning as a farmhouse taking summer visitors, it evolved, with appropriate growth and modification, into a small summer resort, then an important rendezvous for skiers, and finally into a year-round resort with sophisticated and complete facilities for both seasons, particularly noted for fine continental cooking.

Maine's two mountain resorts both command dramatic lake-shore settings, and both are on the threshold of Maine's magnificent forest wilderness. The Mount Kineo Hotel, on the shore of Moosehead Lake, is at the base of Mount Kineo, an extraordinary mountain of solid flint. Developed and opened more than seventy-five years ago as the finest, largest, and most fashionable hotel in the North Woods, Mount Kineo Hotel survived change and development—including several fires—to emerge in the end as a fireproof and modern but historic resort with a magnificent setting and every facility on land or lake to take full advantage of its unique isolation. You can reach it only by boat.

Maine's second forest-lake resort grew from a popular but primitive fishing camp on the east shore of a beautiful alpine lake called Kezar, set among the foothills of the White Mountains. Severance Lodge grew from a joint disaster—fire and bankruptcy—which ended the fishing camp but left its notable setting for the development of a new resort. One of the newest of New England's resort estates, it has grown in thirty years from the ruins of a fishing camp into a rustic but luxurious resort, famed for a fine setting, superb accommodations and facilities, a notable range of guest diversions, and one of the best dining rooms among Eastern resorts.

THE FARMHOUSE THAT GREW AND GREW

Of all the mountains of New England, none are more famous than the White Mountains of New Hampshire, which are part of the great Appalachian system and spread over a thousand square miles of rugged and beautiful country in several great ranges. The most famous is the Presidential Range, so named because particular peaks have the names of presidents of the United States. Among them is Mount Washington, the highest mountain in New England, which towers 6288 feet. The wooded slopes of the mountains are cut with scenic passes called notches and with deep ravines.

The pleasant mountain village of Whitefield is in the northern foot-hills of the Presidential Range at an altitude of about a thousand feet. Whitefield began to draw pioneer settlers in the early nineteenth century, among them an adventuresome Englishman named William Dodge, the third settler of Whitefield. Later he became the town's postmaster and clerk.

Fifty years after William Dodge settled in Whitefield, his son, William Franklin Dodge, moved out of town and built a farmhouse on the crest of a hill north of the village. The site was notable, commanding a stunning view of the sweep of the Presidential Range, to the south, and the Franconia Mountains, to the southwest, a fact that, though not important in running a farm, was the first link in a chain of circumstance that changed the farm into one of the most luxurious resorts in the East. One day during the summer of 1864 a stagecoach was passing along the road just north of Whitefield with several passengers on their way from New Orleans to Montreal. The stage broke down while passing the road leading to the Dodge farm. While the coach was being repaired, passengers went to the Dodge farm, where they were received hospitably and were exposed to the farm's spectacular view. The passengers were so comfortable, the view was so compelling, and the welcome was so warm that they decided to abandon their trip to Montreal and spend their summer at the Dodge farm. At the end of the season they returned to their homes in Louisiana and told their friends of the little farm in the White Mountains of New Hampshire that offered such a comfortable refuge. The next year they returned with friends. The increased influx of summer guests crowded the four-room farmhouse, so Dodge decided that he would convert his farm into a small inn. He did this the next year, giving it the name of Mountain View House.

It is still there, and it is still called Mountain View House, but it bears little resemblance to the frontier farm of 1864. It is now a luxurious, beautifully run, superbly set resort estate, spreading over three thousand acres, which is many times the acreage of the original Dodge farm.

Nothing remains of the original name of the Dodge farm except the word "House." However, there still is the view, a superb panorama to the south of the inn. The resort is still owned by the Dodge family today —the fourth generation of the original settler, William Dodge, and direct descendants of his son, William Franklin, who built his farm on a high hill with a fine view. Also unchanged is the warm hospitality that was first extended to the passengers of the crippled stagecoach.

The succession of changes that converted the farmhouse and the early inn into the present resort never involved tearing anything down. The change—a remarkable structural and architectural evolution—was accomplished by a series of additions, modifications, renovations, and modernizations. The first addition occurred in 1873, with an enlargement of the original farm inn. Another occurred in 1880, and so on through ten successive developments—the final one in 1946, when the resort acquired a beautiful swimming pool and Sports House.

The present managers and operators of the Mountain View House are Schuyler and John Dodge, great-grandsons of the original founder. In a small but charming radio room one can see on the wall a row of pictures of the successive generations of the Dodge family who have owned the inn.

Mountain View House today seems much larger than its 185 guest rooms would suggest, partly because it rambles. There never has been a restriction on space.

The main hotel building is set at the crest of a hill facing the south, so that most of the public rooms and many of the guest rooms share the spectacular view. The building is four stories high and extends along the hill for several hundred feet, with wings extending to the rear and sides. A gabled square tower rises above the main entrance. The whole building is painted in the best tradition of colonial New England design—butter yellow and white with green shutters and a green roof. The resort's thousands of acres of beautifully maintained grounds stretch in all directions from the main building. Hundreds of acres are in natural woods, with hundreds more in wide, sweeping lawns. The nine-hole golf course is one of the best in New England. On the lawn in front of the hotel is a putting green, and beside it are two fast-drying tennis courts. Within easy walking distance of the hotel is the Sports House. Behind the hotel are stables where horses are maintained. A two-acre cutting garden that keeps the rooms glowing with fresh flowers adjoins the stables. A celebrated floral feature of the resort is a wide terrace in front set with hundreds of begonias.

The public rooms of Mountain View House are unusually spacious. In character and appointments they suggest the best traditions of colonial and eighteenth-century décor. One of the exceptions is a striking modern cocktail lounge off the main lobby. The main dining room is large enough to accommodate almost the entire guest register. A big ballroom is a focal point for evening entertainment, which includes dancing, motion pictures twice a week, and a traditional Sunday-evening concert. There are several card rooms, a well-stocked library, and television rooms. Since much of the hotel was built during a period when there was no premium on space, the guest rooms are unusually large, with enormous closets, and are decorated and maintained to provide solid comfort.

Most of the outdoor activities are divided between the Sports House, with its adjoining pool and play fields, and the golf course, which is 2915 yards long, a par 35, designed to take advantage of the surrounding slopes and hills. It has very little level ground, a constant challenge to golfers of all abilities.

Dining at Mountain View House is a notable experience. During the years of their ownership the Dodge family became interested in unusual and outstanding dishes they discovered in their travels. Although the large and varied menus are essentially American, they also contain dishes based on recipes found in Europe.

There are two unusual sight-seeing opportunities at the resort. One is the spectacular view of the mountains. The other is the remarkable cutting garden—an exhibition of growing flowers that can be matched by few gardens in the country for variety and luxuriance.

Less than an hour's drive on U.S. 3 and U.S. 302 is the base for the extraordinary Mount Washington cog railway, oldest in the world, built in 1869—three years after the original Mountain View House was established. The ride to the mountain summit takes three hours for the round trip. The crest, one of the windiest spots in the world, usually offers an extraordinary view. Another sight-seeing novelty, a half-hour drive from Whitefield, is within Franconia Notch. It is a curious cliff variously called the Great Stone Face, the Old Man of the Mountain, or the Profile, a craggy silhouette that strikingly resembles the face of a man, fifty feet from brow to chin. A nearby sight-seeing facility is the Cannon Mountain Tramway, just north of the area of the Profile. In the winter it is used to lift skiers to the tops of the ski run; in the summer it gives visitors an exciting ride. There are scenic drives throughout the mountain area in all directions.

Most guests drive to Mountain View House on good highways that converge on the resort area. It is about 325 miles from New York to the resort by two routes: the New York Thruway to Glen Falls, U.S. 4 to White River Junction, U.S. 5 and U.S. 302 to Littleton, and U.S. 3 to Whitefield and the resort, and the Merritt Parkway and Interstate 91 linking with U.S. 5 leading to Woodstock, thence 302 and the same continuing route as above. The resort is 174 miles from Boston over Interstate 93 and U.S. 3 all the way to Whitefield, and the resort's own road. From Portland, Maine, 110 miles over U.S. 302 and Route 3. Montreal is 174 miles to the northwest over Routes U.S. 2 and U.S. 3. From Whitefield itself, the resort's own road is about three miles north of the village on U.S. 3, where at the crest of a hill a handsome sign and gatepost point the way down a road through a forest to the resort's property.

Mountain View House is open only during the summer, beginning late in June and extending to early October. The rate schedule is American plan, with single-room rates starting at $20 and double-room rates at $36. One exception to these basic rates is a limited number of both double and single rooms with hot and cold water but lacking private baths, all conveniently located near public bathrooms on the floors where they are; these rooms are offered at a minimum rate of $16 per day per person. Greens fees at the resort, for unlimited use of the golf course, are $3 per day.

WAUMBEK MEANS WHITE HILLS

The White Mountains of New Hampshire are a massive cluster of wooded peaks and slopes that include the highest crest in New England. Long ago the Indians who lived among the mountains gave them the name Waumbek Methna, which means the White Hills, or Crystal Hills.

For many years the White Mountains were a frontier little known and unsettled. An early settlement, named Jefferson in honor of Thomas

Jefferson, was made around 1795. Among the earliest settlers was a
Colonel Joseph Whipple, who, sensing that the region was important,
bought the entire township for a sum of $4200 and for many years lived
in the heart of his wilderness domain in semibaronial style. He laid out
roads, built sawmills, and encouraged other pioneers to begin a new
life in the forests of New Hampshire. But it was more than fifty years
after Colonel Whipple established his village of Jefferson that the rest
of the world paid any attention to the settlement and the spectacularly
scenic country where it had been established.

Attention came at last in a curious way, as the direct result of an
articulate preacher named Thomas Starr King, who not only believed
in carrying the gospel to the wilderness, but thoroughly enjoyed traveling. In one of his early trips he visited the White Mountains and was
so impressed he wrote a book in which he translated the Indian name
Waumbek to the White Hills. The book, published in 1859, was enthusiastic and specific and did much to attract wide notice to the charms
and opportunities of the White Mountains. Dr. King made a particular
point of mentioning the little settlement of Jefferson, nestling in a high
mountain valley between the towering ranges. In describing the country around the village he said:

> From no point is a better landscaped picture to be gained. We ride
> in full view of every summit of the chain, seeing Washington in
> the center, dominant over all. For grandeur and for opportunities
> of studying the wildness and majesty of the sovereign range, Jef-
> ferson is without rival in New Hampshire. There is as yet no
> large public house in Jefferson. If a good hotel should be erected
> there, the village would soon become one of the most popular re-
> sorts among the mountains.

Within a year, his proposal for a resort hotel at Jefferson became a
reality with the opening of a remarkable resort called The Waumbek.
The promoter built the largest, most luxurious and fashionable hotel in
the North Woods. For a name he went back to the Indian name for
the mountains, but he gave credit to the influence of Dr. King by naming the resort's own personal mountain—a peak rising 3925 feet immediately behind the resort—Starr King Mountain, thus making the
Reverend Dr. King one of the few ministers of the gospel to have a
mountain named after him.

The Waumbek eventually grew to a size that would accommodate
five hundred guests. It was the largest and most popular hotel in the

New England mountains. The elite of the East arrived at The Waumbek in private railway cars, which were left on a siding in front of the hotel. Today The Waumbek has accommodations for fewer guests than it did during its heyday. But it has become one of the most distinctive resorts in the East, with self-contained facilities for about two hundred fifty guests.

Following the Depression, The Waumbek was managed by Herbert Malcolm, an adroit and imaginative resort operator who had learned practical resort management in Florida. He acquired the whole property, including its own Starr King Mountain, and began converting it into a small but luxurious summer resort. Among its special features is a remarkable swimming pool fed by a mountain stream. He established courts for bowling on the green, built several tennis courts, completely remodeled and modernized public and guest rooms, and developed a fine golf course of championship caliber.

Some of the best trout streams in New England are within easy distance of the hotel. Mountain climbing is especially popular, and there are miles of scenic highways. The Connecticut River, which divides New Hampshire from Vermont, is within fifteen miles of the resort and has scenic roads on both sides of it. A toll road to the crest of Mount Washington begins at Glen House, less than twenty-five miles to the southeast, and the cog railway that climbs to the top of Mount Washington from the opposite side of the mountain begins at Bretton Woods, about the same distance to the southwest. Several of New Hampshire's famed scenic notches are within an hour's drive, including Franconia Notch. Near this is the Cannon Mountain Tramway, the first aerial railway of its type built in this country. Its enclosed cars each lift twenty-seven people two thousand feet above the valley.

The Waumbek, easily accessible by highway, is directly on the most northern of the transcontinental highways—spectacularly scenic U.S. 2, which crosses both New Hampshire and Vermont, linking the resort with many main roads from the south and north. By highway the Waumbek is 175 miles from Boston, 385 from New York City. It can be reached by air to Laconia and Lebanon, New Hampshire, where hotel cars meet guests on advance notice. Rail service is provided by the Boston & Maine railway to Jefferson, or the New York, New Haven and Hartford to White River Junction, Vermont. Taxis meet all trains.

The Waumbek is open for the summer season, generally opening in late June and remaining open until mid-October. Rates are American plan. Single rooms begin at $20, double rooms at $32.

TURKEYS, TURNIPS, AND MORGAN HORSES

The most aptly named mountains of New England are the Green Mountains of Vermont. They *are* green, and they gave their name to the state—*"vert monts,"* or green mountains. They are also one of the most beautifully wooded and easily accessible wilderness playgrounds in the East. Though the roots of the mountains are deep strata of Vermont's most celebrated product—marble—most of the slopes and crests are covered with forests, including the Green Mountain National Forest which covers more than 168,000 acres.

Most of the mountain ridges rise from two to three thousand feet, with the two highest peaks, Mansfield and Killington, only a little more than four thousand feet high. The most famous hiking trail in the East, the Long Trail, extends the entire length of the state for more than two hundred fifty miles. There are dozens of good small lakes well stocked with fish. In the winter the slopes are threaded with ski trails and lifts, offering some of the finest skiing in the East. In the summer the slopes and crests, blessed with an invigorating climate, draw thousands of visitors from over the world to provide brisk business for small inns and resorts that range from the luxurious to the primitive.

In the heart of the mountains is one of the most delightful and luxurious small resorts in the East, with a long and picturesque past. Officially called Mountain Top Inn, Cottages and Club, it grew from a barn built in 1781.

The story of Mountain Top Inn, which involves turkeys, turnips, and horses, began in the last half of the eighteenth century. About 1760 families from the coastal regions of New Hampshire and Massachusetts began to trickle into the mountains of Vermont to establish farms in the valleys. Most of the farms failed, for the land was difficult to work and the growing season was short. But here and there farms were successful. One of them was owned by a rugged individualist named Henry Long, who set his farm on a high ridge in the heart of the mountains and cleared some acreage along the ridge and nearby slopes. He began to prosper and soon had the reputation of being a very shrewd and practical farmer. Among his specialties were turnips—the biggest and best in all the region. Another specialty was that famous Vermont product the turkey. Long claimed that his turkeys were better than others because he fed each one a turnip a day. He also raised Morgan horses, a breed of

great stamina and vitality developed in Vermont with an Arabian blood-
line. Other farmers bred and used Morgan horses, but farmer Long's
horses were better than most and had especially lustrous coats. He
claimed that each horse ate three of his giant turnips a day.

Farming in the area came to an abrupt end in 1816, known throughout New England as "the year without a summer." Frost in July killed
many crops and put most farmers out of business. You can stand on the
porches of the Mountain Top Inn today, look across the sweeping valleys
and slopes of the mountain ranges, and see patches identified as abandoned farms. Eventually Long's farm was abandoned too, not because of
frost, but because of fire. The fire destroyed the farmhouse but left the
great barn at the crest of the ridge. After that the Long farm began a
slow return to wilderness until one day it was visited by Mrs. William S.
Barstow, whose husband had made a fortune in the utility business and
had sold out to the Samuel Insull interests of Chicago for fifty million
dollars. Mrs. Barstow, the daughter of an architect and herself trained
as an architect, was looking for a remote but beautiful place where she
could create her own Shangri-La. Her travels, which had carried her
over this country, throughout Europe, and as far as the South Pacific,
came to an end in the Green Mountains and the abandoned Long farm.

Mrs. Barstow discovered the barn standing alone in the center of a
meadow choked with weeds. She also discovered the view from the crest
of the ridge, looking across a mountain lake to range after range of
forested slope. She was so enraptured with the view that she bought
the barn and the abandoned farm and several other farms in the area.
It wasn't much of a job for a trained architect to convert the barn into
a distinctive and spacious guesthouse, and in 1941 she opened it as the
Mountain Top Tavern, reserved exclusively for her guests. The word
of its unique charm spread rapidly among her many friends, who began
to arrive in such increasing numbers that soon she added a wing to the
barn. A few years later she decided that the effort of running her private
resort was too much, and in 1946 she sold the tavern and all the acreage
to its present owners, Mr. and Mrs. William P. Wolfe, of New York.
Mr. Wolfe conducts a resort and hotel sales agency from New York
City.

The Wolfe Company immediately converted the informal but delightful tavern, with its spectacular setting, into a full-scale resort. The
solidly timbered barn was left as the central part of the resort building,
and wings were added north and south. Wide porches and terraces
were added to the east and commanded the wonderful view of lake and
mountains in that direction, and in a wooded grove to the west, guest

cottages were built. A nine-hole golf course was built—one of the most scenic and challenging courses in New England—and just north of the hotel a swimming pool in a beautiful setting was added. A roadway linked the resort with Mountain Top Lake, two square miles of shining water among forested slopes. At the end of the road to the lake, boat docks were established, and a fleet of craft was provided for the use of guests who might want to boat or fish.

Though Mountain Top Inn was built around a barn, there is nothing barnlike in its character. The resort can accommodate more than a hundred guests in fifty rooms in the main building, and more in nearby cottages. It has an air of intimate charm and informal luxury with the emphasis on comfort. The rooms are spacious and modern, and the public rooms are graced with furnishings that suggest the best of a New England and British tradition. Wide porches opening from public lounges have the inevitable rows of wooden rockers, but lawn terraces are set with modern outdoor furniture. Guest cottages across the road vary in size from one to three bedrooms, each different in décor and construction. Most of them have fireplaces, and with the surrounding lawns they suggest the settings of private homes.

Perhaps the most spectacular room of the resort is the big two-level dining room, with a huge fireplace at one end and enormous plateglass picture windows along one side, framing a stunning view of lake and mountain stretching miles to the east.

Though Mountain Top Inn has a near-wilderness setting and commands stunning views of apparently uninhabited forest ranges, it is actually quite accessible. The nearest community of size is Rutland, Vermont—a city of about eighteen thousand people, ten miles southwest of the resort, at the junction of U.S. 7 and U.S. 4. From either main highway well-marked secondary roads lead off to the tiny and charming mountain village of Chittenden, with a delightful village green from which signs point up a mountain slope along a paved road to the resort itself at the crest of the ridge. The nearest rail passenger service to the inn is the line of the Delaware and Hudson railway at Whitehall on U.S. 4 in New York State, just west of the New York-Vermont line and thirty-eight miles from the inn itself. With advance notice hotel cars meet incoming guests arriving by train at Whitehall. Guests can fly almost to the inn itself by taking Mohawk Airlines to Rutland Airport, fourteen miles from the inn itself, where hotel cars meet passengers. Rutland is served by Greyhound and Vermont Transit Lines.

Mountain Top Inn has been drawing an increasing stream of celebrities from all parts of the world. President Dwight D. Eisenhower visited the inns staying two nights during an official tour of New England. Guests who now occupy the sunny corner room that was the President's bedroom during his stay are invariably informed that Eisenhower slept there.

Mountain Top guests come from Switzerland, Bavaria, Austria, Scotland, and England. They almost invariably compare the extraordinary beauty of its setting to some location in Europe.

Though the view from the inn is spectacular, few guests spend much time absorbing it. Activities run the whole gamut of recreation. For golfers the new nine-hole course to the west of the resort is remarkably scenic, and each of the holes is technically challenging. The course spreads over what were once mountain meadows at the crest of a high ridge. The greens are sculptured to provide deception and unexpected surprises. Another barn—not destroyed in the farm fire many years ago —has been converted into an attractive golf clubhouse.

On the lake the resort maintains a sailboat, canoes, an outboard motorboat, rowboats, a speedboat for water skiing, and a pontoon houseboat chiefly used for weekly excursions around the lake, but available for family trips or group fishing. The variety of fish in the lake—as well as in the many nearby mountain streams—includes rainbow and brown trout, smallmouthed bass, sunfish, and, a unique rarity in the region, fresh-water smelt. Though swimming in the lake is possible, most guests prefer the swimming pool, which is lighted for night use and also is a setting for weekly steak broils.

Many guests hike over the miles of wooded trails that spread through the mountains. The Long Trail, east of the resort proper, is the most famous. The mountains are also popular for horseback riding, and excellent horses are available at Mountain Top's own stables. There is good hunting in season for ruffed grouse, woodcock, deer, and black bear.

In recent years nearby Killington Peak has become famous for its skiing. The slopes provide nine lifts with a capacity of seven thousand people an hour. As a result of the boom in skiing in the area, the inn now stays open in the winter and offers skiers special facilities that include package rates and guaranteed skiing in a "ski week," which means from Sunday to Friday. The guarantee is that if skiing is not available, no charge is made for the room occupied by the guest. But the main season for Mountain Top Inn is still summer, June to August, when the temperature seldom goes above eighty at the peak of daytime heat and usually drops to a point at night when open fires are pleasant and sleeping under blankets is required.

Most summer visitors discover after a few days that there is a good deal to see and do in the general area. About six miles north of Rutland is one of the world's largest marble quarries, where there is an exhibit room that explains the story of marble quarrying and production. At West Rutland is Wilson Castle, an unusual expression of pride and vanity built during the middle of the last century to satisfy a homesick English bride. Set on a hundred fifty acres, the castle and grounds resemble an English estate, it has thirty-two rooms, eleven with fireplaces, and is equipped with an extraordinary assortment of decorative oddities, including furniture, statues, rugs, and objects of art.

Southeast of the inn on Route 100A is the quiet village of Plymouth, which is the birthplace of President Calvin Coolidge. The house where Coolidge was born in 1872 is now a memorial. Nearby is the country store that once was run by his father. John Coolidge, the son of the President, still maintains a home in Plymouth and operates one of the best cheese factories in Vermont, where visitors can sample and buy a variety of cheeses.

A little more than an hour's drive to the east of Mountain Top Inn on U.S. 4 is the celebrated small city of Woodstock, nestling in the foothills of the Green Mountains. One of the most famous colonial villages in New England, it has long been popular as a summer resort and winter sports center. Its unusual oval village green is familiar in the East. On the west side of the town is a famous covered bridge.

About thirty miles northwest of Mountain Top Inn is historic Fort Ticonderoga, overlooking Lake Champlain from the west shore. The historic fort, which Ethan Allen and his Green Mountain Boys took by surprise from the British in 1775, has been restored according to early plans and has a museum.

Organized activities at the inn include weekly golf tournaments, softball games, table-tennis tournaments, and evening square dances called by picturesque Vermont callers.

Mountain Top Inn operates on the American plan. Rates for a single room are from $16 to $30 per day. Double bedrooms and twin bedrooms from $14 to $23 per day per person. Rates for children sharing their parents' room are $10 and $12 per day, depending on the age of the children. Cottage accommodations, consisting of a single bedroom with fireplace, dressing room, and bath, are $23 daily per person for double occupancy. The rate for a suite with sitting room is $30 per day in addition to the rate for the double room occupied. Rates for golfing are nominal greens fees, with caddies and carts available at nominal cost. The rate for horseback riding is reasonable and includes the services of the groom. The charge for boats is $2.50 for a half day for a sailboat, outboard motorboat, or canoe. Rowboats are free for the use of guests. Off-season rates, somewhat lower than those of the regular season, are available from Labor Day until July 1. Special group rates are offered during certain seasons.

ROAD OF THE SMUGGLERS

Among the handsome wooded mountains of Vermont, the highest and most celebrated is Mount Mansfield, in the northwest corner of the state, less than twenty miles east of Lake Champlain and only thirty miles south of the Canadian border. Its slopes rise to a series of unusual crests, the highest being 4393 feet.

The profile of Mount Mansfield, as seen from the valley below, resembles an upturned human face. The highest points of the ridge, which forms the mountain's crest, have been called the Forehead, the Lips, the Chin, and finally the Adams Apple. Of the group the Chin is the high point. A three-mile strip of the crest has been set aside as a special preserve because of the many botanical rarities found in the area. One feature of the mountain, a deep cleft between Mount Mansfield and adjoining Sterling Mountain, accounts for the title of this report. For more than a hundred fifty years a forest trail ran through the cleft. During the War of 1812 smugglers found it a safe route over which they could bring contraband into the United States. Caves located close to the trail were useful for hiding themselves and their illegal freight. It was logical that in time the cleft in the mountains would come to be known as Smugglers' Notch. Along that ancient forest trail, now supplanted by a secondary highway, is a small but remarkable resort estate —one of the most sophisticated luxury resorts to operate year round in New England, called the Lodge at Smugglers' Notch.

The reason why the Lodge at Smugglers' Notch grew to be an important resort is linked to the nearby village of Stowe. As a winter sports center, Stowe, Mount Mansfield, and the entire surrounding region have become the most important ski and winter sports area in New England, drawing eager participants from hundreds of miles. For them the Lodge

8. Wentworth-by-the-Sea, at Portsmouth, New Hampshire, is the most celebrated resort on the coast of New England. Its porches command a wide view of sea and shore.

9. Clambakes and lobster roasts on the shore are a favorite dining adventure at Wentworth, which uses more lobsters than any other resort in the country.

Carlton Gould

Edward D. Hippl

10. At York Harbor, Maine, the unusual setting of the Marshall House, once an island in the center of a rocky cove, offers the advantages of agreeable climate and seclusion.

Douglas Armsde

11. Mountain View House, near Whitefield, New Hampshire, began as a farmhouse with a superb view. The present extensive resort still offers guests the same wide vista.

12. Mount Kineo Hotel, one of the few resorts in the country reached only by boat, fills the peninsula at the base of Mount Kineo, Moosehead Lake, Maine.

13. Though most guests at the Lodge at Smuggler's Notch, near Stowe, Vermont, go there in the winter to ski, there are some, like this daring young man, who do a little mountain scaling in the summertime.

Bob Bourdon

14. At Severance Lodge, on lovely Kezar Lake, in Maine, the most popular dining occasion is the weekly mountaintop cookout, featuring chicken broiled over a wood fire.

at Smugglers' Notch is a rendezvous uniquely equipped to provide all that the most fastidious winter sports fan could ask. But it did not become an important resort quickly. Its growth was gradual and, in a sense, unintentional.

About the middle of the last century many New Englanders began to discover that the mountain valleys and slopes of Vermont's Green Mountains had a cool and invigorating climate and offered pleasant relief during the summer. Summer hotels of various types were built in the mountains. At about the same time an enterprising group of promoters contrived to build a road to the top of Mount Mansfield. It was one of the first mountain roads of its type in the East, and the building of it involved engineering problems of unique character, with log bridges spanning the ravines and gullies along the route, a toll road leading to the crest. With the road finished the promoters built the Summit House, at the base of a peak called the Nose. The Summit House was owned by the same company that operated the larger and more fashionable Mount Mansfield Hotel, in Stowe. The Summit House was finished in 1858 and served as a lure to venturesome visitors for about twenty-five years. Then, in 1883, the large hotel in Stowe suffered the fate of so many wooden resort hotels: it burned to the ground. The owners decided not to replace it, but to continue operating the Summit House. But accommodations were limited, and the increasing number of visitors were housed in converted farmhouses for several years. One of the most popular of the farmhouses evolved into a regionally famous and increasingly popular small New England inn, called the Lodge at Smugglers' Notch. It continued as a New England inn, drawing its patronage from summer visitors to the mountains for almost fifty years.

Beginning about 1940, with the building of a single chair lift on Mount Mansfield, scattered ski enthusiasts began to grow into an army of winter sports fans. They soon found that the trails and slopes of the mountain offered some of the best skiing anywhere in the East. The Mount Mansfield Company was formed and operated a succession of lifts on Mount Mansfield and the adjoining Spruce Peak. The next step for the ski-lift operators was to accommodate the skiers who came to the area. They bought the Lodge in 1949 and made many changes and additions, one of which was to convert its kitchen into one of the finest in New England. They imported French chefs and a European staff. A wine cellar was stocked with the best vintage wines. The Lodge at Smugglers' Notch became increasingly renowned, not only as a ski center, but for the excellence and character of its food. Few resorts in the country can claim a better or more interesting dining room.

In the early fifties, it was realized that, though Stowe was a winter sports center, the area was still popular with summer visitors. The management decided to attract summer guests as well and added a heated swimming pool, tennis courts, riding stables, and other recreational facilities.

The cycle of year-round patronage was completed when many companies found that in the spring resorts offered a unique setting for executive meetings. The Lodge has been used by atomic scientists from thirteen countries and by other scientific groups. It has sixty guest rooms in the main house and adjoining buildings. Though small, it is quite complete.

Part of the Lodge's success as a ski and summer resort is because of its setting. The resort spreads over several hundred acres of mountain slope and high valley. South of the resort is the toll-road entrance up Mount Mansfield, and just north ski runs converge at the highway, where chair lifts operate from a parking area. To the east is a double chair lift to the crest of Spruce Peak, second only to Mount Mansfield as a skiing area. Across the road from the resort is a clear, fast-moving mountain stream with foaming rapids and small waterfalls. Behind the main building is a heated swimming pool flanked by a sun terrace. On the east side of the road are tennis courts and lawn games. The stables are nearby. The main lodge has two attractive lounges, a well-stocked library, card rooms, game and television rooms, and a cocktail lounge. Guest rooms are spacious, several have open fireplaces, all are furnished in Early American style. The resort also has guest golfing privileges at Stowe's eight-hole country-club course.

Many guests at the Lodge are likely to describe with joy the quality and character of the meals. Most of the dishes are French in origin, although an outstanding New England specialty will crop up occasionally on the extensive menus.

The Mount Mansfield and Stowe area is one of the most scenic in New England. Mount Mansfield, with its sixty-four miles of ski trails, has dozens of things to see and do year round. In the summer many guests drive up the toll road. This four-and-a-half-mile trip through heavily forested slopes is spectacular and thrilling. The slopes are steep and the turns sharp. It is not intended for the inexperienced driver. The reward at the crest is a marvelous view of seventy-five miles of mountain scenery, including an unusual view of Lake Champlain, twenty-five miles to the west. The route to the north through Smugglers' Notch as far as the Canadian border, thirty miles away, passes the birthplace of President Chester A. Arthur, who was born in a cottage on a farm about four miles west of the route of Route 108, two miles south of the village of Enosburg. The cottage has long since disappeared, but the site is marked by a massive single block of granite standing in complete isolation in a wilderness setting.

Vermont's famed granite district is southwest of Stowe near the city of Barre and Vermont's capital, Montpelier. The world's largest granite quarry is in this area.

To the southwest of Stowe on the shore of Lake Champlain is Vermont's largest city, Burlington, where the University of Vermont is located. A ferry operates from the city, and an unusual highway runs north of the city along a chain of islands in the center of the lake to the Canadian border.

The Lodge at Smugglers' Notch is easily accessible by automobile. It can also be reached by air. Mohawk and Northeast airlines fly to Burlington and Montpelier, each about thirty-five miles away from the resort. New York is three hundred miles to the south. You can take the New York Thruway to Albany, then Route 9 to Saratoga Springs, then a succession of connecting routes to Burlington, from which Route U.S. 2, Interstate 89, and Route 108 lead to the Lodge. An alternate New York route is the Taconic State Parkway and Route 22 and U.S. 7 north to Burlington, thence U.S. 2 and 108 to the Lodge. Boston is 230 miles to the southeast, and a succession of excellent highways lead northwest from that city to Waterbury through Montpelier, and at Waterbury Route 100 and 108 to the Lodge. The nearest large city in Canada is Montreal, 120 miles to the northwest. The most direct route from the west would be through Albany and the New York Thruway, then the normal New York route to the Lodge from Albany.

Rates at the Lodge are American plan, beginning at $15 per day per person, and up to $40 per day per person for the larger suites.

THRESHOLD OF THE WILDERNESS

One of the true primitive areas that remain in the United States is the vast wilderness region of northwestern Maine, which covers several thousand square miles. It is a spectacular land of low, craggy mountains, an immense primeval forest, and hundreds of lakes. Few roads or railways penetrate its heart. The land is a paradise for hunters and fishermen who trek through it on forest trails or paddle canoes up the clear little rivers and across the hundreds of lakes.

The largest lake is Moosehead—an extraordinary body of water forty miles in length and ranging in width from one to twenty miles. Its surface is at an elevation of a thousand feet. Moosehead Lake is one of the largest fresh-water lakes in the country, and one of the most ruggedly beautiful bodies of water anywhere. It has been a favorite base for hunters and fishermen for more than a hundred fifty years. Rugged wooded mountains rise around it. One of the mountains, a solid mass of flint called Mount Kineo, almost fills a promontory that thrusts into the lake from the east and rises to an elevation of 1806 feet, about 800 feet above the surface of the lake itself. At the base of the sheer cliffs of Mount Kineo a flat peninsula thrusts two miles into the lake. At the tip of the peninsula, spreading over 1500 acres is one of the oldest resorts in North America. On the site, one hotel or another, called Kineo House or Kineo Hotel, has been serving guests who sought wilderness isolation since Captain Joshua Fogg built the first primitive lodge there, in 1848. It was followed by a half-dozen successive Kineo hotels, each more elaborate than the preceding one. Fire usually dictated the need for a replacement.

Kineo reached its climax in 1912 with a huge, rambling wooden building that claimed to be colonial in design. Long wings extended behind a seven-story façade projecting toward the lake.

The whole thing was a Victorian monstrosity that was the pride of its builders and the talk of the resort world. An advertisement issued at the time to describe its features and facilities ended with this statement: "All this makes the new Mount Kineo House the largest and most luxurious inland water hotel in America, with ample accommodations for over 500 guests."

For a number of years after its grand opening in 1912, the new Mount Kineo House was an increasingly popular haven for the rich and fashionable who wanted a luxurious but isolated summer refuge. No highway approached it. All guests arrived by steamer from Greenville, at the south end of the lake.

But the inevitable occurred—the hotel burned to the ground. For the first time in its history the owners did not replace the destroyed building with a bigger one. Instead they built a small hotel with accommodations for about two hundred people. It is the present, modern, luxurious resort in the wilderness with eighty guest rooms and suites and an assortment of facilities, some of which the proprietors of the 1912 hotel never dreamed of. One thing hasn't changed: Mount Kineo Hotel is still isolated. Guests reach it only by boat, although the trip is much shorter now than it was in 1912. It's only a mile across the lake from Rockwood, which is at the end of Route 15 along the lake's west shore. The hotel provides a garage at Rockwood for the cars of its guests, and has its own ferry across the lake.

Another thing that hasn't changed since 1912 is the setting: the wide, beautifully landscaped finger of land thrusting into the lake from the base of Mount Kineo, which lifts its sheer cliffs above the lake in a spectacular rampart. The clear blue waters of Moosehead, its wooded shores and islands all add to the unspoiled wilderness setting.

There is nothing primitive about the resort itself. The guest rooms are as luxurious as could be asked. In addition to the main hotel, there are housekeeping cottages for groups near the lake shore. A large heated swimming pool is set in a wide sun plaza of paved and sheltered terraces. The golf course is actually two separate nine-hole courses. There are a trapshooting range and a tennis court. But, more important, there is a fleet of small craft for guests to take full advantage of the lake.

As in the beginning, the chief activity is fishing. Tackle, bait, and guides are provided. The catch is usually salmon, trout, togue, and almost every fishing trip is rewarded. Guests also may take sight-seeing trips in one of the hotel cruisers. Other excursions include picnics on the beach at the base of Mount Kineo, where steak cookouts are held.

An important asset of the resort is the unique purity and pollen-free character of the mountain air, which makes Mount Kineo a special haven for those who suffer from hay fever and other respiratory ailments.

Mount Kineo Hotel is fairly easy to reach. The nearest community of any size is Bangor, ninety-five miles to the southeast. From Bangor, U.S. 2 leads west twenty-six miles to Newport. Maine Route 7 leads north to its junction with Route 15 at Guilford, where the real wilderness, the Maine northwoods country, begins. Route 15 leads north through the forests and along the west side of the lake for about fifty miles. Alternate routes include: U.S. 2, leading from the west to its junction at Newport with Route 7; Interstate 95, a limited-access freeway along the Atlantic coast to a junction with U.S. 2 at Skowhegan, twenty-four miles west of Newport.

You can fly into Bangor on Northeast Airlines, where taxi service at moderate rates is available direct to Mount Kineo Hotel. Car-rental service is also available. Private planes can land on the paved Greenville airport, where rental cars are available. Or guests can be met by the hotel. The Canadian Pacific Railway provides service to Greenville Junction from Montreal and from St. John, New Brunswick.

Mount Kineo Hotel is open for the summer season only, June 15 through Labor Day. Rates are full American plan. Single-room rates are $20 per day and up; double-room rates begin at $34. Two-room suites with connecting bath begin at $58 for four persons.

LUXURY IN THE NORTHWOODS

On the wilderness border between New Hampshire and Maine, the slopes of the White Mountains drop down steeply into Maine from the crests of the Presidential Range. In Maine, five miles from the border, where the mountains merge with the foothills, is a small but stunning lake named Kezar. It's about ten miles long and from a half mile to a mile and a half in width. Part of it resembles a wide river. From its southern end one of Maine's famous little rivers, the Saco, flows southeast to the sea. The west shores of the lake are quite rugged, rising in abrupt slopes in a series of terraces toward lofty summits, and the eastern shore is gentler and less rugged. The lake is almost entirely surrounded by forest.

As the lakes of western Maine go, Kezar is neither large nor famous. There are better known and larger lakes among the thousands that mark the wilderness forests of Maine. To the north is a lake with an incredible name—Mooselookmeguntic. Twenty-five miles to the southeast is big, booming Sebago Lake, which is rimmed with resorts. But Kezar, on no main highway, and a little hard to find, needs neither size nor fame. There are those who regard it as one of the most beautiful lakes in Maine, or for that matter in the East. It has been described as having a special quality, an "intimate softness of the land." Geologists say that the "intimate softness of the land" is the result of glacial action more than ten thousand years ago—the slow sculpturing and grinding of ice a mile deep that scooped out the bed of the lake. Besides shaping the land, the glaciers left the immediate region with one unique heritage: a great variety of minerals and gem stones, over two hundred, which can be found in rock outcroppings and along stream beds.

Kezar Lake first gained local fame because of the fishing, which was superb. The lake was once alive with hungry, landlocked salmon, and there were trout and bass in the lake and the streams that fed into it. Admiral Peary, the discoverer of the North Pole, was an early fisherman. He is said to have kept a bateau on the Saco River just south of the lake. At any rate, so many fishermen began to flock to Kezar Lake that fishing camps (like hundreds of others scattered through the Maine wilderness) began to be established along its shores. One of the most popular was started in 1903 by an enterprising gentleman named Benjamin Brown, who obviously had an eye for beauty. He established his camp on the eastern shore of the lake where two small coves framed a wooded point. One of the widest stretches of the lake spread in front of the camp to the steep western shore, with the majestic ranges of the White Mountains standing as a backdrop.

Brown's Camp prospered, but today this remarkable resort is now called Severance Lodge. How Brown's Camp evolved into Severance Lodge is a unique tale. By 1924 Brown had built his fishing camp into a profitable enterprise. Then he decided to extend his activities to Florida. He took his profits and everything he could borrow and lost most of it in the 1926 crash of the Florida land boom. The rest of his money he lost in the early stages of the Depression. His camp, heavily mortgaged, went bankrupt. The next year two banks that held a joint mortgage on the property failed. Then the main lodge at Brown's Camp burned down. It seemed a final and sorry end to a once prosperous enterprise. Curiously, it was a beginning.

In the meantime Harold Severance, who loved Maine and its unspoiled wilderness, had decided that someday he wanted to own and run a resort. It seemed a more exciting way to live than the real estate business, which he was in with his brother. Through a succession of jobs ranging from the Harvard Club in Boston to the Newport House at Bar Harbor, he began training himself to become a resort operator.

He had heard about the fire at Brown's Camp, and he visited the site, which he found beautiful. The wreckage of the camp was shabby and dismal, but the price of the property was a bargain. That was in 1934. With such resources as he could command, Severance put in five years of hard work to convert the devastated camp into a comfortable lodge. The next step was to make the lodge into a true and complete resort, luxurious enough to satisfy the most fastidious guest without offending or marring the wilderness charm of the setting. This took another twenty years, although it continues, with improvements each year.

Severance Lodge spreads over a hundred acres, all heavily forested. Set within the forest and almost invisible from the lake are the guest cottages, which can accommodate 132 guests. The cottages are linked by forest trails that are carefully lighted for night use. The resort faces the lake shore, where most of the facilities are. The shore swings in and out of the two original coves that made the Brown fishing camp so convenient. Off a point of land that goes into the lake between the two coves is a tiny island that is crested with a miniature forest of tall pines and linked to the land by a causeway built of boulders. In the center of the island is one of the larger guest cottages—Everbreeze. The central lodge building is across the cove from the island. It has lounges, a dining room, a few guest rooms, and a kitchen. Flanking the central lodge on either side are cottages, almost all with a lake view. Along the lake are two bathing areas, a shuffleboard court, tennis court, an outdoor grill and amphitheater, and a nine-hole putting green. At the head of the cove near the main lodge is the resort's boat dock, with slips for more than a dozen craft, including the resort's own large fleet of power boats, canoes, skiffs, and sailboats.

In converting Brown's primitive camp into a luxurious wilderness resort, Harold Severance has been careful to build nothing that in design or décor, either inside or out, would be out of harmony with the rustic, sylvan beauty of the forest setting. All the buildings are constructed of log or stained timber and are similar in design to buildings often found in national parks. Severance once described his resort as "an inconspicuous blending into a softened landscape." Most of the cottages are wood-paneled. The furniture and fittings are made of native woods.

Three of the guest lodges are noted for their distinctive character. Everbreeze has a large paneled living room, an enclosed sun porch, and eight bedrooms. Tam Glen, near the bathing beach, has a huge living room with a picture window, and six corner bedrooms. A brook, waterfalls, and a flower garden are on the immediate grounds. The Chalet, on the lake shore, is Swiss in design. It has a two-story living room, a huge fireplace, balconies, a wide porch, and six bedrooms.

Though the resort has the appearance of rustic simplicity, there is nothing primitive in the comfort and luxury. Each guest cottage has a living room with a fireplace. All of the bathrooms are modern and complete. Every appointment and accessory is designed for comfort. There are dozens of little extras. The enthusiastic staff adds nice touches of service. Many guests returning to their cottages at night are delighted to discover that the lights have been turned on, the fire replenished, and the beds turned back. Early each morning a houseboy starts a fire, fills the wood box, and stocks the refrigerator.

Though guest life at Severance Lodge is informal, there is seldom a lack of activity. The lake is, of course, a base for sailing, all water sports, and sight-seeing in one of the several speedboats. Organized canoe trips are frequently held on the Saco River. Each week the resort stages its most celebrated diversion—a forest cookout on a ridge high above the lake. Guests are ferried across the lake in speedboats and are shuttled up the mountainside in jeeps. Dozens of chickens are broiled over a vast open fire with special equipment.

Superb food is a specialty of the resort. It is international and is prepared and served with gourmet touches that seem astonishing in the North Woods. Many guests relish snails at the Lodge, where they are served in the manner of the best Parisian restaurants. Oftentimes guests will tell you that the resort's cheese fondue is better than can be found in Switzerland. The resort's beautifully prepared salads are matched in few restaurants anywhere.

Some dishes are typical of Maine, such as the lobster suppers featured at a buffet each week. A dining accessory that late risers relish is a wheeled vehicle called the Sleepy Head Buffet, which is trundled into the main lobby after the closing of the dining room for breakfast, and guests may forage for themselves. Complete breakfasts, with hot dishes hot and cold dishes iced, are available.

Guests who want exercise will find plenty of it. The resort's nine-hole putting green is generally filled. Those who want a full round of golf can drive to the nearby Lake Kezar Club, where there is a nine-hole course, designed by Donald Ross, that is regarded as one of the most interesting and challenging in Maine. It has water hazards, gullies to pitch over, and well-trapped greens. One hole, the second, has a pine tree in the middle of the fairway behind a gully and a brook, making the 314-yard hole a probable five. The course is 2988 yards long and a par 36. Severance Lodge guests have all privileges on the course.

The lake is an endless source of activity. Fishing for black bass is good enough to challenge most guests, trout fishing is fine in nearby streams, and pickerel and white perch are caught in many nearby ponds. The resort can arrange for guides, tackle, bait, and boats. Sailing and canoeing on the lake take place every day. Often a group charters one of the resort's speedboats.

Some Lodge guests become enthusiastic collectors of semiprecious and precious stones as a result of their visit. With guidance from Harold Severance and his staff, they hike over forest trails hunting quartz and garnets. The general region has produced the world's largest beryl crystal, as well as the largest aquamarine gem ever found in North America.

Part of the special charm of Severance Lodge is its isolation. Thousands of acres of forest and the waters of Kezar Lake insulate the resort from the sights and sounds of the world. But it is actually easy to reach the resort by highway, and there are express highways not far away. Portland, Maine, is one and a half hours away; Boston (157 miles) is three and a half hours; Montreal, six hours; and New York (375 miles) seven hours. From New York and Boston the shortest and most scenic route is along the shore to Portsmouth, New Hampshire, Route 16 to Conway, New Hampshire, then U.S. 302 to Fryeburg, and Route 5 north along the shore of Kezar Lake to Centre Lovell. The slightly obscured entrance gates to the resort are on the left-hand side of Route 5, just past Centre Lovell going downhill through the forest. A faster but less interesting route is straight up the coast on the Maine Turnpike to Portland, then U.S. 302, Route 93 to Centre Lovell, and Route 5 to the resort gates.

Guests arriving by train usually go to Portland, where rental cars are available, or a bus will take you to Fryeburg. On advance notice a Lodge car will meet the bus at Fryeburg, Maine, or Conway, New Hampshire.

Guests arriving by air usually fly to Portland, rent a car there, or take the bus to Fryeburg, making the same arrangements to be met as do guests arriving by train. An alternate possibility is scheduled service to Portland (Northeast Airlines) and air taxi to the Maine airport at Fryeburg.

Severance Lodge is a summer resort, its normal season running from June 14 to October 14. Because it has an extremely high rate of occupancy by a small army of regular guests who return year after year, advance reservations are required. All rates are based on full American plan, which includes accommodations, meals, use of all sports facilities, cookouts, canoe trips, and other diversions. Nominal additional charges are made for golf at the Lake Kezar Club and the use of some of the boats. Variations in rates are based on the type of accommodation. Single-room cottages for two are from $18 to $20 per day per person. Cottages with living room and bedroom are from $21 to $23 per day per person. Rooms in the main lodge are $17 per day with private bath.

CHAPTER 4

PINELANDS AND
SAND HILLS

By any standard, that region of North and South Carolina between the coastal plain and the mountains to the west would be an improbable place for a fine resort. A geological accident that occurred hundreds of millions of years ago left the soil of the region almost pure sand in which the only thing that grew was the longleaf pine tree. The area has little scenic appeal—there aren't any mountains and there are few lakes.

But today the sand-hill region is the setting for one of the most celebrated resorts in the country—Pinehurst, in North Carolina. Clustered about Pinehurst are resorts of lesser renown. The establishment of Pinehurst as the greatest golfing center in the world began in New England, and one of the major factors in its development was the appetite of the American people for ice-cream sodas.

After the early settlement of North Carolina, settlers began to drift west toward the mountains. On the way they found superb forests of towering pines growing from a soil so sandy that it was useless for farming. But the trees themselves were an abundant source of naval stores, turpentine, pine pitch, and timber. Settlers cut down the trees with such abandon that at the end of the Civil War the great pine forests had been reduced to a bleak wilderness of stumps and sand dunes. What the ravagers of the forest didn't know was that for some odd meteorological reason the region of the sand hills had an extraordinarily good climate—dry, mild, and healthful.

About the time the North Carolina settlers were busily cutting down the forests, the second decisive element in the destiny of Pinehurst took place. In 1835 a child named James W. Tufts was born in Charlestown, Massachusetts. He was a boy of energy, determination, and imagination—qualities that endured through an eventful and remarkable life. When the boy was sixteen years old, he was apprenticed to a local druggist, and by the time he was twenty-one, he had branched out for himself and soon owned three drugstores. In addition to being apothecary stores, selling drugs and patent medicines, drugstores were community centers for serving ice cream. Noting the increasing appetite of his customers for such concoctions, Tufts decided that there was a bright future in concentrating on soda fountains. He started making extracts, then began to make the soda-water apparatus used in drugstores. Before long he had developed a line of silver-plated accessories such as pitchers, dishes, and vases, which every soda fountain worthy of the name had to own. He also invented a machine for making and dispensing soda water at soda fountains. Before long he was rich. In 1891, when he was fifty-six years old, his company was consolidated with several other firms to become the American Soda Fountain Company, the largest in the world.

In 1895, Tufts turned the management of his company over to others and began using his fortune to do things that he had always wanted to do. He had never been a particularly robust man and for reasons of health had taken many vacations. He had traveled south and was one of the early pioneers in recognizing the advantage of Florida winters. Tufts had long cherished the idea of starting a colony where people of modest means could live pleasantly in a warmer climate during the cold New England winters. He began searching for the perfect setting. After investigation he decided on the North Carolina sand hills.

One day in 1895, Henry Page, who lived in the village of Aberdeen, North Carolina, in the heart of the desolate sand-hills country, was visited by Tufts, who explained that he wanted to purchase a large tract from Page, who owned most of it. The deal was quickly concluded: Tufts paid a dollar an acre for five thousand acres of desolate sand-hill land. The price, in terms of real estate values of the region, was outrageous, since the land without its timber was regarded as worthless. As Tufts' grandson wrote many years later: "The soil was so poor that it was said to be necessary to bury a person with commercial fertilizer in order to afford some prospect of his rising on the day of judgement."

But Tufts was not interested in burying people. On the contrary, he wanted to help them live more abundantly. He began developing his colony with unparalleled energy, good judgment, and imagination. One of the experts he hired was the distinguished landscape architect Frederick Law Olmsted, who had gained a national reputation for his imaginative use and development of land. One of his achievements had been the conversion of a rock-strewn wilderness on the edge of New York City into Central Park. Basing his North Carolina development on the ideal New England village, Olmsted proceeded to lay out a complete village among the sand hills. It had a village center, a church site, and delightfully curving streets. To restore the original verdancy of the land, Olmsted bought more than two hundred thousand plants, nearly fifty thousand of which were imported from France. Pinehurst today has a natural forest cover in addition to thousands of flowering plants and trees bordering the curving lanes.

The Pinehurst settlement was first opened to guests six months after Tufts had made his deal with Page. Rapid completion of the new village was an incredible achievement in planning and development. Streets had to be graded, public utilities provided, cottages and stores built, and an electric railway built to the nearby village of Southern Pines. Tufts first built a small hotel called Holly Inn, which was opened in 1896. Holly Inn, at Pinehurst today, a direct outgrowth of the first inn, is one of two luxurious resort hotels now owned and managed by the descendants of Tufts as a part of the resort village of Pinehurst. When the village opened, there was, in addition to the hotel, a store, several boardinghouses, and about sixteen small cottages. Although the streets had been built and a water system installed, it still was a bleak town. There were few trees except for a handful of stunted, twisted pines that had been regarded as worthless for lumber. The tract had been swept by repeated forest fires, adding a note of ruin and desolation. The buildings stood naked along the streets and lanes, and it would take several years before the landscaping miracle that Olmsted and his associates were to accomplish would begin to show results.

But Pinehurst did have something to offer, as its early guests quickly learned: climate. The climate can best be described as benign, with dry mild air and an aromatic quality derived from remnants of the piny forests of the region.

Tufts proved to be as good a promoter as he was a planner and builder. He sent out innumerable letters and booklets—many going to physicians—stating the case for his village. One of his letters said:

My choice of a location in North Carolina was made after careful consideration. There are curative virtues in the aromatic breath of the pine of whatever variety and wherever found, but there is abundant proof that the long-leaf pine far surpasses all other kinds in healing power.

Those whose health is impaired must have such comforts and conveniences as they have at home—good nourishing food, well-cooked and daintily served, pleasant surroundings, and agreeable companions, interests, amusements and occupations. But how few such places there are where people of moderate means can go to spend the winter. It is not intended to be a sanitarium. It has no hospital features. It is a bright, cheery village, artistically laid out, possessed of all modern conveniences. I desire it to attract only a refined and intelligent class of people. To such, whether of large or small means, it offers advantages absolutely unequalled.

Early Pinehurst visitors had to entertain themselves. They were nearly all people of modest means—retired schoolteachers, army officers, ministers, and a few of Tufts' associates and business friends. They had strong cultural and religious interests. They gave recitals, played cards, danced, walked, took carriage trips around the country, and, when they felt the need of more strenuous exercise, they played roque—a variation of croquet played with a mallet and ball. Some guests occasionally rode bicycles, others went quail hunting, but nobody played golf.

In fact, there was little golf played anywhere in those days. Golf was just beginning to cross the Atlantic and find favor here and there. In the United States the first golf country club was established on Long Island in 1891. But more and more golfing enthusiasts were beginning to describe the joys of the great Scottish game. One of these enthusiasts came to Pinehurst by chance in 1897 with a set of golf clubs, and extolled the pleasures of playing. Soon Pinehurst residents were enthusiastically annoying the cows in the village pasture by banging away at little white balls. Tufts was an early convert and promptly set about building a proper golf course. In 1898 a nine-hole course was laid out, with Tufts giving his personal attention to its construction. The course was designed by Dr. Leroy Culver, one of the few people in the country who knew what a golf course should be. The early holes consisted of no more than built-up tees; greens were a few feet of rolled ground surrounding the hole. The first clubhouse was built in 1899. The next year two Europeans visited Pinehurst with results that became decisive in the community's destiny. One of the visitors was Harry Vardon, the British golf champion who played the nine-hole Pinehurst course in 1900 and was so enthusiastic that he began to tell all his friends about the fine golfing facilities there. That same year Donald Ross, a young golf professional from Scotland, visited Pinehurst and met Tufts, who was seeking a professional to take over the golfing responsibilities at Pinehurst. The two men struck up a friendship and made a deal that was to last many years. Donald Ross became a resident of the Pinehurst community and there he died in 1948. During his lifetime he was instrumental in transforming the New England village set among the sand hills into the most famous golfing center in the world, with five great golf courses. Ross served as a designer and a consultant on golf-course design, and worked on more than six hundred golf courses throughout the country.

Although the game made Pinehurst famous throughout the world and provided the chief activity for visitors, it was only one of a number of Tufts' special interests.

Another of his specialties was religion. One of Tufts' closest friends and associates in Boston had been the great religious leader Edward Everett Hale, who was the grand-nephew of Nathan Hale, the martyr-spy of the Revolution. Dr. Hale had been minister of the South Congregational Church of Boston and for several years was the chaplain of the United States Senate. His fame rests mainly on a slender book called *Man Without a Country*, which is known to nearly every schoolboy. Dr. Hale was a frequent visitor at Pinehurst and often preached there. His influence on the community and on Tufts was profound. It resulted in the construction of the community-sponsored chapel, which is one of the loveliest churches in America.

By 1901 the fame of Pinehurst's climate and its renown as a golfing center had spread so widely that the resort community was a huge success. The original Holly Inn could no longer accommodate the number of guests who flocked to it. Thus the larger and more luxurious Carolina was built. It was called Queen of the South and became a social and vacation center with more than two hundred fifty rooms and the kind of spacious elegance that well served the leisurely life at Pinehurst.

However, golf was the magnet that drew guests and golfers from everywhere. Many played at Pinehurst for the first time. They would take a few lessons, buy a few clubs, and return to their homes determined to organize a local golf club. It is impossible to say how many community golf clubs today had their inception at Pinehurst.

The first nine-hole course was opened in 1898. One year later the nine holes were extended to eighteen. The first nine holes of the second course were built in 1901; in 1903 nine holes were added to that course.

In 1907 the first nine holes of the third course were added; in 1910 that course became eighteen holes. By 1919 a fourth eighteen-hole course had been completed. Over the years the courses were constantly changed and improved, a process that is still going on with the present redevelopment and redesigning of a number of Pinehurst's now famous golf holes. The fifth course was built in 1961.

Tufts died in 1902 at the age of sixty-seven, with his dream of a healthful resort community developed far beyond his first hopes and expectations. It became the most important golfing center in the world and a resort that drew guests from every corner of the country for the fall and spring seasons, which glittered with social occasions, golfing, and other sports events. Pinehurst, while a village in the actual sense, was not a village in the political sense. In 1911, though, Pinehurst was granted a special charter as a private business enterprise operating under the laws of North Carolina. The charter granted the owners the right to exercise police powers. A special legislative act established the geographic limits, which are a perfect circle approximately two miles in diameter, so Pinehurst is probably the only community in the country established legally within a true circular border.

Today it is a community of great charm. Over the years its landholdings have been increased to preserve the village and to ensure the character of its surroundings. No longer is the land a bleak, stump-strewn wilderness. The years also have brought maturity to Olmsted's plantings, so that not only has the longleaf-pine forest been restored, but the forest cover of the whole region has been greatly enhanced. Driving along the winding roads of the village in the spring is an adventure in floral splendor. Olmsted's roads are as he planned them: all of them curve, some wind and turn, and still others form circles around special areas. As a result most visitors inevitably get lost, but in doing so discover sections that they had not expected to see. Hundreds of houses face the roads throughout the village. They range from modest cottages to luxurious estates, and many are opened year round. Owners have discovered that the summer climate of Pinehurst is not nearly as hot as it is in other places.

Pinehurst has several distinctive features as a community. One is the village center, with the usual cluster of shops and civic buildings, all controlled to preserve the general air of casual charm. The main office of Pinehurst, Inc., the Tufts family corporation by which two generations of the family manage their unique property, is in the heart of the village. They divide up the chores. Richard S. Tufts, grandson of the founder of Pinehurst, supervises the golfing activities and is considered one of the foremost golfing authorities in the world.

Facing the village green is the Holly Inn, one of the two hotels maintained by the Pinehurst company. It developed from the original Holly Inn, but since 1896 has increased its facilities, one of which is a handsome new swimming pool, beautifully screened behind the towering holly trees that give the inn its name. There are ninety guest rooms and suites and a variety of public rooms. Guests have the use of all Pinehurst facilities. A few years ago the policy of the resort was changed to permit the opening of the Holly Inn in the summer, and this met with such notable success that the inn is usually filled during those months when the rates are substantially lower.

The other hotel is the Carolina, huge and rambling, with extending wings and fringes of wide, covered porches. It dominates extensive landscaped grounds and is larger, more spacious, and more luxurious than the Holly Inn. The Carolina has rooms and suites enough to accommodate about four hundred fifty people. Its rooms are Georgian colonial in décor and include one of the handsomest dining rooms in the South. Special facilities include a shopping arcade, a billiard room, and a ballroom for nightly dancing in season. The Carolina opens about mid-September and closes about May 15.

South of the village center stands the graceful village chapel, whose design suggests the meetinghouses of New England. The church is a favorite subject for artists and photographers. Across the road is a cluster of log cabins which has become a curious Pinehurst institution. Called the Woman's Exchange, it is a clearinghouse and shop for locally designed products, particularly needlework, and for antiques.

About two blocks south of the chapel is Pinehurst's famed country club. It dominates the recreational life of the community, with the fairways of its five great golf courses spreading from the colonnaded porches that surround the clubhouse building. Construction was begun in 1901. It is filled with a fascinating clutter of souvenirs and pictures of great golfing events at Pinehurst over the years. The clubhouse stands on a low hill, and below it are beautifully kept lawn-bowling greens that have been the scene of several annual tournaments. Clay tennis courts are nearby. Beside the clubhouse is a special fairway called Maniac Hill, the driving range for golf practice. The fairways spread over the sand-hill terrain between avenues of tall, dark pines, each fairway tipped with its immaculately manicured green.

The five courses vary in character and challenge. Some holes are remarkably scenic—delightfully rolling land set against backdrops of forest, jeweled here and there with little lakes that are water hazards. In the spring of the year the floral glory of Pinehurst is at its peak.

The Number 2 course is regarded as the most demanding at Pinehurst and is one of the truly great professional courses of the world. Donald Ross, who designed it, regarded Number 2 as the best he ever built. One golfing writer wrote:

> What makes it great is its marvelous design, the skillful trapping and the genius with which each hole has been shaped. The course is eminently fair, can be played by the average golfer without pain, yet stretches out to be a magnificent challenge to long-hitting golf stars.

Pinehurst's most scenic course is Number 5, which stretches south from the clubhouse. A cluster of holes with greens and approaching fairways is built around a small lake. But the most scenic of all Pinehurst holes is probably Number 15, on the fifth course, called the Cathedral Hole, where an oddly shaped green is set like an emerald among the towering pines.

Professional golfers and golf-course architects consider the Pinehurst terrain the best in the world for golf because of the combination of sandy soil and climate. One can play at Pinehurst thirty minutes after a drenching rain. The courses vary in length. Number 2, the championship course, is the longest—7051 yards, par 72. The shortest course is Number 4, traditionally regarded as a beginners' course—5990 yards, par 70. Number 4 also has the shortest hole at Pinehurst, par 3, 130 yards. The longest Pinehurst hole is Number 10, on the championship course, a tremendous 596 yards, par 5, regarded by experts as one of the most challenging golf holes anywhere.

Another distinctive Pinehurst facility is a famous race track with stables for several hundred horses. For more than thirty years the Pinehurst track has been an important training camp in the South for the winter training and racing of horses. The reasons that make Pinehurst a great golfing center—a mild and invigorating winter climate—are apparently equally good for horses. Owners and trainers welcome the pure water and the resiliency of the sandy soil, which is valuable in breaking in yearlings. Some of the great record-setting trotters and pacers in the country have been trained at Pinehurst. During the winter season, when the stables are full and the track in constant use for exercising and trial racing, watching the horses run is daily diversion for Pinehurst guests. Races are held almost every afternoon during the spring season.

In its early days Pinehurst was famed as a center for quail hunting, with the resort supplying guides and dogs for hunting on fifty thousand acres of leased land. Though changing conditions of land ownership and farming have sharply reduced the land area suitable for quail hunting, Pinehurst in recent years has re-established its hunting preserve on about two thousand acres. The quail season runs from October 15 to Thanksgiving, and from February 17 to March 31. Dove shooting is good; trapshooting and skeet-shooting ranges also are maintained.

For those who prefer to ride horses rather than watch them, the resort has a stable full of saddle horses and maintains many miles of all-weather riding trails through the pine forests. Pinehurst guests attend horse shows, steeplechases, and fox hunts.

Most people go to Pinehurst because of the climate and facilities and never stray beyond its limits, but those who do wander discover that the surrounding region is pleasant to drive through and has some attractive things to see. Just west of the Pinehurst property is a nursery called Clarendon Gardens, which has one of the finest collections of exotic shrubs and flowers in the South. Not far away is Fort Bragg, the home base of the 82nd Airborne Division. Pinehurst guests are welcome to watch practice jumps, and many do. Tobacco auctions are held in most nearby towns.

Pinehurst is easily accessible by automobile, train, or plane. Several main north-south highways pass nearby. Interstate Highway 95 passes through Fayetteville, thirty miles east of Pinehurst. The nearest main highway is U.S. 1, which passes through Southern Pines and Aberdeen a few miles east of Pinehurst. The route of U.S. 220, running almost due north and south, is about fifteen miles west of Pinehurst.

Guests arriving by train are met by a hotel bus at the nearest station, Southern Pines. Pinehurst has its own airport, with service by Piedmont Airlines and connecting flights at Charlotte, Raleigh, and Fayetteville. Regular service begins in October and continues through April. All flights into the Pinehurst airport are met on advance notice by the hotel bus, and at Charlotte, Raleigh, or Fayetteville when convenient connections to the Piedmont schedules cannot be made.

Guest-room rates at Pinehurst's two hotels vary seasonally. At the larger, more luxurious Carolina, lowest rates are from December 1 to January 31, when a single room, American plan, costs $14 and up, and a double room, American plan, $26 and up. The highest rates are charged during the fashionable spring season, from March until closing, when single-room rates begin at $18 and double-room rates at $38. At the smaller and less pretentious Holly Inn, the lowest rates are from November 26 to February 1 and again during the summer season, June 1 to September 21, when a single room, American plan, costs $12, and a double room, American plan, costs $22. Highest rates at the Holly are from February 16 to April 27, when a single room, American plan, is $15, a double room $30. During the summer there are special package rates for golfers—seven days and six nights, American plan, $87; three days and two nights, $34. The package includes greens fees at the Pinehurst Country Club.

Pinehurst golf fees during the early, late, and mid-season run $4 per day, $17 per week. During the fall and spring seasons the fees are $4 per round. Caddie fees for eighteen holes are $3 for one bag, $5 for two. Tennis and lawn-bowling fees run from $1 per day to $15 per month. Saddle horses can be hired at $4 for the first hour and slightly lower rates for successive hours. You can hire a double team with driver for $10 for a half day, $15 for a full day; a horse and buggy with no driver, $6 for a half day, $10 for a full day. Hunting fees are $3 per person for dove shooting. Quail shooting runs $30 for a half day and $40 for a full day, including services of a guide and dog. Pinehurst stocks a number of private ponds for the exclusive use of guests, with a nominal fee of $1 per day per person for their use. The catch is usually bluegill or bass.

OTHER SAND-HILLS RESORTS

Though Pinehurst is the only self-sufficient and self-contained resort estate in the Carolinas, there are a number of good small resorts nearby offering the same advantages of climate and terrain that have made Pinehurst so celebrated. Two worthy of note are just outside the small city of Southern Pines:

Mid-Pines Club and Golfotel, a pleasant combination of small resort and motor inn, with seventy-three rooms, operated on the American plan, and a good dining room. It features a fine eighteen-hole golf course, 6800 yards long, par 70. The resort is two miles west of Southern Pines on Route 2. Rates start at $22 per day for a single; $36 per day for a double.

Almost next door is the *Pine Needles Lodge and Country Club,* even smaller than the Mid-Pines Club, with thirty-four American-plan rooms offering golf, fishing, and a heated swimming pool. Its beautifully maintained eighteen-hole golf course is rolling but not too hilly, 6412 yards long, par 71. American-plan rates start at $33 per day for a single; double at $40 per day. Both resorts are open year round.

From the region of Southern Pines the sand-hill zone stretches into South Carolina.

Aiken, South Carolina, near the border of Georgia about fifteen miles northeast of Augusta, is a town of about eleven thousand people. It has been popular for a generation, particularly among horse lovers. Each year polo ponies, trotting, steeplechase, and riding horses are wintered there. Aiken calls itself the polo capital of America. It has three excellent golf courses, offers tennis, trapshooting, quail and dove hunting in season, fishing on dozens of ponds and small lakes set among the pine forests and sand hills.

CHAPTER 5

TIDELANDS AND
GOLDEN ISLES

The tidewater lands of the Atlantic seaboard—in the north the shores of Virginia and Maryland, and in the south portions of the coast of South Carolina and the whole coast of Georgia—are among the most pleasing and useful associations of land and water in the world. Along the shore, in the Maryland-Virginia section, great tidal rivers such as the Potomac, the Rappahannock, the York, and the James flow southeast into that extraordinary arm of the ocean Chesapeake Bay. Between the rivers are the tidewater peninsulas where the first English settlements in America began, starting with Jamestown, on the James River. On the shores of the tidewater peninsulas developed a graceful way of life—the prosperous tobacco plantations.

Farther south a somewhat different form of plantation life, based first on rice and indigo and later on cotton, developed among the sunny, semitropical, and verdant chain of islands that fringe the coasts of South Carolina and Georgia.

The land itself provided wealth. But the wide waters of the rivers, the great bays, the channels, coves, and island chains helped create a special way of life. The centers of the tidewater life were the busy little colonial towns that in time grew into cities. A whole chain of these cities flourished down the coast—Baltimore, Annapolis, and Georgetown in Maryland; Alexandria, Fredericksburg, and Williamsburg in Virginia; Charleston in South Carolina; and Savannah and Brunswick in Georgia. Williamsburg, Virginia's colonial capital, became the most elegant and enlightened capital in the New World. Maryland's Georgetown and Virginia's Alexandria were to give special character to Washington.

But the tidewater shores and islands were more than just a pleasant and a prosperous region. They were a seedbed of history. Great men of colonial days were born on the plantations of the tidewater lands. The Revolutionary War ended at tidewater in the surrender at Yorktown. Several of the great battles of the Civil War were fought on tidewater lands.

Many residents of tidewater were wealthy and had ample leisure. It would seem that the classic combination of wealth and leisure should have resulted in the establishment of resorts. However, none were developed until after the beginning of the twentieth century.

The explanation is simple. From colonial times on, many tidewater residents could afford the luxury of resort life, but when they sought it they headed for mountains to the west or went abroad. The reason for this involves a combination of factors. The climate during the summer months in the tidewater country was muggy, encouraging wealthy natives to leave. Another factor was transportation, and for about two hundred years the main way to travel along the Atlantic seaboard was by boat. Roads, such as they were, ran far inland or west into the mountains. It was easier to ride in a carriage toward a summer sanctuary in the cool mountains than it was to seek dubious escape in one's own sweltering back yard along the shore.

Eventually notable resorts did come to the lands of the tidewater. Established within recent years were two fine and distinctive resort estates. The Cloister, of Sea Island, has thousands of acres on two of Georgia's coastal islands. The Tides Inn has a commanding setting at the tip of Virginia's tidewater peninsulas and overlooks a wide reach of shining water where the Rappahannock River meets Chesapeake Bay. Both The Tides Inn and the Cloister are year-round resorts.

Their recent establishment may be explained by the wider use of automobiles and the extension of good highways, the general adaption of air-conditioning to mitigate the traditional humidity and heat of tidewater summers, and the growing popularity of pleasure boating.

There was one remarkable exception to this late-blooming of tidewater resorts—the Jekyll Island Club, owned and patronized by some of the richest and most influential families in America. It was established on one of Georgia's offshore islands. Its season was a brief winter period. It was established in the last quarter of the nineteenth century, before automobiles were widely used and good highways existed. But it needed neither automobiles nor highways, for its members and their retainers invariably arrived and departed by yacht. The resort has finally succumbed to the pressures of changing times, but while it existed it was one of the most curious and exclusive resort estates the world has ever known.

THE GOLDEN ISLES

Compared with other Southeastern states, Georgia's coast is relatively short—about a hundred fifty miles. Wedged between South Carolina, on the north, and Florida, on the south, the coast is a strip of low tidal land with three river-mouth harbors that give Georgia access to the sea. The almost flat coastal strip is laced with channels where small rivers twist and turn between wide stretches of salt marsh. There are two important coastal cities—Savannah, in the north, and Brunswick, to the south. The marshy tidal shore is fringed with a chain of remarkable islands called the Golden Islands or, in the language of geographers, the Sea Islands.

The Sea Islands are unique novelties that are the result of separate geologic and meteorological forces that just happened to converge on this particular patch of topography. The infinitely slow movement of the earth's crust over hundreds of millions of years submerged the Georgia coast and chopped the islands free of the mainland, creating the network of tidal channels that separate them. Another geologic force, based on continental characteristics thousands of miles away, set the Gulf Stream in motion and brought it close enough to the coast of Georgia to give the islands a semitropical climate and invest them with a luxuriance of plant life unmatched anywhere else on the Atlantic shore.

Georgia's coastal islands have had a long and vigorous history marked with odd and colorful events. The islands began to be regarded as an important resort area almost a hundred years ago, when some of the richest men in America established Jekyll Island. The island is a fascinating relic of wealth and leisure but is no longer a resort itself. To the north lies St. Simons Island, on the seaward side of which is a quite small island called Sea Island, the central area of a magnificent estate, one of the finest and most distinctive family resorts in the country or, for that matter, anywhere.

The story of Sea Island is the end product of a pattern of history that goes back for hundreds of years. The Spanish colonists of the New World—Franciscan priests—built the first Christian chapels in North America in 1566. One of these chapels was the center of the first settlement on land that is now the state of Georgia. At one of these settlements a Spanish priest named Brother Domingo wrote the first book on what is United States soil—a catechism and grammar translated into the Indian dialect.

In the seventeenth century the islands became havens for British buccaneers preying on Spanish treasure ships. Blackbeard, one of the islands on the northern end of the chain, is named for the notorious pirate. In 1736, three years after the establishment of the British colony of Georgia under James Oglethorpe, the British built on St. Simons Island the most expensive fortification in America—Fort Frederica—and established around it a frontier settlement. The first fort, built as a defense against the encroachments of the Spaniards from the south, was a base from which they were driven from the land following the Battle of Bloody Marsh a few years later. The battlefield, the only one on the North American Continent in which British and Spanish troops were engaged, is at the southern end of St. Simons Island. At about the same time that Fort Frederica was built, John and Charles Wesley came to America as aides to James Oglethorpe and missionaries of the Church of England. They preached to a wilderness congregation and laid the foundations for Methodism in America. The site of their religious pioneering is now marked by a charming little church near Fort Frederica.

In 1793 a Connecticut mechanic named Eli Whitney, while visiting Georgia, invented a piece of machinery called the cotton gin, which was to revolutionize the South.

In the next few years cotton plantations on Georgia's coastal islands were the first in America to grow a fine, long staple variety of cotton which originally grew in the valley of the Euphrates, near the Persian Gulf. Grown on the Sea Islands, it made the island planters rich and took the name of the islands—Sea Island cotton.

The first six naval vessels built by the new United States Government were built of timbers cut from the great live-oak trees growing on the islands. The first ship of that early navy was the frigate *Old Ironsides*, which took its nickname from the strength of the Sea Island timbers in its hull.

All of these events are a part of the fascinating historical mosaic involving the beautiful Golden Isles of Georgia. Each event in one way or another is marked by a memorial, a monument, or a carefully preserved ruin. And all contribute a sight-seeing bonus to visitors to the Sea Island resort. Its establishment is the direct result of the growth of the automobile industry in the early years of this century. One of the pioneers of the industry was a young automotive engineer named Howard E. Coffin, who was a man of dynamic energy and great imagination. He helped to organize the Hudson motorcar company and became its vice-president and consulting engineer. Coffin was intensely interested in automobile racing and in 1911 went to Savannah, Georgia, to take part in the Vanderbilt Cup Races. He was entertained by local authorities and one day joined a hunting and fishing party on Sapelo Island, one of the northern islands of the Sea Island group. Fascinated with the rich natural beauty of the island, Coffin started to acquire it the next year. He began to develop a plantation and shooting preserve and also rebuilt a historic mansion on the island for an occasional home. During the next ten years he made frequent visits to his retreat, often bringing friends along to hunt and fish. On one such occasion it was learned that the state of Georgia proposed to build a causeway and highway east from a main north-south coastal road at Brunswick, Georgia, to link the mainland with St. Simons Island. It seemed reasonable that when the new road was finished land values in the coastal islands would skyrocket. Coffin and his friends began buying land on St. Simons Island. The first tract purchased was a former cotton plantation now known as the Retreat Plantation, once one of the richest and most beautiful in Georgia. Years later it was to grow into the Sea Island Golf Course. One day, while scouring the area for suitable land to buy, Coffin discovered Sea Island.

One of the smallest islands of the coastal group, it lay immediately to the east of St. Simons Island, and was separated from it by the narrow channels of Black Banks River and Village Creek. It had a five-mile ocean beach on one side and was covered by a semitropical growth of ancient trees and shrubs and great pines, of enormous live oaks fringed with Spanish moss, and of hollies, magnolias, and junipers. Fascinated by his discovery, Coffin bought the island. It was five miles long and varied in width from a few hundred feet at its southern tip to a mile and a quarter at the northern end—in all, about twelve hundred acres of wilderness with a magnificent beach and rolling dunes. The idea was to build a family resort on Sea Island that would appeal to middle- and upper-bracket families, surrounded by a residential colony of cottage homes. In keeping with similar grandiose projects that were blossoming all over Florida during the booming twenties, the first plans called for an elaborate, ornate complex of Spanish-type buildings with indoor and outdoor pools, sunken gardens, fountains, and all the trappings of splendor which Florida land developers liked and sold.

Fortunately the first plans were not carried out. It was decided to build a much smaller, simpler, but still elegant hotel and put it at the southern end of the island. To build it, Coffin engaged an eccentric genius of an architect named Addison Mizner, whose work in Palm Beach had transformed that community with Spanish and Mediterranean dwellings and hotels. Mizner later went bankrupt building Florida's vast and fabulous Spanish resort that is now Boca Raton. Fortunately for Coffin, Mizner restrained his exuberance of design and planned a small hotel of forty-six guest rooms in the Mediterranean style. It included architectural elements that gave it a name—the Cloister. It is still regarded as a good example of Mediterranean architecture and one of Mizner's most tasteful achievements. The original Cloister, now much enlarged and greatly modified, opened its doors in 1928. It is now the core of a luxurious resort estate with 169 guest rooms and more than 175 cottages filling the central part of Sea Island, with holdings of more than six thousand acres.

Coffin's Sea Island family resort had immediate success. An early development was a golf course at the southern end of St. Simons Island, using the first large tract that Coffin had bought in 1925—the historic Retreat Plantation. A series of beach-front houses was built on Sea Island for transient guests. To utilize the island's superb beach—one of the longest and best on the Atlantic coast—a beach club with many facilities was developed. A unique feature of the resort has been its attraction to newly married couples. More than a thousand couples a year honeymoon at the Cloister. In recent years many couples beginning their honeymoons at the Cloister are the children of newlyweds who stayed there a generation ago, and more than twenty thousand couples have visited Sea Island and the Cloister. Famous guests include celebrities from almost every country in the world. Queen Juliana and Prince Bernhard of the Netherlands have been guests. President Calvin Coolidge was a guest, and so was President Eisenhower.

Throughout its history, the Sea Island management has stuck to the original concept: an informal family resort where life is casual and unpretentious. There are no signs telling you where or where not to go.

Despite its casualness, the Cloister is a mature and sophisticated resort estate, taking maximum advantage of a marvelous year-round climate in a luxuriant setting and offering guests a wide range of diversion. One of the few things guests cannot do at Sea Island is climb mountains.

The Cloister, with its adjacent residential and service buildings, fills most of the southern end of Sea Island and is surrounded by beautifully landscaped lawns and gardens, six tennis courts, a croquet court, a nine-hole miniature golf course, and a softball field. Opposite the main entrance is an eighteen-hole putting green, and a fishing dock on the Black Banks River is close by. Two hundred yards east of the hotel is the Beach Club, with two swimming pools and five miles of wide beach. North of the Beach Club are beach-front accommodations for guests. From the cluster of buildings at the southern end of the island Sea Island Drive leads north through the residential colony. The road, flanked by moss-hung oaks, is one of the most picturesque drives in the country. The "cottages" facing it range from small cottages to elaborate residential estates. Sea Island Drive ends at the Hampton River, which divides Sea Island from Little St. Simons Island. The entire beach is fine for surf casting, and the tidal rivers and creeks offer excellent fishing from skiffs and small power boats. Deep-sea fishing is good in the summer. Less than a mile from the Cloister, across the Black Banks River, is Sea Island's gun club, with two skeet fields and a clubhouse. A little farther on are the resort's extensive riding stables. The Sea Island Yacht Club is about five miles from the resort, just south of the causeway over Frederica River, on the west edge of St. Simons Island. The river, incidentally, is a section of the Intracoastal Waterway, the small-boat channel along the Atlantic coast between Florida and the northern Atlantic states. It carries a steady procession of yachts and pleasure craft whose owners often stop at Sea Island.

The most distant of the resort's facilities, the golf course, takes in much of the southwestern end of nearby St. Simons Island. The course is unique in its combination of historic association and scenic setting. It is also technically challenging and is widely regarded by skilled golfers as well worth playing. It was an eighteen-hole course until a few years ago, but nine more holes have been added. The original eighteen, consisting of two quite different nines, make a course of 6541 yards and a par of 72. The course is level but has large tees and well-trapped, beautifully sculptured greens and is kept in superb condition year round. Eight lakes provide scenic interest and challenging hazards. Eighteen of the twenty-seven holes are inland. The nine holes by the ocean are reminiscent of an English seaside course, with ocean winds making shots vary every day. On the seaside course, the sixteenth hole, a par 4, is generally regarded as the most challenging. The most scenic is Number 2 on the inside course, where the green nestles among great arching live oaks festooned with Spanish moss. One of the holes is called Bald Eagle, another Alligator. One is named Noah's Ark (a water hole) and another is named Swan's Lake, though the swans who originally lived on the lake have been eaten by alligators.

The course suggests those historic days when the entire area was part of one of the most beautiful and successful plantations in Georgia. The main drive, leading into the resort from the public highway, was the original Plantation Drive, a dramatically beautiful stretch of roadway under curving, moss-hung trees. The original plantation house, built in 1838, was destroyed by fire in 1903. Every timber was of handhewn live oak put together with handmade nails, but no trace of the main house or its garden remains. But parts of the other buildings, which were built with a type of cement using oyster shells, survived the fire and have been incorporated into the golf clubhouse.

Although golf at the island is popular and the course is excellent, the Beach Club is by far the most frequented part of the resort. It is both a day and night social and recreational center for the guests and cottage residents. Diving and swimming take place in the hugh kidney-shaped pool; colorful dinners are held on a wide terrace flanking the pool. The clubhouse contains a lounge, grill, and snack bar. An open dining terrace overlooks the sea. A sailing catamaran and an air boat are on the beach, available to the guests.

Fishing at Sea Island is as varied as the most ardent angler could wish. At the dock, boats, tackle, and guides are available for fishing in the web of salt-water channels that thread the island group in all directions. The catch is usually trout, bass, sheepshead, whiting, and drum.

The 169 guest rooms and apartments at Sea Island are air-conditioned, ranging in size from double rooms, in the main hotel building, to beach-house suites that have double exposure toward the sea and land, with either a private roofed balcony or open terrace overlooking the sea.

Dining at Sea Island is varied. All guests have regularly assigned tables in one of the three dining rooms in the Cloister, and all meals are on the American plan. Since the nearby city of Brunswick is known as the shrimp center of the world, shrimp, and many other seafoods, are always on the menu. On occasions a plantation supper will be held at twilight in a wooded area north of the main resort, and there are gala suppers at the Beach Club.

Although the facilities of the resort can fill all of one's waking hours, most guests soon discover that the nearby area has dozens of sight-seeing opportunities, many on St. Simons Island, only a few minutes' drive from Sea Island. Of these the most important are the ruins of Fort Frederica, a national monument, with the ruins of Frederica Village, where archaeological excavation by the National Park Service has uncovered the old town. The story of Frederica is retold by exhibits at a museum.

Just outside the Fort Frederica area is charming Christ Church, built in 1884 on the site where John and Charles Wesley first preached in the United States. Also on St. Simons Island is Epworth-by-the-Sea, a Methodist center for the South Georgia Conference. It was established on the grounds of the Hamilton Plantation, which once was one of the largest cotton plantations in the South.

At the south end of the island is St. Simons village, in which there is a small but first-rate fine-arts center that attracts many resort guests. A monument overlooking the sea marks the site where the British ended the struggle with Spain for control of what became the Southeastern United States.

Many guests visit Jekyll Island State Park, where the winter homes of some of the richest men in America are preserved. The island is a seventeen-mile drive from Sea Island, and on the way you pass through Brunswick, Georgia, a city with a rich and historic past. A gigantic oak called Lover's Oak, said to be over nine hundred years old, is one of the town's special sights. The Brunswick fishing docks generally draw a crowd of onlookers. A shrimp fleet and crab boats usually come in around three o'clock each afternoon.

Even though Sea Island is several miles away from the main routes of travel, it is easily reached by highway, rail, or air. It is linked to the mainland by a causeway. Brunswick, the nearest city, is twelve miles away and is midway between Savannah, Georgia, and Jacksonville, Florida. For those traveling by automobile the best route is U.S. 17 along the coast. The Sea Island causeway connects with U.S. 17 at Brunswick. For visitors from the west U.S. 82, 84, and 341 all converge at Brunswick. Interstate 95, paralleling U.S. 17 along the coast, will be available with completion of the interstate system. Guests arriving by train have a choice of the Southern Railway to Brunswick, from the west. From the north or south you can take either the Seaboard, with the nearest station at Thalmann, Georgia, thirty miles away, or the Atlantic Coast Line to Jesup, fifty miles away. For guests arriving by rail, the Cloister will have motor transportation meet trains if notified in advance.

One can fly almost directly to the hotel. Delta Airlines flies to Brunswick. Additional service is provided by National and Eastern airlines jets to Jacksonville, Florida, where connecting flights by Delta or charter service to the Brunswick Airport can be made. Many guests rent automobiles at the Jacksonville airport for the ninety-mile trip to Sea Island.

Rates at Sea Island, all on the American plan, vary with the season and type of accommodation. There are three seasons: summer, June 1 to August 31; fall, September 1 to January 31; and winter and spring combined, February 1 to May 31. The lowest rates are available during the summer, and the highest are charged during winter and spring. All rooms are equipped for double occupancy, although single-room rates are available. Rates during the summer for a single room with meals are from $20 per day; two-person room rates are $30 per day and up. In the fall season single-room rates are $22 per day and up, and two-person room rates are $32 per day and up. The spring season rates: single-room rates are $26 per day and up; two-person rooms are $38 per day and up. The most elaborate and luxurious accommodations that the resort provides are the beach houses. Each unit has its own terrace or balcony, dressing room-bedroom, and living-room area. The rates start at $40 per day for two in the summer, $42 per day in the fall, and $48 per day in the winter and spring season. In addition to the rooms available at the Cloister and its associated buildings, about half of the cottages among the 160 owned on Sea Island are available for rental when not occupied by their owners. There are completely furnished two- to five-bedroom houses. The rates range from $600 to $1500 per month. All the Cloister facilities are available to cottagers.

Fees for various special facilities and services at Sea Island: golf fees for eighteen holes are $4.25 June through January and $5.25 February through May. All the facilities of the Beach Club are free to Cloister guests except locker rental, which is 50 cents per day or $2.50 per week. Fees at the gun club for skeet shooting are $3.85 per round, including shells, or $2.50 per round, targets only. Rates for fishing on inside waters are $28 for a half day for rental for two persons of a power cruiser; $45 for a full day, with $7.50 each for additional passengers over two. Small boats and outboard motors are available at lower rates. Tackle and bait are furnished. Charter boats for deep-sea fishing are available during June, July, and August: one to four persons $50 per day, six persons $60, tackle and bait furnished. Saddle horses can be rented at $4 for the first hour, $2 for the second hour. The use of the tennis courts is $1 per hour, with weekly and longer period fees available. Bicycles can be rented for $1 per half day, $1.50 all day, or $9 per week.

Transportation rates to airports and railway stations vary with distance. The rate to the Brunswick Airport on St. Simons Island is $1.50 for one person, $1 each for additional persons. The resort will meet guests at either the Savannah or Jacksonville airports on notice for a fee of $30 for one or two persons, and each additional person costs $5.

MILLIONAIRES ONLY

Jekyll Island is the smallest of the six islands in the Golden Isles of Georgia. It is only nine and a half miles long and from a quarter to one and a quarter miles wide. It lies immediately east of Brunswick and is connected to the mainland by a causeway. The island is shaped like a giant foot. The big toe of the foot points north to St. Simons Island, two miles away across St. Simons Sound. A fringe of palms and live oaks shelters thousands of visitors' cars to Jekyll Island. As a state park, Jekyll attracts and provides facilities for hundreds of thousands of visitors each year. But a relatively few years ago the only visitors to Jekyll were its millionaire owners. The rich men and their friends reached it only by yacht. Although Jekyll Island today is not a resort, it was a remarkable colony for fifty years and its story belongs in this chronicle. Visitors glimpse the life of exclusive opulence that began in 1886.

Jekyll Island resembles the others in the island group in topography and physical character. It has groves of enormous live-oak trees draped with moss. It has a fine beach on its seaside, and it has the same mild climate that graces other areas of the coastal islands.

The history of Jekyll Island is uncomplicated. It was named for Sir Joseph Jekyll, a close friend and supporter of James Oglethorpe, founder of Georgia. After Oglethorpe's victory over the Spanish at the Battle of Bloody Marsh, one of Oglethorpe's officers, Major William Horton, became the first resident of Jekyll Island as commander of a small garrison there. He built a house, the walls of which are still standing, and cleared the fields for a small farm. Among his crops were hops. Horton established the first brewery in Georgia on Jekyll, where rum was prohibited but beer was not. The beer was unusually good, because it was made from the superb artesian well water, which was abundant

15. At Pinehurst, the Carolina is one of two resort hotels of this remarkable North Carolina resort estate.

16. Greatest golfing resort in the world, Pinehurst maintains five eighteen-hole professional courses. Shown here is the seventh green of Number 3 course.

17. Pinehurst, in addition to being a golfer's haven, is a winter training center for harness racing.

John G. Hemmer

18. One of the most charming buildings on the Pinehurst estate is the village chapel.

19. The Beach Club at Sea Island, Georgia, on a marvelous five-mile ocean beach, is one of the best facilities of its type anywhere.

20. Fort Frederica National Monument, preserving a stronghold built in 1736, is one of many sights of note near Sea Island.

21. Boating is a way of life at The Tides Inn, near Irvington, Virginia. There guests have the use of a flotilla of craft ranging in size from ocean-going yachts to sailing skiffs.

on the islands. More than fifty years later the island was acquired by a French family named Du Bignon, who were refugees from the French Revolution. They and their descendants owned the island and cultivated indigo and Sea Island cotton there until 1886. Several generations of the family are buried in a tiny walled cemetery on the island.

The next owners made the island famous throughout the world, for the period was one of booming wealth and great financial power, when industrial tycoons built railways and controlled financial empires. It was a period when the very rich and socially elect spent their summers at Newport, owned houses in Tuxedo Park, and attended the races at Saratoga. It was the era of New York City's elegant town houses.

Among the very rich of the day was a small group of men who had been summered together at exclusive places in the East but who felt that they needed a pleasant place to go in the winter to escape the bad weather and to enjoy each other's company. The group, numbering less than a hundred, included such families as the Pierpont Morgans, the Astors, the Goulds, the Harrimans, the Hills, the Stillmans, the Vanderbilts, the Rockefellers, the Pulitzers, the Pullmans, the Marshall Fields, the McCormicks, the Drexels, and the Biddles.

They commissioned two doctors to roam far and wide and find their Shangri-La. The two men finally reported that they had found an ideal spot—Jekyll Island off the coast of Georgia. It fulfilled all the specifications: mild, semitropical climate, distinctive natural beauty, excellent water, isolation, and reasonable proximity to New York and other business centers. The group organized the Jekyll Island Club and bought the island. They established a village center that was dominated by the club, which was the center of social activities, providing accommodations for some members who did not build their own cottages, and meals for all members. About a dozen members of the club built "cottages," that were cottages in name only, for nearly all were Victorian in design and spacious and luxurious, though not as opulently ornate as the Newport "cottages." They were given odd and romantic names. The club became busy early in January and remained so until late spring. During that period it was not uncommon for the channel, which the village center and the club faced on the west side of the island, to be clustered with giant yachts. Morgan's *Corsair IV*, the largest yacht afloat, and the *Liberty*, the Pulitzer yacht, the publisher's floating home for many years, were among the yachts anchored there. In the village center club members built a charming small chapel called the Faith Chapel, which still stands today. On the east side of the island, facing the ocean, one of the earliest golf courses in the country was built, designed by the great Scottish golf architect William J. Travis. It was reminiscent of the dunes courses of coastal Scotland. They imported bowling on the green from England. Club members found good hunting in the wilder areas of the island, shooting deer (including a rare albino species, the only one of its type found in the East), wild turkey, quail, and other native game. To improve the hunting, members imported pheasants from England. J. P. Morgan added zest and danger to hunting on the island by turning loose three hundred wild boars he acquired from the King of Italy. Most members maintained their own stables.

Dining was mainly at the club, where a master chef with a full staff was imported each year from Delmonico's, in New York, to prepare the most elaborate menus that his skill and supplies imported from the mainland could provide. Dinners ran from eight to twelve courses and usually lasted three hours. Occasionally they were made notable by the presence of a distinguished guest. One memorable dinner honored Andrew Carnegie, who was not a member of the club but who had his own private retreat on Cumberland Island, to the south. At another dinner President William McKinley was the honored guest. There were other noteworthy occasions on Jekyll. In 1915, Theodore Vail, a member of the club and then president of A.T. & T., arranged to have a thousand miles of cable run to the island so that he could take part in the first transcontinental call from San Francisco through New York and Washington to Jekyll Island. During the call, Vail talked with President Wilson, in Washington, and Alexander Graham Bell, the inventor, who was in New York.

The full story of Jekyll Island, told in all its detail, could fill a book crowded with anecdotes of the eccentricities of the wealthy. The guest of one former member, for example, remembers a particular beach picnic served by a half-dozen white-jacketed waiters on tables spread with linen cloths and a menu including lobster Newburg, oysters Rockefeller, baked Alaska, and crêpes Suzettes. It is said that Joseph Pulitzer, whose most celebrated eccentricity was his detestation of noise, offered a dredge captain operating in the channel opposite the Pulitzer cottage one hundred dollars a day to *refrain* from blowing his whistle while in front of the cottage.

The last season of the Jekyll Island Club was the spring of 1942. Early that spring a German submarine torpedoed a tanker in St. Simons Sound just north of the island. The incident made the Government fear that the concentration of power and wealth on the island among club members might be an additional target and ordered evacuation. The Coast Guard was left in charge.

The club was never reopened. Members sold out in 1947 to the state of Georgia for the paltry sum of $650,000. In 1954, Georgia built a causeway and bridge across the Intracoastal Waterway along the west side of the island, linking the island with the mainland and making it easily accessible to automobile traffic. The island has been a distinctive and popular state park ever since. The millionaires' village, on the west side overlooking the sound, appears much as it did during its heyday. Some buildings are unchanged; others have been converted to provide public accommodations. The Rockefeller cottage has been converted into one of the most remarkable and delightful museums imaginable, filled with relics and souvenirs of the island's great days, including many of the original furnishings of the cottage itself. On the east side of the island are the public facilities, including a public beach, a casino, and large motor hotels. Another beach casino has been built at the south end, and all parts of the island have been linked with adequate highways.

TIDEWATER SHOWCASE

A majestic arm of the sea called Chesapeake Bay stretches along the eastern flank of Virginia, extending north to south for about two hundred miles, a superb reach of useful water. The narrower, northern half of the bay is within the state of Maryland, but the southern half, where the tremendous bay widens to almost thirty miles, is in Virginia. Four famous rivers flow into the Virginia end of the bay. The most northern is the Potomac, which Virginia shares with Maryland and Washington. The next river south is the Rappahannock, then the York, and then the southernmost, the James. Each of them, as it nears its junction with Chesapeake Bay, widens into a great tidal channel. The four rivers separate long fingers of fairly rugged land varying in width from ten to twenty miles. These fingers of land, divided by the four rivers, make up the distinctive tidewater region, which in many ways is the most historic part of the United States.

From the beginning of the English settlement in Jamestown to the Civil War, the tidewater played a decisive part in North American history. The great rivers, which give it its unusual geographic character, helped to make it one of the most easily settled and pleasant places to live in the New World. Along the shores of the rivers developed the colonial plantation estates. One of them was Mount Vernon, the home of George Washington. Another was Stratford Hall, where Robert E. Lee was born. Nearby is the former plantation where Washington was born and lived as a boy. Dozens of other great manor houses overlook the wide waters of these rivers.

The land of the tidewater region itself is not particularly scenic. It is a pleasant land, fertile, low-lying, and deeply cut with channels and bays of quiet water. Its charm lies in this association of water and the land—a friendly, practical, and constant union. Nearly all the residents of the area are skilled in the use of boats. Nowhere else in this country has boating—both for profit and pleasure—developed the way it has along the tidewater rivers and the shores of Chesapeake Bay.

On the north shore of the Rappahannock River is The Tides Inn, a charming small resort that has made boating a way of life to delight and beguile its guests. The inn is set on the crest of a knoll facing the Rappahannock, which at this point is only six miles upriver from the Chesapeake. The Tides Inn is remarkable in many ways. It maintains and uses more boats than any other resort in the country. It is one of the few resort estates developed entirely after World War II, and probably is the only one planned and developed by complete amateurs with no experience at all in resort management.

The story of The Tides Inn actually was begun by an energetic gentleman named E. A. Stephens, who operated a successful automobile agency. One of his hobbies was boating, and his family did a good deal of it on the wide waters of Chesapeake Bay and the tidal rivers of Virginia. One day while his family was scooting along in a speedboat on the Rappahannock, they noticed a low headland thrusting into the river. It seemed like an unusually attractive patch of land that might make a pleasant homesite for a boat-loving family. The land had become overgrown with a tangle of honeysuckle, briars, and vines. But in walking over it Stephens decided that he wanted the land, and he bought it. The tract had been known as the Ashburn Farm, an abandoned homestead that had been in the same family for more than a hundred years. The house had fallen in. Stephens hired men to clear the land, and in the process his enthusiasm for the property increased. The family decided to build, not a private home, but a small inn that might serve the many pleasure-craft owners who did their boating in the area. An architect produced plans for a relatively simple, three-story frame building that was similar in design to those that had been built by English settlers. Stephens decided to use local timber. He bought trees from the surrounding region, had them cut and hauled, often by a yoke of oxen, to a small sawmill where they were sawed and racked for drying. Much of the charm of The Tides Inn today is the result of that effort. Wood for the cyprus paneling in one of the lounges was found in a swamp twenty miles away and hauled to the mill by oxcart. Some fine black walnut paneling was cut from fallen trees on the property itself.

With timber and plans in hand, Stephens started to build in the spring of 1946. He acted as his own contractor; Mrs. Stephens supervised the decorating. He hired three local men—a carpenter-foreman, a plumber, and an electrician who in turn hired a crew of laborers—and everyone went to work, with Stephens himself pitching in from time to time.

As their inn rose on a strategic point of land overlooking the finest boating water in the East, they made an important decision. Stephens says, "We decided that our little inn would be the finest thing that could be developed and still keep the rural atmosphere. Having in mind that the Northern Neck was originally settled by the English and has kept many of the English customs, we decided that the smart thing to do would be to go to Europe and secure unusual and attractive furnishings for the inn."

This decision resulted in a whirlwind buying spree in Europe. An assortment of unusual and beautiful antiques was brought back to Virginia and now graces the inn. Notable prints were bought in Belgium and France; fine antique silver was acquired in England. Two giant wine coolers supposedly used in Stratford-on-Avon when Shakespeare lived there are among the treasures that were imported.

The Tides Inn opened for business in 1947. Guests came from two directions—by automobile down the long, narrow Northern Neck, and by water down the rivers and coves that the inn faced. The fully equipped pier built for its seagoing guests began to acquire a small fleet, and this has grown into a most remarkable flotilla, ranging from two ocean-going yachts to a catamaran barge.

In the beginning there were only forty-seven guest rooms in the inn, for Stephens had had no plans for other than a small inn dedicated to the pleasures of boating. Its development in fifteen years into a small but elegant resort estate was the result of its success as an inn. A handsome swimming pool was built on a lower slope in front of the hotel overlooking the bay. A glass-enclosed house was put up alongside the pool so buffet luncheons could be served. As the inn's fame spread, guests kept coming. To accommodate them, two luxurious buildings with guest rooms and suites were added to the rear of the main building. Many of the new rooms and suites had balconies and terraces overlooking the channel, which looped around behind the peninsula on which the hotel was situated.

It soon became evident that the guests who liked boating also wanted to play golf. Stephens took a major step and hired the resident golf architect of St. Andrews, Scotland, to design an eighteen-hole championship golf course. There was not enough land near the inn itself, so additional land was acquired on a nearby peninsula. The new course is one of the best in Virginia and has scenic charm and challenging holes. Golfers reach the course by a catamaran ferry with a canopied top.

The two ocean-going yachts owned by the inn are constantly used by guests for sight-seeing trips and frequent beach picnics nine miles away down Chesapeake Bay. On Wednesdays a fish-fry cruise is held for the guests. Other water activities include water skiing, sailing, and outboarding. Boats and gear are provided by the resort. Each fall the inn sponsors the Frostbite Regatta, for members of yacht clubs in the area.

The Tides Inn also has become celebrated in the East for its unique menus and its dining room, which is a spacious and elegantly appointed room with a fine view of the bay. The cuisine is basically American and boasts some notable New Orleans dishes. Seafood of every variety is generally featured, but roast beef is a specialty, as are certain Continental dishes. The most famous meal, however, is breakfast, which offers a great variety of tempting and unusual dishes. One of these superb dishes is Hangtown fry, made from a recipe of the gold-rush towns of California and consisting of oysters and scrambled eggs.

Service and appointments in the main dining room are reasonably formal. Informal buffet luncheons are served on board the inn's yachts, and at the Bubble House, by the swimming pool. An ornate and extensive seafood buffet is held every Sunday evening in the main dining room.

The inn's unique location in the heart of one of the most historic regions of the East gives guests an opportunity for ample sight-seeing. The birthplaces of two presidents—James Monroe and George Washington—are on the peninsula north of the inn and are reached on Route 3. Stratford Hall, the beautiful birthplace home of Robert E. Lee, is nearby at Fredericksburg, on the main route of U.S. 1 and Interstate

95, fifty miles south of Washington, D.C., is a fascinating small city, close to many Civil War battlefields. Colonial Williamsburg, the superb restoration of the colonial capital of Virginia, is fifty miles from the inn. Jamestown, the site of the first permanent English settlement in America, has many exhibits of ruins and relics of that historic village. Colonial Yorktown is also near the inn. It was there that George Washington defeated the British at the close of the Revolutionary War. The battlefield of the final engagement is today preserved as a memorial. Most Tides Inn guests see Yorktown, Williamsburg, and Jamestown on a single trip, as the towns are linked by the scenic Colonial Parkway, which begins at Yorktown, passes through colonial Williamsburg, and ends at Jamestown.

The Tides Inn is easily reached by boat or car. Motorists coming from the north can leave Interstate 95 or U.S. 1 at Fredericksburg, and then follow Virginia Route 3 down the peninsula approximately seventy-five miles to Irvington. An alternate route from Fredericksburg is U.S. 17 along the west bank of the Rappahannock River, crossing to Route 3 thirty miles north of Irvington and the inn. From the south take U.S. 17 through Norfolk, Hampton, and Yorktown to a junction with Virginia 33, which leads east across the Rappahannock River from Saluda. From the west come through Washington or Fredericksburg, then follow the suggested routes.

An increasing number of guests arrive in their own boats, which can be docked at the inn's pier. The Intracoastal Waterway passes less than fifteen miles from the dock.

Guests can fly to The Tides Inn by taking scheduled air service to either Richmond or Newport News, Virginia, where a car will meet them on advance notice. The fee for this service is $7.50 per person one way—a minimum of two people.

For several reasons, the resort operates as a club, which is called the Chesapeake Club. Membership and advance reservations are required. Once membership in the club is established and reservations are accepted, rates are full American plan, from $20 to $28 per day per person, double occupancy. When children share a room with two adults and are under twelve years of age, the additional rate is $10; if over twelve years, $16. Rates for the small suites in the new building near the main inn start at $26 per day per person. From November 1 to January 1 there is a 20 per cent reduction in rates. In addition, the inn offers fall package weekends at bargain rates. Greens fees for eighteen holes on the new golf course are $4. Tennis fees are 75 cents per person per hour, with rackets and balls available at the sport shop. Fees for boating and fishing depend on the size of boat required and the duration of the trip. The frequent yachting excursions are provided at no extra charge.

CHAPTER 6

GOLD COAST AND
GULF SHORE

Before the railroads began to push through Georgia into what now is
the state of Florida, that vast and unique peninsula was a relatively unsettled and lonely land. It was a curious region dotted with innumerable lakes, pine forests, ancient oaks hung with Spanish moss, and vast
tropical swamps. Its shores were fringed with islands on the seaward
side of which were some of the best and most beautiful surf beaches
in the world.

Two railroad pioneers who had made fortunes in the North began to
change Florida into a resort region of unique character and unparalleled popularity. One was Henry Flagler, who first visited Florida in
1883, when he was fifty-three. His wealth came from an association
with John D. Rockefeller. He took over the east coast of Florida as his
special zone of influence, and began to string rail lines south through
the wilderness of scrub pine and palmetto. A few years later Henry
Plant, a steamship tycoon, made the west coast of Florida his domain.

Flagler moved first into St. Augustine, a sleepy southern village that
had been an ancient outpost of Spanish dominion, and transformed it
almost overnight into a remarkable resort community by building two
extraordinary hotels, the Ponce de Leon and the Alcazar.

Pushing the tracks of his Florida East Coast Railway far south along
the shore, Flagler discovered a beautiful offshore island with a superb
ocean beach. He acquired this tropical Eden and renamed it Palm
Beach. The resort community that he planned and built soon became
the place to go or be seen in. Eventually it became one of the most
luxurious resort cities in the world. To help make it so, Flagler built
two hotels. The Royal Poinciana was the largest resort hotel in the

world. The other, through successive stages of development, grew into the elegant Breakers, the most renowned resort hotel in the most celebrated of Florida's resort communities.

Meanwhile, Henry Plant had pushed the Atlantic Coast Line Railway into western Florida and began building hotels that he hoped would rival in magnificence the Flagler resorts on the east coast. One of these attempts was in the Spanish city of Tampa. It turned out to be an incredible cluster of onion domes, spires, and pinnacles and is now a tourist curiosity and part of the University of Tampa. Another hotel, huge, rambling, but less ornate, was built near the Gulf and was first named The Belleview. The Belleview-Biltmore, as it was later called, has become the largest resort hotel of Florida's west coast.

Beyond the limits of Florida, farther to the west, another resort had been established on a pleasant point of land thrusting into Mobile Bay. The Grand Hotel was opened in 1844, long before the development of Florida. For its day it was truly grand, serving the rich plantation owners along the Gulf between New Orleans and Mobile. They arrived by boat and made the Grand Hotel a center of wealth and society for many years.

When the Flagler-Plant railroads opened, a growing stream of holiday seekers and homesteaders moved into Florida. New towns sprang up and so did resorts of every size and type. Flagler started Miami, and before long it began to take on the aspects of a metropolis. Across the bay sand bars sprouted with the most amazing assortment of resort hotels the world has ever seen—Miami Beach.

Part of the development of Florida was a boisterous boom in real estate and town development. The dream of the gifted architect Addison Mizner was the development of a fabulous new city. He made a start toward his dream with opulent and beautiful Boca Raton Hotel, one of the crown jewels of the Gold Coast, which stretched from Palm Beach to Miami Beach.

Florida's gaudy land boom collapsed in time, but growth and change continued. The state now has a number of remarkable resorts and resort communities of every type flanking the Atlantic and Gulf shores. Miami Beach has huge and colorful resort hotels. Palm Beach is exclusive, elegant, and beautiful. The west coast has a hundred-mile resort strip, with St. Petersburg at its core, that lures visitors of all ages and means. Among them all are distinctive resort estates that are self-contained centers of ease and luxury. Mizner's Boca Raton is vast, colorful, and ornate. Flagler's aristocratic Breakers towers above Palm

Beach. Ponte Vedra has its shining beaches and golf course built around lagoons. Plant's Belleview-Biltmore rises above the quiet shores of the Gulf.

And dominating its unique setting on the shore of Mobile Bay is a new Grand Hotel, the proud heir to the oldest and most celebrated resort on the Gulf shore.

THE GOLDEN CITY OF THE GOLD COAST

A chain of slender barrier islands extends more than five hundred miles along Florida's east coast. The surge of the open Atlantic has created some of the finest ocean beaches in the world on the seaward side of the chain. About halfway between Palm Beach and Miami a bay lies between the waterway and the ocean. The inlet was named Boca de Ratones on early Spanish maps. Literally translated, it meant Mouth of the Rats because the channel mouth was fringed with sharp, toothlike rocks. Pirates found the bay a handy place to hide in because the sheltered water was difficult to approach from the sea. Captain Edward Teach, better known as the pirate Blackbeard, is supposed to have used Boca Raton as a favorite rendezvous, and was buried nearby with treasure.

After Florida became a winter haunt for the well-to-do, the channel was developed by the Government as an official waterway and became part of the Intracoastal Waterway. Pleasure craft—from palatial yacht to tiny skiff—travel the Waterway in great numbers.

Boca Raton is an amazing sight when viewed from the Intracoastal Waterway. The western shore of the bay is a wide and beautiful lagoon, fringed with palm trees and other tropical growth. An incredible building rises above the lagoon. It towers pink and white above the shining water, among emerald lawns and luxuriant gardens. Four medieval-looking towers rise above acres of red tile roofs. The extraordinary building is like a gigantic Spanish castle, like nothing else in the Western world, one of the most exceptional resort estates in this or any other country.

The story of Boca Raton Hotel involves the labors and ambitions of three unusual men. The first was Addison Mizner, a talented architect and dreamer. Boca Raton was a part of a Mizner dream, but only a part. He died bankrupt before the dream became reality. The second man was Clarence H. Geist, once a farm boy from a small town in

Indiana. In the freewheeling days after World War I, Geist, who built a fortune estimated at more than fifty million dollars developing and manipulating public utilities, was a man with an overwhelming inferiority complex that expressed itself in arrogant pomposity. He acquired the Mizner dream as a real estate bargain and turned it into the most exclusive and expensive private club in the world.

The third man was a tycoon of American industry, Arthur Vining Davis. After Davis retired as head of the Aluminum Company of America, he moved to Florida. The empire that he built included Boca Raton. Davis and his associates turned the private club into the luxurious resort it is today.

Mizner arrived in Florida during the first land boom of the twenties. He had no formal training as an architect, but began designing architecturally radical houses in Palm Beach. They were his own adaptations of Spanish colonial design, which once had fascinated him on a visit to Guatemala. Later he went to Spain, where he refined and improved his efforts. His neo-Spanish houses in Palm Beach soon won him fame as a designer of elegant dwellings for the rich.

His reputation as a brilliant designer and builder established, Mizner hatched his grandiose dream. Studying the land between Palm Beach and Miami, he chose Boca Raton as the site for a dream city that would surpass in splendor anything seen before. He proposed to build the largest hotel in the world on the beach. On the lake behind the sheltering island he planned a small and elegant inn modeled after a Spanish building. He planned to lace his project with twenty miles of Venetian canals. Visitors in his new city would travel over El Camino Real, The Royal Highway, which would be the widest and most splendid boulevard in the world.

There would be three golf courses, and Mizner's own home would be an actual Spanish castle, built on an island in Lake Boca Raton and connected to the mainland by a drawbridge. He proposed to sell lots in his new city, and with the help of an enthusiastic corps of promoters and salesmen he managed to dispose of $26,000,000 worth of them. Actress Marie Dressler was a member of the Mizner sales staff. While the lots were being snapped up by fascinated purchasers at prices sometimes running to $40,000 apiece, Mizner started work on the first unit of his new city—the small, elegant Cloister Inn. He lavished everything he knew about design and decoration on it and produced a distinctive architectural gem, appropriate to its lakeshore setting. Each suite was furnished in a different style. Every room typified an Old

World spot with New World luxury. To decorate his elegant little hotel, Mizner imported tapestries and antiques from Spain and set thirty craftsmen to work in a furniture factory making copies of rare Spanish pieces. The landscaping of his grounds was to be the most beautiful ever attempted. Hundreds of acres were planted with rare and exotic plants. Mizner's Cloister Inn opened in February 1926, the Ritz-Carleton Hotel of New York managing the property. The inn was finished, the grounds immediately around it had been spectacularly landscaped, and the extraordinary road, El Camino Real, leading west from Florida's main north-south highway, was completed—a broad boulevard lined with stately royal palms.

About that time balloons began to burst all over Florida. The biggest bang was Boca Raton. Most of the $26,000,000 invested in lots went down the drain. The Mizner dream was broken, with nothing left but a beautiful small hotel.

The chain of events then moved to Chicago, where Charles and Rufus Dawes owned a company called the Central Equities Company. It took over Boca Raton's assets. One of the brothers' associates was Clarence Geist, whose fortune in 1928 was estimated at about $54,000,000.

Geist decided to build his own private club in Florida, so exclusive and so opulent that the handsome premises of the famed Everglades Club, in Palm Beach, would look like a shanty town. The Dawes brothers suggested to their friend Geist that maybe they had just the thing for his millionaire's club. So Geist took over all the Boca Raton assets for $200,000 and proceeded to invest $8,000,000 in turning the charming little hotel into a huge, luxurious Spanish hotel with four hundred rooms that could accommodate more than seven hundred people.

Fortunately for Boca Raton today, Geist had the good judgment to hire reputable architects for the expansion. With the Mizner building as the core, the architects maintained the traditions of design and décor throughout the whole building.

Geist's ultraexclusive millionaire's club opened in 1928. The annual dues were five thousand dollars, a sum that Geist had planned to double the next year but didn't because of the first shock waves of the Depression. But in 1928 there were still enough rich men who could afford the Boca Raton dues and who liked the privacy and the luxury offered by the club, which he ran like an Oriental potentate. No affair started without his command. He liked to play golf but hated to walk, and since electric golf carts had not been invented, he had his chauffeur-driven limousine trail him around the golf course, down the fairways, and up onto the greens.

Geist ran his club for ten years until his death in 1938. The Depression resulted in mounting deficits, which Geist met from his own resources. He left a sum of $500,000 to keep the club going. But the ranks of millionaires were dwindling and the club went deeper and deeper in debt. Finally, the Army took over the property in 1942 and established a radar-training school there. After World War II, Boca Raton was acquired and run for a few years by another self-made man, J. Meyer Shine, head of the Shine Theatrical Enterprises, who turned it into a public resort. But the Shine control was an interim stewardship and did not fully develop Boca Raton. That achievement was reserved for the remarkable Arthur Vining Davis, who had come south to Florida on his retirement and had begun putting together a real estate empire. Boca Raton and eleven hundred acres of adjacent land cost Davis $22,000,000. He promptly set about developing it into an extraordinary resort. On five hundred acres of land south of the club, he developed the Royal Palm Yacht and Country Club. He completely refurnished and redecorated the hotel itself, restoring much of the original Mizner charm. He completely rebuilt the golf course, making it one of the best championship courses in the South. On the beach of the barrier island just east of the hotel, he built what is probably the largest cabaña club in the world. Davis and his staff restored the manicured tropical splendor that had been part of the Mizner dream. Thus the great entrance drive, El Camino Real, which Mizner had proposed to make the widest and most splendid boulevard in the world, is almost that. It ends at a magnificently landscaped circle where enormous wrought-iron gates open onto the immediate grounds of the hotel and club. Five hundred acres of superb gardens provide a tropical setting.

If Mizner were alive today he would doubtless agree that Boca Raton now approaches his dream.

Boca Raton is concentrated in two buildings—the main hotel and the cabaña club. The hotel is huge and rambling and spreads over acres of ground. Its extending wings enclose two vast tropical patios in true Spanish style, and many of its guest rooms have balconies overlooking Lake Boca Raton.

The resort itself is a riot of color. Outside the hotel color is found in the pink and white walls of the building and in the flowering of tropical plants. Color is everywhere inside the building in the décor of a bewildering cluster of rooms with exotic names. The Cathedral Dining

Room, for example, the resort's main dining room, presents a spectacle of golden columns ending at a pale-blue vaulted ceiling. The floor is covered with a plum-colored rug. The Patio Royal, another of the several dining areas, is decorated in light blue and crimson. The Loggia, a favorite rendezvous for cocktails, is done in blue and green. The wall of the men's locker room is graced with a two-hundred-year-old Gothic carving, more appropriate to a monastery than a meeting place for golfers. Many rooms that Mizner or Geist planned for other purposes have been converted to provide convention facilities.

Thus, an auditorium theater is housed in an indoor swimming pool room, built during the Geist era. The Mizner Room, also used for meetings, resembles a medieval cloister.

The second building of the resort, the cabaña club, overlooks the ocean about a mile away from the main resort building and is reached by a road leading over the Intracoastal Waterway and through the luxurious new homes called Boca Raton Estates. The club is built in a great semicircle facing the wide white beach. It has two hundred private cabañas, a solarium, two dining rooms, a cocktail lounge, an outdoor bar on the beach, the inevitable enormous swimming pool, and several meeting rooms.

The cabaña club is a three-minute drive from the main building. Practically all of the other outdoor facilities of Boca Raton are within walking distance of the hotel. The resort boat dock, on the shore of Lake Boca Raton, can accommodate twenty-five large yachts up to a hundred thirty feet in length. Several slips are equipped with electrical and telephone facilities so that owners can live aboard. Boca Raton is a favorite stop for yachts passing along the Intracoastal Waterway, a few hundred yards from the marina. The resort maintains a water-ski school, and just south of the hotel on the shore of the lake is a huge fresh-water swimming pool.

Other facilities include tennis courts, archery, bowling on the green, and shuffleboard. The resort's notable golf course has its first tee just a few steps from a rear entrance of the hotel. The present course, bearing little resemblance to the earlier one, was completely redesigned with the aid of Robert Trent Jones a few years ago. Greens were rebuilt and three lakes have been added to the course. The total yardage is 6690, a par 71. The course is not difficult, and it favors average players. It is fringed with palm trees and other tropical plants. The club pro is Sam Snead.

Polo matches are held every Sunday between January and April at the Royal Palm Polo Grounds, not far from the hotel.

The meals at Boca Raton are extremely varied. Dinner in the Cathedral Dining Room can be a full-fledged Continental meal. Lunch at the cabaña club is often an informal but extensive buffet. The Polo Lounge, linked to the golf-course area by an outdoor dining terrace, is a frequent setting for steak roasts.

Boca Raton is very accessible by car. Its grounds flank the right of way of U.S. 1, and the resort's own spectacular entrance drive leads off that busy highway at the village of Boca Raton, which is twenty-two miles south of Palm Beach and thirty-five miles north of Miami. It is equally accessible from the seaward side by Florida Route A1A. Passengers arriving by rail come by either the Florida East Coast or the Seaboard railways. There is a train station in Boca Raton Village, where taxis are available. The resort is also accessible by boat through the Intracoastal Waterway, and by air from commercial airports at Miami, Fort Lauderdale, and West Palm Beach.

Rates at Boca Raton, based on full American plan, vary with the season and type of accommodation. The lowest rates are in two periods from October to mid-December and from mid-April to the closing of the hotel for the summer. The low rates run from $22.50 per day per person, with two occupying a room. Special holiday rates are offered from December 14 to January 13, when the rate for two guests in a room is $50 per day. The high-rate season is from mid-January to March 1, when the minimum rate per person for double occupancy of a room is $25 per day. Cabaña rates start at $12 per day, depending on location. Greens fees for registered guests on the golf course are $5 for eighteen holes. No charge is made for the use of many facilities, such as table tennis, shuffleboard, tennis, the nine-hole pitch-and-putt course, a nine-hole putting green, or practice on the club's driving fairway, for which clubs can be rented from the Pro Shop. The resort maintains charter boats for guests at $50 for a half day for four persons, $90 for a full day.

PONCE DE LEÓN AND MINERAL SAND

Some historians contend that the first land sighted by Ponce de León, in 1513, was a strip of beach midway between the present cities of Jacksonville and St. Augustine. There seems little doubt that after sighting land the Spanish explorer who discovered Florida veered a little to the south and came ashore at what is now St. Augustine, seeking the Fountain of Youth. There is no evidence that Ponce de León ever visited the beach he first sighted. Eventually that beach acquired a Spanish name, Ponte Vedra, probably derived from Spanish communities and regions of the same name.

About four hundred years after Ponce de León first saw Ponte Vedra from the sea, the beach became a vital aid to the World War I effort. It was discovered that the white and shining sands of Ponte Vedra beach were rich in minerals urgently needed. The beach itself and the deep sandy soil behind it were found to contain appreciable quantities of zircon silicate, monzonite, and titanium—all useful in the war. The Government sent great dredges to the area that gouged ragged ditches in the sandy soil. It is ironic that the massive disfiguration left by the dredging is now one of the most distinctive and attractive features of the Ponte Vedra Inn and Club. The huge trenches today are shining lagoons that wind along behind the beach, flanking the golf course.

Ponte Vedra beach was a route for troops in the long and bloody struggle between Spanish, French, and English forces for the southern Atlantic coast. In 1565 the Spanish destroyed a French invading force that was coming up from the south. The savage massacre took place along the banks of the Matanzas River, a few miles south of St. Augustine. More than one hundred years later the Spanish, desperately trying to hang onto Florida, were defeated and driven from the area by the English in a battle on one of the coastal islands of Georgia early in the eighteenth century, a few miles north of Ponte Vedra. The first notice given to the beach in modern times was recognition of the high mineral content of the sands. Then in 1928, when Florida was in the news, the Ponte Vedra area was recognized as having opportunities for development. A log clubhouse was built on the beach and a nine-hole golf course laid out. When the state of Florida built a shore highway a few years later between St. Augustine and Jacksonville—famous Route A1A—Ponte Vedra beach began to grow. The golf course grew to eighteen holes, then to twenty-seven. The beach-front log clubhouse became a handsome central lodge, with villas stretching along the beach in both directions, and Ponte Vedra assumed the character and proportions of a true resort estate.

Today more than twenty buildings stretch along the beach. The main lodge has an assortment of spacious public rooms and facilities. Most of the guest rooms are in groups of cottages and villas, either facing the beach or near it. Also facing the beach is the Surf Club, and there are two huge swimming pools flanked by a wide paved sun terrace. Adjoining the pool is the Patio, a favorite setting for nighttime dining and dancing.

Two features of the resort are distinctive: the private beach, a mile long of glistening white sand, one of the finest in the world; and the twenty-seven hole golf course along both sides of the lagoons. The lagoons help give the resort its remarkable character, providing both a scenic setting and a series of dramatic challenges to golfers. The course is designed to hold the interest and tax the skill of par players, but it will not discourage the weekend duffer. One golf writer described it recently like this:

> Ponte Vedra is tough; some people find it fascinatingly tough. Others regard it as unduly tricky and unfair. It can get you an argument in any group of experienced golfers. The holes are so tricky that they eat up balls, and some skilled players feel that the course does not respond fairly to an accurate game of top golf. But for most people it is a fascinating course, one on which every hole is the satisfying result of brains, money and loving care.

The lagoons traverse the whole length of the course. At least half the holes cross them or are trapped by them. Several holes are unique. The green of Number 9 is on an island in the middle of a lagoon and is reached by a wooden walkway. Number 4 also plays across a lagoon. The greens of Numbers 2 and 10 have a lagoon behind them on three sides. Overplay is disastrous. An arm of a lagoon extends into the fairway of Number 3, making sure losses of the balls of dubbed drives. The first eighteen holes, a par 72, add to 6786 yards from the long tee. The additional nine holes are a par 36, 3618 yards.

An unusual sport offered by Ponte Vedra is quail hunting. The club has its own quail preserve, fifteen minutes' drive from the inn itself, which has a hunting lodge with every convenience at the preserve. Duck and wild turkey are also hunted there. The inn makes all arrangements for hunting, including guns and ammunition for guests.

Dining at Ponte Vedra Inn is noted for the variety of its menu and the quality of the food. There are a number of dining areas available, including a handsome, semiformal dining room, the golf club, and the Surf Club, where diners are seated overlooking the ocean. Southern cooking, some Continental specialties, and a wide variety of the fine seafood for which Florida is famous are available.

The most popular city of interest in northern Florida is the historic city of St. Augustine, which is less than twenty-five miles south of the inn on Route A1A. St. Augustine is crowded with historic sites, including the magnificent Castillo de San Marcos National Monument, which was built by the Spaniards to defend the coast of Florida in 1672; it is a fine example of a masonry fort. Other historic sights include the oldest wooden schoolhouse in the country, the original city gates, an old Spanish treasure, and the presumed site of the Fountain of Youth, which Ponce de León didn't find.

The resort city of Daytona Beach is sixty miles south of St. Augustine on the shore. Its famous beach is one of the widest in the world. The St. Johns River, which flows north to Jacksonville roughly parallel with the shore several miles west of Ponte Vedra Inn, provides some of the finest fresh-water fishing in the country. Boat docks and boats, tackle and bait are available at various points along the river.

Ponte Vedra Inn and Club is easily reached by automobile, train, or plane. It's about fifteen miles southeast of Jacksonville, with express highways from Jacksonville to the shore and Route A1A south along the shore. Jacksonville itself is a hub of main express highways coming in from the north, west, and south: from the north U.S. 1, 17, and 23 and Interstate 95; from the west Interstate 10; from the south U.S. 17 and U.S. 1. It is possible to reach Ponte Vedra from the south on U.S. 1 by leaving the express road at Durbin, about fifteen miles south of Jacksonville, and following 210 to its junction with Route A1A just south of the inn.

Several airlines, particularly Eastern, National, Northeast, United, and Delta, provide regular service to Jacksonville. Rail service to Jacksonville is provided by the Atlantic Coast Line and Seaboard Railway. From Jacksonville taxi or car rental service is available at airport and railway terminals.

Ponte Vedra Inn and Club operates on the modified American plan (which includes breakfast and dinner) between October 1 and March 1. The rates begin at $24 per day for a single room, $32 for a double room. Larger rooms and suites vary in rates according to location; thus, a penthouse room is $24 single, $42 double; an ocean house is $34 single, $42 double; a studio bedroom is $36 single, $44 double. Rates on all accommodations are about 20 per cent higher between March 1 and June 1, the most popular season at the resort. There are lower rates during the summer, from June 1 to October 1. Fees at the golf course are $6 per day per player. Tennis-court fees are $1 per person per hour.

PALATIAL LUXURY AND COCONUT PALMS

Among the pioneers who helped transform Florida none accomplished more than Henry Morrison Flagler. Over a period of about thirty years, he developed a railway empire that made Florida accessible to the rest of the world. He built a half-dozen huge and celebrated hotels, and he helped to develop communities such as St. Augustine, Palm Beach, and Miami.

An enduring monument to Henry Flagler is one of the world's most palatial resort hotels, the majestic Breakers, which dominates the beautiful resort of Palm Beach. Flagler died in 1913 and never saw the Breakers as it exists today, but it is the direct product of his dynamic career in Florida.

The Flagler story began in true Horatio Alger style. He was born in 1830, in northern New York State. The son of a poor Presbyterian minister, Flagler left school at the end of the eighth grade to improve his family's meager income. He saved his money, moved from job to job, and bettered himself with each move. Some years later he found himself in Ohio in the grain-commission business.

In the grain business he met a young man named John D. Rockefeller, who was one of his Cleveland customers. The two men became friends and then partners. The result was that Henry Flagler retired from business when he was fifty-three, and went to Florida to relax. He was a millionaire many times over from his association with Rockefeller and the founding (in which Flagler shared) of the Standard Oil Company.

In the winter of 1883 and 1884, Flagler turned up in St. Augustine, Florida, which then was a tiny but delightful community steeped in history. Flagler, delighted with the Florida climate and the beauty of old St. Augustine, decided to go into business again, planning to build a new kind of resort hotel there that would help to draw the thousands of rich Americans to Florida who were going elsewhere for their winter holidays. The Ponce de Leon was begun in 1885 and is still there, one of the most remarkable and ornate in the country.

Flagler's primary interest was hotels to serve winter visitors who could afford tropical luxury, but he soon realized that, to get them to Florida, he would have to provide reliable transportation. Before long he controlled more railroads than anyone else in Florida and was extending the tracks of his lines south along the east coast. That process inevitably brought him to a region then called Lake Worth, which was actually a wide channel between the mainland and an island chain. The only town in the area was the tiny hamlet of Jupiter, which was at the head of Hobe Sound, just north of Lake Worth. From Jupiter a railway only eight miles long led to the lake itself. It was known as the Celestial Railroad because it linked the communities of Jupiter, Mars, Venus, and Juno. Juno was at the head of Lake Worth.

Flagler first visited the area in 1893. With the imagination of an inspired land developer, he saw that the island flanking the ocean on the east side of the lake was a unique site for a new hotel and community. Its uniqueness was in part the result of an ancient accident. Many years before, a Spanish ship, the *Providencia,* had been wrecked on the coast. Its cargo of coconuts was washed ashore, and the pioneer settlers planted them, hoping to establish a thriving copra business. Instead they covered the whole area of the island to the north and east of Lake Worth with a forest of palm trees. It was the palm groves, combined with the delightful winter climate, that attracted Flagler. He set about establishing a resort community on the island, linking it to the mainland with a causeway and building a monumental resort hotel.

Flagler's plans leaked out, and although he managed to acquire the real estate he wanted before a boom set in, the inevitable inflation in land prices occurred, boosting values from $100 to more than $1000 an acre. The same land is now probably worth at least $100,000 an acre.

Flagler broke ground for his immense new hotel in May 1893. The problems of logistics and construction were monumental but were solved with incredible efficiency. Nine months later the new hotel was completed—painted, furnished, and open for guests. Flagler is usually credited with naming the community. The name was inspired—Palm Beach. It became the most sumptuous resort community in the world. The name of the hotel—the Royal Poinciana—was fanciful, one of the few hotels named for a flowering vine. It was the largest wooden building in the world and had more guest rooms than any other resort hotel —more than a thousand. For its grounds Flagler set aside a complete slice of the island. The resort was an immediate success. Flagler bridged Lake Worth with a causeway that permitted his railroad to run a spur line into the resort, and it was soon filled with the private cars of millionaires of the country. With the Royal Poinciana filled, Flagler started another hotel on the opposite side of his property, overlooking the ocean. He called it the Palm Beach Inn, which commanded a marvelous stretch of ocean beach. The inn was soon renamed the Breakers.

A pier was built so that steamers could dock near its main entrance. Flagler promptly established a steamship line running between Palm Beach and Nassau.

In 1905, the first Breakers, which only had ninety rooms, was destroyed by fire. It was rebuilt the next year with two hundred fifty rooms. The second Breakers burned to the ground in 1925 and also was rebuilt the next year.

Today the Breakers is a massive fireproof building with classically ornate rooms that fill its lower floor. Its four hundred fifty luxurious guest rooms and suites can accommodate about six hundred sixty people. Since its opening in 1926, it has dominated the ocean shore of Palm Beach island. But for the first eight years of its existence it was subordinate to its huge and nearby neighbor, the tremendous Royal Poinciana. Then the 1934 hurricane devastated the sprawling wooden building. It was impossible to rebuild, so the hotel was torn down, leaving the Breakers as the dominant resort on Palm Beach.

The Breakers is much more than a hotel. It is a magnificent self-contained resort estate of more than two hundred acres. The main structure is essentially the same in design and character when its doors were opened to guests in 1926. Throughout the years it has been remodeled and modernized so that while it is still classically ornate its appointments and facilities are thoroughly modern. A regal Roman pool and a tremendous cabaña club owned by the hotel are on the beach front. The Breakers casino is nearby. West of the hotel is the celebrated Breakers golf course. It is 6008 yards in length, a par 70, and was designed by Donald Ross. It is faultlessly maintained and provides adequate challenge for the most exacting golfer and opportunity for the novice.

There are several great and elegant dining rooms at the Breakers. Menus are traditionally Continental. Its proprietors, heirs to the Flagler railroad and resort empire, describe their great resort as one that offers "luxurious comfort in an atmosphere of refined exclusiveness." Most guests at the Breakers don't use the resort as a sight-seeing base, but there are places to go in the area. Palm Beach itself is a good beginning. It is one of the most beautiful communities in the world and is the northern gateway to the whole Florida Gold Coast.

From the Breakers itself a highway leads south, closely following the shore, to a chain of pleasant towns and resort communities, climaxed by Miami Beach, a city unique in color and character. Hotels of extraordinary design and remarkable facilities vie with each other for attention. The booming metropolis of Miami itself has dozens of sights from horse racing to alligator wrestling. Beyond Miami, U.S. 1 leaves the mainland to leapfrog over a chain of tropical islands—the Florida Keys—and at the end of the chain is the city of Key West. This highway is one of the most spectacular overwater automobile journeys in the world.

Less than two hours from Palm Beach is the Everglades National Park, the great amphibious wonderland. For guests who prefer fishing to sight-seeing, Lake Okeechobee, one of the world's most unusual lakes, is less than thirty miles from Palm Beach. There is superb black-bass fishing, and hundreds of boats with tackle and guides are available. A half day's drive north of Palm Beach is the Cape Kennedy complex.

The Breakers is easily reached by rail, air, or highway. U.S. 1 passes through West Palm Beach, across the channel from Palm Beach. Florida's north-south toll road, the Sunshine State Parkway, has a West Palm Beach exit. Travelers from the west usually enter Florida from the northwest on U.S. 90 or 27, the latter angling southeast through the state to a point west of Palm Beach. Route 441 then leads east to West Palm Beach and Palm Beach. Flagler's original Florida East Coast Railway comes in from the north to a West Palm Beach station. Both communities are served by several airlines. Service is, of course, available into the Miami International Airport.

The Breakers is open only during the winter, starting about mid-December and closing April 15. It is operated on the full American plan, and rates start at $26 per day for a single room, and $48 per day for a double room. Two-room suites begin at about $60 per day for two.

QUEEN OF THE GULF

As Henry Flagler was developing Palm Beach and Miami, Henry Plant, who owned the Atlantic Coast Line, was building up the west coast of Florida. Its tracks cut into and through central Florida to St. Petersburg Bay and helped to develop Tampa and St. Petersburg. Perhaps the best-known monument that Plant left is the University of Tampa. He constructed its main building as a hotel to rival those put up by Flagler on the east coast. Plant, using florid examples of Moorish magnificence, built a grotesque, minareted pile that is astonishing in size, shape, and ornamental detail. Today it is a sight-seeing landmark in the heart of Tampa.

Plant's most successful operation was another hotel, the huge Belleview, just west of the present city of Clearwater. He had in mind a luxury resort where he could entertain business associates and friends and increase the patronage of his newly established Atlantic Coast Line Railway. About 1895 he decided that his hotel should be built on a thousand acres of property he had acquired near Clearwater. Two factors influenced his decision: climate—Clearwater had more days of sunshine during the year than any other city in the state; and topography—the particular tract chosen was an elevated bluff with rolling land cut by natural ravines, and springs and creeks cut through the land to the Gulf, an unusual condition on Florida's west coast.

With his usual zest for getting big jobs done quickly, Plant brought large crews of workmen to the site to clear away the palmetto thickets, clumps of oak, and Florida pines that covered the site. Construction began in 1895. The grand opening was held on January 15, 1895.

The original building contained 145 guest rooms, described in a brochure as containing:

> three incandescent electric lights, a mantle of polished cedar with handsome tiling surrounding the fireplace, polished floors and oak or cherry furniture, large rugs in many of the rooms, and entire carpeted floors for those who prefer them. There are several suites of rooms with bath connected.

In addition to general advertising, Plant made sure that anyone who rode his railroad in a private car would have a place to park it while a guest at the resort. Plant's zeal and advertising paid off. The Hotel Belleview was an immediate success, although Plant did not live to see it develop into the popular resort it would become within the next two decades. He died soon after the grand opening.

By 1909 the Belleview had become so well established as a winter resort that a new wing was added, doubling the hotel's capacity. And a few years later its name was doubled in size when its new owners added Biltmore to the Belleview. The hotel still continued to grow; another wing was added in 1924, which brought its total number of rooms to four hundred fifty. It also developed a resort colony with "cottages" ranging in size from eight to sixteen rooms, including quarters for large staffs of servants. The cottages were occupied in the winter by wealthy industrialists who were chiefly from the Midwest.

Then came the Depression of 1929, and virtual bankruptcy. Control reverted to bondholders, most of whom were residents of the Clearwater area. For years a succession of managers struggled to keep the vast property open and operating, but without much success. In 1942 the entire property was requisitioned by the United States Government and made into an auxiliary barracks for Air Corps personnel from nearby training bases. At the end of the war the tremendous property was acquired by a new set of owners, who represented a variety of interests. Many of them were local to the area, but the combine was headed by a group of Detroit men. They began the gargantuan job of refitting, restoring, remodeling, and reopening the great hotel. It took several years to finish the job. In convenience and comfort the big resort was modernized, but the spacious elegance of its early days also was restored.

In addition to the main building itself, changes were made on the grounds. The golf courses were redesigned to provide two eighteen-hole courses of championship quality. They begin and end near the hotel's east porch. A thirty-six-hole putting green was added close by the main building. Several new tennis courts were built. A fishing and boating dock was extended into the bay. A long stretch of private Gulf beach was equipped with appropriate cabañas. On the immediate grounds of the hotel a huge tiled swimming pool, first built in 1916, was remodeled. The resort's transformation was a fascinating blending of modern functionalism with its elegant Victorian ancestry.

Today the Belleview-Biltmore owns more than six hundred acres of waterfront property facing the secluded waters of Clearwater Sound. The two adjoining golf courses are beautifully maintained and provide enough challenge for top-flight golfers. Each course is a par 72. In addition to its fine private beach, the resort has its own cruiser available for deep-sea fishing.

For those guests who wish to explore the area, the old Spanish Quarter of Tampa, twenty-five miles to the east, is fascinating. The Greek sponge-fishing settlement at Tarpon Springs, north of Clearwater, attracts many visitors. The handsome little city of Sarasota is about an hour's drive south of the resort, through St. Petersburg on U.S. 19. Most of the town is devoted to the circus, including the museum of the Circus. The elegant Ringling Museum houses the largest collection of paintings by Rubens in this country. Big-league baseball games are played near Clearwater almost daily in March and early April. An assortment of nature and historic exhibits is scattered throughout the area. Everglades National Park, reached over the Tamiami Trail, is a half day's drive to the south.

The Belleview-Biltmore is easy to reach by most modes of transportation. It is two miles from Clearwater, twenty miles from St. Petersburg, and twenty-four miles from Tampa. Main highways converge from all directions. For travelers from the Atlantic seaboard, Interstate 4 leads diagonally across the state directly to Tampa. For travelers from the west the main routes of U.S. 19 and U.S. 41 lead into Tampa and Clearwater. The Atlantic Coast Line and Seaboard Line railroads have direct trains to Clearwater. Delta, Northwest-Orient, Trans-Canada, United, Eastern, and National airlines fly into Tampa International Airport, nineteen miles from the resort. Guests arriving by plane are met at the airport on advance notice.

The Belleview-Biltmore is open from early January to late April. It operates entirely on full American plan. Rates vary with the type of room, starting at $20 per day per person for two or more in a room. Suites are available at higher rates.

"DAMN THE TORPEDOES! FULL SPEED AHEAD!"

One of the great natural harbors of North America is Mobile Bay, which extends from the Gulf of Mexico thirty-five miles north to the mouth of the Mobile River. It is from eight to eighteen miles wide—a large and safe enough ocean harbor for a vast fleet. The big bay meets the open Gulf of Mexico between Florida on the east and Mississippi on the west. A cluster of deep rivers reaches the bay through a fertile delta. Mobile is at the northwest corner of the bay. The old, proud city claims a heritage of culture and civilization that goes back further than the Gulf's great port of New Orleans. The vast bay is bell-shaped—narrow at its head and wider toward the Gulf. Two slender sandspits thrust out from either shore, almost closing the bay. Low wooded bluffs rise from the shore, cut here and there by the quiet water of a bayou.

For more than four hundred years Mobile Bay has been a focus of history. One historical event involves the Grand Hotel at Point Clear, which is on the eastern shore of the bay.

The event was the Battle of Mobile Bay, during which Admiral David Farragut, who was in command of a massive Union fleet, overwhelmed the guardian forts at the entrance after a nineteen-day bombardment. The admiral, who had himself lashed to the rigging to ensure better vision, sailed toward Mobile with his fleet. His gunboats shot cannon balls in all directions. Warned that the bay was full of torpedoes, that is, mines, the admiral issued that now famous command: "Damn the torpedoes! Full speed ahead!"

The command has a unique significance for the Grand Hotel, for just about the time the admiral gave his command, one of his cannon sent a shot through a wall of one of the hotel buildings. The jagged cannon-ball hole is still there, carefully and proudly preserved by the proprietors of Point Clear. An extraordinary mural of the Battle of Mobile Bay hangs from one wall of the hotel's cocktail lounge. It clearly shows that Admiral Farragut lost the battle.

Mobile Bay was an important place long before Admiral Farragut put a shell through the hotel's wall. Few regions around the Gulf have had a more vigorous and colorful past.

Seventeen years before Admiral Farragut won the Battle of Mobile Bay, the first hotel on the site was built. Guests discover very quickly why this particular site was chosen. The whole eastern shore of Mobile Bay has a far better climate than any nearby area. Point Clear, in particular, has a superb climate, and a prevailing breeze makes even the hottest summer day comfortable and provides temperate weather in the winter, too.

In the nineteenth century rich plantation owners who found the summer in the Gulf area humid and oppressive began to hear about the unique atmosphere of Mobile Bay. They began to build summer homes near Point Clear, and before long there was a row of them stretching several miles in two directions. Boats traveled between New Orleans and Mobile, bringing the summer cottage owners to the area and taking them back again. So it was natural that some kind of resort would develop. The first Grand Hotel at Point Clear was completed in 1847, built with timbers brought from Mobile on sailing boats. Soon regular ferry service was operating between the two points. The hotel drew the elite of the South and became a social center for the rich and leisured. An early report of life there said: "It was the gathering place for the merchants of the South, and poker games with high stakes and billiards enlivened with the best of liquors were their pastimes."

The booming prosperity of the first Grand Hotel was sharply broken by the Civil War. The hotel was deserted; Mobile Bay itself became a base for Confederate blockade runners. Several ships were built in yards on the bay. The same yards built Confederate warships, including one that is claimed to have been the first submarine, sunk while attacking a Union warship in 1864. The Confederate ironsides *Tennes-*

see, flagship of the fleet that opposed Farragut in 1864, also was built on the bay.

As the war deepened, the deserted resort was taken over for military purposes. One of the larger buildings was turned into a hospital. Another became an officers' residence. Then came the Battle of Mobile Bay, with Farragut's powerful fleet fighting its way north toward Mobile. A fire leveled most of the resort a few years later. In 1875 it was rebuilt and for some years enjoyed a brisk new prosperity. It again became the leading resort of the South, drawing distinguished families from all along the Gulf. The hotel's dock at Point Clear became a regular stop for steamers from New Orleans.

In the late 1930's the second Grand Hotel was torn down and the present one built, opening in 1940. The adjacent cottages were completed in 1952. The new owners represented shipping interests, so it is one of the few resorts in the United States owned by a shipping company. Naval architects helped design the building, with the result that the profile of the hotel suggests in a vague way the shape of a ship. Timbers in the big dining room overlooking the bay were brought from sturdy wooden ships and ocean piers.

The Grand Hotel at Point Clear today is notable in many ways and unusual in several. It is the only resort on the North American Continent which was actually involved in a Civil War battle. It is the oldest resort anywhere in the South below Virginia, and certainly the most famous resort in the whole Gulf Coast area. Its setting is extraordinary, filling the sharp triangle of Point Clear and extending for several hundred acres behind the point. The resort has 122 guest rooms and suites, both in the main hotel and in a cluster of cottages suitable for group and family use. Nearly all the rooms are distinguished by an unusual feature—paneling of lustrous golden-brown cypress, a wood for which the Gulf Coast region is famous.

The main hotel building is beautifully adapted to its setting. A central core rises three stories, and long, two-story wings extend in four directions. Guest rooms in the wings have maximum exposure to the breeze, the sun, and the view of the bay, which sweeps away on both sides of the point. The central core of the building contains a lobby with an enormous six-sided stone fireplace. A tremendous stone chimney rises through the building. Public rooms open from the lobby. The main dining room has huge picture windows on three sides overlooking the bay. The massive beamed ceiling is built from former ships' timbers. In front of the dining room at the precise tip of Point Clear is a pavilion called Julep Point, a favorite nighttime spot for cocktails and dancing.

From one side of the point the resort's excellent sand beach lies, a favorite place for ocean bathing. A long, slender pier extends at the end of the beach and is used for casual fishing. Poles and bait are provided by an attendant. On the opposite side of the point is a cluster of guest cottages, each with a living room, porch or terrace, and from one to four bedrooms. They extend along the point to a yacht harbor and small-boat anchorage that lead inland from the point itself and provide berths for craft up to the size of an ocean yacht. Boat-servicing facilities are available for almost any request or supply. Beyond the boat harbor is the resort's incredible swimming pool, probably the largest pool maintained by any resort anywhere. It is a hundred forty feet wide, flanked with paved terraces and a succession of roofed shelters. Opening into the pool from the hotel side is a picturesque lagoon that is fed by a fountain at one end. Built of authentic Spanish tile brought from South America, the fountain commemorates the fact that Mobile Bay once was a Spanish possession and was discovered by a Spaniard.

Other recreations include bowling on the green, croquet, horseshoe pitching, tennis, two courts, and shuffleboard. The resort's most celebrated recreational area is its championship golf course—the Lakewood Golf Club. Developed in a grove of towering pine trees a half mile inland from the point, it is one of the best courses in the South, 6713 yards from the long tees, and a par 70. Its big, handsome clubhouse building, with facilities for dining and a golf shop, resembles a Swiss chalet. The course is highly scenic, with most fairways running between groves of tall pines and masses of blooming, semitropical shrubbery. Twelve of the eighteen holes are dog-legs. The course was designed by Perry Maxwell, one of the leading golf architects of the country. It calls for accuracy and will penalize long hitters who lack control. The greens are small but superbly maintained, and they at first startle some players when they discover that tee flags are miniature Confederate flags.

On the Fish River, eight miles northeast of the resort, is the hotel's fresh-water fishing camp. Skiffs with power, tackle, and bait are available. Speckled trout and fresh-water bass are the catch. The resort offers deep-sea fishing from its own power cruisers.

The Grand Hotel's menus are richly varied, and seafood is a specialty. French and Creole dishes are featured too, suggesting the resort's historic heritage in French and Spanish settlers of Mobile and New

Orleans. There is a snack bar at the pool, and a full menu of short-order specialties is available at the golf clubhouse. An extraordinary buffet in the main dining room is often held, where twenty-three kinds of fish are served in thirty-three different ways.

There are a number of unusual and rewarding nearby places to see. Two historic old forts are on opposite sides of the entrance to the bay from the Gulf. On the east side is Fort Morgan, now preserved as a state park. The fort was begun in 1813 as a defense during the War of 1812. It is a copy of an ancient Italian fort. Fort Morgan held out for nineteen days against Farragut's Union fleet and still bears scars of that battle. Opposite Fort Morgan is Fort Gaines, near a fine ocean beach and casino.

One of the showplaces of the South, Bellingrath Gardens, is across the bay from Point Clear, reached by car or boat. The luxurious home is now a museum open to the public with an extraordinary collection of Americana. The garden spreads over many acres and is one of the finest exhibits of flowers, trees, and shrubs in the South, superbly displayed in a series of formal and informal arrangements, linked by walks leading through groves of ancient trees.

At the head of the bay is the city of Mobile, Alabama's only seaport, twenty-three miles northwest of Point Clear. Founded by the French in 1710, it has an unmistakable imprint of French culture. Beautiful ante-bellum mansions line the residential streets. Mobile's annual Mardi Gras, although not as famous as New Orleans' Mardi Gras, is older in origin and was first staged in 1704.

The Grand Hotel at Mobile Bay is one of the most accessible resorts in the country, by air, highway, and boat. Interstate 10, U.S. 90, and U.S. 98 parallel each other along the Gulf through Mobile, with U.S. 98 leading past the front gates of the resort. New Orleans is 174 miles to the west; Pensacola, Florida, less than fifty miles to the east. Interstate 65 leads northeast to centers of population along the Atlantic coast, and U.S. 43 leads north to the Midwest and Chicago, 893 miles away.

United, Eastern, National, and Southern airlines fly to Mobile. The hotel will meet guests arriving at the Mobile airport on notice, bringing them to Point Clear for $6 per person. For private plane use the well-equipped new municipal airport at Fairhope, a four-minute drive from the Grand Hotel. Railway service to Mobile is offered by the Louisville and Nashville Railway. The hotel will meet guests on notice and bring them to Point Clear from the railway station for $4 per person. Many guests at Point Clear arrive in their own boats along the Intracoastal Waterway, a channel of which crosses Mobile Bay a few miles south of Point Clear.

Guest rates at the Grand Hotel are all American plan and vary slightly with the season. The main, high-rate season is in two sections, from February 15 to May 31, and from October 1 to November 15. During that season double-room rates start at $40 per day, with a double room reserved for single occupancy starting at $30. Small suites start at $46 per day for two, or $52 per day for a corner suite with a parlor and one bedroom. Cottage accommodations for four people, including two twin bedrooms, two baths, and living room, are $94. The rate for a third person in any two-person room is $12 per day. Slightly lower rates are available in the off seasons: June 1 to 14, September 4 to 30, November 16 to February 14. Then a double room, American plan, is $36. European-plan rates are available starting June 15 through Labor Day, starting at $17 per room, either single or double occupancy.

Special rates for various activities include $4 per day for greens fees on the golf course. Bicycles can be rented for $1.50 per day. Sailboats are rented for $4 for the first hour, $3 for each additional hour. Deep-sea fishing cruisers can be chartered by the hour or day. The rate is $12 for the first hour, $10 per hour after that, or $80 for a ten-hour day.

CHAPTER 7

MIDDLE LAKES AND
MOUNTAINS

From northwestern New York extending southwest about three hundred miles is an inland zone of mountains and lakes. The mountains, divided by broad fertile valleys, are in distinctive groups. The lakes are within the mountains and on their foothill fringes. In the area are several unusual topographic regions, each dominated by a resort estate of special character.

The ancient, wild, and wooded ranges of the Adirondacks fill the northeast corner of New York, protected from despoilment by a two-million-acre forest preserve. There, Lake Placid is a jewel at the center of a forest wilderness. An alpine resort called Whiteface Inn, the most celebrated resort in the Adirondacks, overlooks Lake Placid. It was established during the resort boom of the last quarter of the nineteenth century, and it has survived, grown, and prospered because of skilled management, its superb setting, and its fine climate.

About 125 miles to the southwest is a narrow lake of great charm, which the Indians called Glimmerglass and the map makers call Otsego. On the lake shore, set among the rolling hills of the Mohawk Valley, is the Otesaga Hotel, a resort of individual character that grew and prospered for quite special reasons, involving neither setting nor climate (although the setting is handsome enough), but events of history and the habits and treasures of people. The village where the resort is situated is named for the father of James Fenimore Cooper, a gifted writer of stories about Indians. His home, the village of Cooperstown, is full of relics of him and his Indian heroes. Another man, who made Cooperstown even more famous, was named Doubleday. He in-

22. The main entrance to Florida's opulent Boca Raton resort combines Spanish architecture and tropical palms.

23. With its boat docks and golf course Boca Raton's landscaped tropical grounds spread over several hundred acres.

24. Bordering wide lagoons, the unusual golf course of Florida's Ponte Vedra Club has one famous hole on an island.

25. Largest and most extensively gabled wooden resort hotel in the world, the Belleview-Biltmore, at Clearwater, Florida, has an impressive shore setting.

26. The Belleview-Biltmore's new Beach and Cabaña Club commands an important stretch of beach and gulf shore.

27. A geological oddity, Point Clear, in Mobile Bay, Alabama, makes an unusual setting for the oldest resort on the Gulf Coast, the Grand Hotel.

28. A remarkable painting in the cocktail lounge of the Grand Hotel proves that Admiral Farragut must have *lost* the battle of Mobile Bay, a few years after the resort was founded.

29. In the wilderness heart of forested mountains, on the shore of lovely Lake Placid, Whiteface Inn is both one of the oldest and most celebrated resorts in the Adirondacks.

30. Whiteface Mountain, second highest in the Adirondacks, rises above Lake Placid. A stunning view of both the mountain and lake are part of the scenic dividend for guests at Whiteface Inn.

31. Few resorts have a more impressive entrance than the Otesaga Hotel, in the museum village of Cooperstown, New York.

32. Largest and finest resort in the Poconos of Pennsylvania is the Inn at Buck Hill Falls, set among several thousand acres of forested slopes.

33. Excellent courts for bowling on the green are maintained by the inn.

34. Some guests at Buck Hill Falls combine sight-seeing with riding, include an inspection of the resort's most famous scenic novelty, a tumbling waterfall.

35. Commanding a hilltop overlooking the town of Hershey, Pennsylvania, an unusual memorial to a remarkable man that chocolate made famous is the Hershey Hotel.

vented baseball at Cooperstown. Today the village has the National Baseball Museum and Hall of Fame, one of several museums in the unique treasure village of Cooperstown. One is about farming, another about New York's history. They all draw a stream of curious visitors for whom the Otesaga Hotel, a complete resort estate on the lake shore, offers luxurious sanctuary.

About a hundred miles south of Cooperstown in eastern Pennsylvania are the Poconos, a cluster of rugged, isolated hills that rise above the west shore of the Delaware River. They have three special qualities that have made them the most popular resort district for miles around, and the setting for one of the largest and most unusual resorts in the East: climate, easy access to urban centers, and isolation. Main routes of travel by-pass them, so that for many years after the rest of the region was settled the Poconos were almost empty until the Quakers from Philadelphia discovered that they had a pleasant and invigorating climate in winter and summer. The Quakers started a summer colony called the Inn at Buck Hill Falls. It has grown into a baronial resort estate, with a great central lodge rising like a castle on the Rhine above the crests of thousands of acres of wooded hills. Surrounding the Inn at Buck Hill Falls are other resorts—large and small, luxurious and primitive—which draw swarms of visitors year round to golf, swim, hike, fish, and ski.

The fourth resort of the "Middle Lakes" region—seemingly one of the most improbable in the country—is for several reasons very unusual. Its setting hardly suggests a likely resort locale. Although mountains are visible, they are miles away. There are no lakes or nearby rivers. The countryside is rich, rolling farm country, but the closest town is a small industrial center. The secret is chocolate.

The resort is the Hotel Hershey. The town also is named Hershey. Both town and resort are named for their founder, a man of curious genius who learned how to make candy so successfully that he amassed a vast fortune from the largest chocolate factories in the world, built near his birthplace in the Pennsylvania Dutch country of eastern Pennsylvania. The hotel, with a hilltop setting of some of the finest gardens in the East, is another product of the chocolate millions. It overlooks the buildings and grounds of the richest orphan boys' school in the world, the final heir to the Hershey fortune, which now owns the hotel and the chocolate factories.

AT THE HEART OF THE ADIRONDACKS

The Adirondack Mountains, which spread over more than eight thousand square miles of New York State, are composed of the most ancient known rocks in the world, and are different in aspect and character from neighboring ranges such as the Catskills and the Green Mountains and White Mountains of New England. For the average traveler, unconcerned about the age of mountains, the Adirondacks are a paradox. Though close to such important urban centers as New York, Buffalo, and Boston, the mountains are wilderness. Within their borders is a vast forest tract of more than two million acres. It is a wild and beautiful wilderness with more than a thousand alpine lakes, hundreds of miles of mountain streams, and a great green blanket of primeval forest with more than forty peaks rising to above four thousand feet, several to about five thousand feet.

The spectacular alpine heart of the Adirondacks extends west from Lake Champlain and south from the St. Lawrence, an enchanting wonderland of green forest slopes and shining blue lakes, pierced by a few scenic highways. Here are the highest mountains—Mount Marcy, the highest point in New York State, rising to 5344 feet, and Mount Whiteface, 4872 feet. Near the base of Mount Whiteface, on the shores of Lake Placid, is one of the oldest and most sophisticated resorts in the state: Whiteface Inn, a resort with about seventy buildings scattered over a thousand acres. It has been beguiling guests with its lake and mountain scenery since 1888.

Three factors are responsible for the building of the first Whiteface Inn. One was the development of the passenger elevator by Elisha Graves Otis and the subsequent organization and growth of the Otis Elevator Company. The second factor was the growth of resorts during the last half of the nineteenth century, a boom that saw the building of resorts in almost every section of the land, from Florida to northern Maine, in the Rockies of Colorado and on the shores of the Pacific in California. The third factor was the theory among physicians that the climate of the Adirondacks, particularly near Lake Placid, was helpful in the control and cure of consumption and tuberculosis.

By 1888 the Otis company had grown into a substantial and prosperous concern. Its vice-president was a Colonel A. G. Mills. The resort boom was in full swing that year, and by then the medical world had agreed that the Adirondack climate was helpful. So Colonel Mills and some friends organized a company to take advantage of the popularity of resorts and of the benevolent climate. The shore of Lake Placid struck them as ideal. The lake, four miles long and a half mile wide, was beautiful, set among wooded mountains of which Whiteface Mountain, at the northern end, was the highest and most impressive. Saranac Lake, with its sanatoriums, established only a few years earlier, was only ten miles away. Colonel Mills and his group selected a choice site on the east bank of the lake. It had a fine view of Whiteface Mountain, so they called the new resort Whiteface Inn. A large wooden building of about a hundred fifty rooms, it was a big hotel for its day and region. Two other resorts were started on the shores of Lake Placid that same year. One became the celebrated Lake Placid Club; the other, no longer there, was the Grand View Hotel.

The prosperity of Whiteface Inn was rudely interrupted twenty years after it had opened by the same kind of disaster that inevitably seemed to beset wooden hotels. In 1908 it burned down. Four years later another hotel of approximately the same size and type was rebuilt, and it opened on the same site. Those who do remember it today say that, unlike the first Whiteface Inn, it had large porches encircling it, like the celebrated U.S. Hotel at Saratoga Springs. The second Whiteface Inn had a brief career. It burned down in 1917. New ownership and management raised another building, the nucleus of today's Whiteface Inn. In 1930 a remarkable man named Henry Haynes took over its management.

Haynes was born on the banks of Kentucky's Green River in 1890. The son of a poor family, he had to make his own way from the time he left grade school. At night he attended a business school in Evansville, Indiana. While working there as an office boy in an investment company, Haynes met a real estate developer who got him a job at a small hotel called the Princess Issena at Daytona Beach, Florida. The job didn't amount to much, nor for that matter did the hotel. When young Henry Haynes went to work there, it was little more than a glorified boardinghouse. He did everything needed to keep the hotel running, from firing the furnace to acting as bellboy and night clerk. He was so successful that four years later he was offered a chance to buy the hotel. He soon began to develop his property so successfully that it became one of the celebrated early hotels of Florida. A few years before the end of the Florida boom, he sold out for a substantial fortune.

The Princess Issena then covered a city block, with a main inn, sixteen cottages, and an apartment house, totaling 225 rooms.

In 1930, when hotels everywhere were beginning to slip into bankruptcy, Haynes was offered the summer management of Whiteface Inn, which was also having difficulties. His efforts proved so successful that he was asked to remain as the permanent manager of the resort. He later was taken into the company as a partner.

He stayed for twenty-five years, during which time he greatly expanded and improved the resort, turning it into the luxurious place that it now is. When he arrived it had room for a hundred fifty guests, but only thirty-eight private baths. When he left in 1955, the hotel had a capacity for nearly three hundred fifty guests. Haynes's development program involved building cottages, luxurious suites, and one of the finest eighteen-hole golf courses in the East. He also was a pioneer in making his resort a center for conventions and business meetings, a phase of resort activity greatly developed under the succeeding management, a syndicate headed by an experienced hotel manager, F. Burton Fisher.

Thirty more lakeshore cottages have been built, the resort's golf course was redesigned and given a new golf club, and new lounges were built in the main hotel, by the pool, and at the golf club.

Today Whiteface Inn is easily the largest and most notable resort in the Adirondacks. Its grounds cover more than a thousand lake-shore acres. Many visitors are reminded of Swiss resorts when they visit the inn. The main lodge has accommodations for about a hundred fifty people. Another fifty-six guests can be housed in a unique lake-front chalet called the Wigwam, which has thirty-six rooms and luxury suites. The rest of the guest accommodations are in more than forty attractive cottages, many of which are on the lake shore. Nearly every cottage has a living room and from one to nine bedrooms, and a terrace or porch overlooks the lake. Few resorts offer cottage accommodation of such luxury and variety. In front of the main lodge are a handsome boathouse and a dock—a base for sight-seeing trips around the lake. A large swimming pool and a sun terrace are on one side of the inn.

Whiteface Inn's golf course is eighteen holes, 6700 yards, a par 72. Spreading over a rolling tract, it extends from the lake shore back into the foothills. It is beautifully maintained and of championship quality, and relatively narrow fairways tend to make the course challenging to all players, including experts.

Other facilities include tennis, shuffleboard, paddle tennis, bowling, horseshoe pitching, archery, each with its own area on the grounds. The resort maintains a stable with riding horses and many miles of forest trails through the hills and along the lake shore. Fishing is generally excellent, the catch usually being bass, rainbow trout, and various other fresh-water fish. Boats, tackle, and guides are supplied by the resort. Several speedboats are available for charter, as well as a sight-seeing boat carrying up to a hundred people.

Dining at Whiteface Inn is famed for its variety and quality, with meals served in several areas. A handsome main dining room overlooks the lake, the boathouse, and the golf clubhouse. Specialties include a number of Italian and French dishes and notable American dishes. Sumptuous indoor and outdoor buffets are regular features.

Few resorts in the East are better equipped for handling group meetings and conventions. The inn has its own convention hall, which can accommodate up to five hundred people.

Since Whiteface Inn is in the heart of a mountain and forest wilderness, it is not particularly noted as a base for general sight-seeing, but many guests soon discover that within easy driving distance there are a number of historic sites. South of the village of Lake Placid, on Route 73, is a memorial called John Brown's Farm, where a monument marks the grave of the celebrated abolitionist whose dramatic adventures just prior to the Civil War helped bring on that conflict. Sterling Game Farm, an exhibit of quite a different character, is two miles west of Lake Placid on Route 86. It has exhibits of furs and many animals from all parts of the world.

There are dozens of highly scenic drives over excellent mountain roads in the immediate area. The toll road to the crest of Whiteface Mountain, a summit 4872 feet high, is a notable one. On the slopes of the mountain a chair lift for winter skiing is operated in the summertime as a sight-seeing novelty, a trip that takes about one hour and lifts visitors 3660 feet to the summit.

The resort village and health center of Saranac Lake is about ten miles west of Whiteface Inn on Route 86. A cottage occupied by Robert Louis Stevenson when he was trying to recover from tuberculosis is now a memorial exhibit. Twenty-five miles east of Lake Placid, in Elizabethtown, is the Adirondack Center and Colonial Garden, a beautiful formal garden and a museum filled with relics of Adirondack history. Ten miles east of Elizabethtown is Lake Champlain. A scenic drive along the lake on Route 22 leads south to the village of Ticonderoga and Fort Ticonderoga, which have been restored as a historic site. The fort, captured by Ethan Allen and his Green Mountain Boys from the British in a bloodless surprise attack, is open to the public daily between mid-May and mid-October, and exhibits a notable collection of weapons, relics, and military gear.

Whiteface Inn is easy to reach despite its isolated wilderness setting. It is 294 miles by highway from New York City, 260 from Boston, 350 from Buffalo, and 110 from Montreal. The best route from New York City is the New York Thruway to Albany, then Interstate 87 to Lake George, and the extension of that interstate express route, U.S. 9, to its intersection with Route 73, which leads to Lake Placid village, on Route 86. The resort is about six miles to the north of Lake Placid. From the west the best route is the New York Thruway to Utica, then Routes 12 and 28 north through the heart of the Adirondacks to Blue Mountain Lake, then to Saranac Lake and Lake Placid. From New England the route to follow is the Massachusetts Turnpike to its junction with the New York Thruway just south of Albany.

Rail transportation to Whiteface Inn is by New York Central from New York City, a train leaving each night at 10:30 P.M. and arriving at Lake Placid at 8:15 the next morning. The New York Central trains coming from the west connect with the Lake Placid train at Utica or Albany.

Mohawk Airlines services the Lake Placid-Saranac airport, twelve miles from the inn. Fare on the airport bus to the inn is $2.50 per person.

Whiteface Inn is open for the summer season only, from May 15 to October 15. The period from opening to about mid-June and from Labor Day to closing is often given over to conventions and special groups. The normal summer social season starts about June 15. Rates are full American plan, single rooms beginning at $23 per day, double rooms at $44. The cottages, which are comparable to two-room suites of conventional hotels, start at $54 per day for two.

ON THE SHORES OF GLIMMERGLASS

Lake Otsego is set among the pleasant small mountains of central New York, with wild ranges of the Adirondacks to the north and crests of the Catskills to the southeast. Otsego is not, as many people think, one of the more famous Finger Lakes, which lie to the west. It is eight miles long and about a mile wide, and the Susquehanna River emerges at its south end and winds through southern New York into Pennsylvania. The village of Cooperstown, at the point where the river leaves the lake, has only 2500 residents, but it is one of the most famous villages in America. It has been called a museum village and a treasure town, and either description fits. It has five remarkable museums, each created to house different exhibits and to appeal to a different audience.

The Otesaga Hotel is in Cooperstown, with grounds that sweep along the shore of the lake. It serves the constant procession of visitors to the village. The name Otesaga is of Indian origin and, loosely translated, means "Welcome" or "This Is a Good Meeting Place," a uniquely appropriate name for this resort hotel.

Cooperstown was founded by Judge William Cooper when the Mohawk Valley was being developed. He was a man of substance and importance who eventually built one of the handsomest houses in central New York; he called it Otsego Hall. But he is more famous for another reason—he had a son named James Fenimore Cooper. James went to Yale but never graduated, leaving college to begin a life of wandering as a sailor and an adventurer. Eventually he returned to Cooperstown and began writing novels. Among the stories he wrote was a group about the Indians and the new frontier which have come to be called the *Leatherstocking Tales*. The locale of many of the stories is the region of Cooperstown. In them the name of a lake called Glimmerglass often appears. It is, of course, Lake Otsego.

Cooperstown would have had moderate fame simply because Cooper lived there and wrote his stories about the region. But many years later, long after his death, the fame of the village gained a new facet. In 1907 it was decreed by the National Baseball Council that the most famous of all American games—baseball—had been invented there in 1839. While a student at the military academy in Cooperstown, young Abner Doubleday devised a completely new game that was to become baseball. It was perfectly natural that Cooperstown would be selected as the site for the establishment of the National Baseball Museum and Hall of Fame.

The second museum established in Cooperstown, the Farmer's Museum, exhibits the skills and crafts of frontier farming and re-creates a frontier community. The third museum is Fenimore House, a gracious old mansion that is the New York State Historical Association headquarters and houses American folk-art exhibits. The Indian Museum describes the story of the Indians from earliest days. And, finally, the fifth museum is the Woodland Museum, set in a forest tract three miles north of Cooperstown, with a unique assortment of nature and pioneer exhibits.

Long before the fifth museum opened in Cooperstown, the Otesaga Hotel had been planned and built. It opened its doors with a fanfare of regional publicity. One feature widely noted and reported was that the hotel was actually fireproof—an important novelty in 1909.

The Otesaga today is a full-scale resort estate with all the accessories that have come to be important in the comfort and diversion of resort guests everywhere. It is still the handsome modern building it was in 1909. Though remodeled in various ways and at different times, it still presents an imposing high-pillared façade to Lake Street in Cooperstown, and from the opposite side dominates an extensive section of the lake shore. The resort's design is colonial Georgian, the most gracious architectural style this country has known. It is set among wide lawns and is beautifully shaded with old trees. The eighteen-hole golf course stretches north along the shore of the lake. Immediately beside the hotel is a heated swimming pool surrounded by a wide sun terrace. Near the pool are a putting green and courts for tennis and shuffleboard. The hotel has 135 guest rooms and suites, most of which have fine views of the lake. The handsome and spacious public rooms carry out the colonial elegance of the Georgian period. Most guest rooms are unusually large, and many have open fireplaces.

The Leatherstocking Corporation is the owner and operator of the Otesaga Hotel. It also operates an inn of great charm called the Cooper Inn, which is a few blocks away. The inn has twenty guest rooms, a dining room and cocktail lounge, and its guests have privileges at the Otesaga Hotel.

The first tee of the eighteen-hole golf course is a few steps from the hotel itself. It is not difficult to play, yet offers reasonable challenge to golfers of all skills. It is rated as a championship course of 6554 yards, a par 72. Two holes are distinctive: the seventeenth, shortest hole on the course, is a par 3 of 180 yards. Its green is directly on the shore of the lake, with the result that overplay or underplay means a lost ball. The eighteenth hole presents a different water hazard—the tee is on an island in the lake and is reached by a causeway. It is a 550-yard par 5. The hole is technically a dog-leg with normal play to the nearest point of the lake shore, but daring players try to cut the corner with a very long drive.

The hotel has a dock extending from its own grounds and provides boats and facilities for water sports of every variety. Fishing tackle and bait can be obtained from the hotel. The most common catch is the Otsego bass, named for the lake. The hotel and inn are probably the only ones of their type in the country where guests can go ice fishing in the winter, using fishing shanties erected all over the lake.

Lake sight-seeing is available to resort guests in the summertime from a public pier about six blocks east of the hotel. A picturesque stern-wheel steamer makes an hour-and-a-half trip up the lake and back.

Almost all of the historic exhibits of Cooperstown are within easy walking distance of the hotel. The National Baseball Hall of Fame and Museum is an easy ten-minute walk. Near it on the lake shore is the Indian Museum. A short walk in the opposite direction from the hotel is the Farmers' Museum, and just beyond it is Fenimore House. Only the Woodland Museum, about three miles north on Route 80, is not within walking distance. But a unique shuttle bus links the hotel and the museum.

Cooperstown and the resort are easily reached by rail, air or highway. It is two hundred miles from New York City by the New York Thruway and connecting highways. The most direct route is the Thruway to Exit 21, at Catskill, then Route 145 to its junction with U.S. 20, U.S. 20 to Route 80, which leads south along the west shore of the lake to Cooperstown. Those traveling from the Albany-Schenectady area or from New England would follow the Thruway to Exit 30 at Herkimer, south on Route 28 to Cooperstown. The nearest airports offering scheduled airline service are at Utica and Albany, where bus or taxi service is available. The Kingston Pinehill Bus Line leaves New York City's Port Authority Bus Terminal and goes directly to Cooperstown. The most convenient rail service is by train to Utica or Albany, and then bus or taxi.

The Otesaga Hotel is operated on a modified American plan during the normal summer season, from June to October, and on a much more limited basis the rest of the year. Cooper Inn operates on European plan year round. At the Otesaga, the limited American-plan rate, which means breakfast and dinner, varies with the type of room. Single rooms start at $20 per day, double rooms at $32 per day. Suites and parlor-bedroom combinations start at $50 per day. A third person in a double-occupancy room is charged at a rate of $12 per day. Rates at the Cooper Inn start for single rooms at $9 per day, double rooms $16 per day.

THE CONVENIENT POCONOS

The Poconos of Eastern Pennsylvania cannot match the rugged beauty of the Green Mountains and White Mountains of New England, or the primitive wilderness of New York's Adirondacks. Few of the crests or ridges rise to more than two thousand feet. Geologists don't classify the Poconos as mountains, but call them the eastern escarpment of the Allegheny Plateau, which fills much of Pennsylvania. The area of the Poconos is limited. The Delaware River Valley is on the east, from which the Pocono hills and valleys extend west about fifty miles. There are few outstanding natural features, only a few small lakes, some waterfalls, small rivers and streams, and a dense forest cover.

The Poconos are not cut by natural valleys that would have invited highway and rail construction. When Eastern Pennsylvania was being settled, towns grew up in other areas along river valleys, such as Scranton, on the Lackawanna River, and Wilkes-Barre, on the Susquehanna. In the Delaware Valley is Stroudsburg, now the largest community near the Poconos, a shopping center for the entire region. The Poconos remained relatively uninhabited for more than fifty years after nearby regions had been settled. There was brief industrial activity beginning about 1860, when mining tycoons discovered that the forests of the Poconos were a handy source of mine timbers. Thus much of their fine cover was cut down by 1870.

When routes of travel skirting the Poconos were established in 1890, a few venturesome people from New York and Philadelphia realized what was almost on their doorstep. Only a hundred miles from each city were rugged hills that, though despoiled of their trees, were still attractive and had fine summer climate. A Philadelphia Quaker named Samuel E. Griscom, who had inherited a tract of several thousand acres in the Pocono region, was one of the early pioneers. In exploring his heritage, Griscom found that his patch of wilderness had many pleasant features—high ridges, deep valleys, and a gorge where a fine waterfall tumbled. The slopes of the gorge were covered by a hemlock forest—one of the few remaining in the region.

Griscom was so impressed that he urged his friends to join him in making it a summer vacation site for Quakers. He persuaded a group of Quakers to visit the land in the summer of 1898. The group, headed by Howard M. Jenkins, editor of a Quaker newspaper in Philadelphia called the *Friend's Intelligencer,* was stirred by the fresh and natural beauty of the site. They bought the land, organized a company, capitalized at twenty thousand dollars, and announced their plans to build a "large inn."

Work was begun in 1901. The site of their inn was on a high ridge above the tumbling waterfall. Roads along the slopes of the hills wound in and out among the trees. The inn was named Buck Hill Falls.

The "large inn" contained eighteen rooms, without private bath or heat. Lighting was by kerosene lamp. When the inn opened in the summer of 1901, it had no golf, swimming, bowling, riding horses—not even green grass, and about the only diversion guests enjoyed was hiking. But there was the light, dry, pleasant mountain air. Perhaps the air turned the trick, for the Inn at Buck Hill Falls, perched in the Pocono hills, was an immediate success. The next year it was enlarged to forty bedrooms that accommodated sixty people, and a dining room for a hundred twenty guests was added. Many diners were owners of cottages built along drives of the inn property in a growing settlement of summer homes.

The Inn at Buck Hill Falls has been growing ever since. It is now the largest resort estate in Pennsylvania, and one of the largest in the country, with 380 guest rooms and suites, including a luxurious eighty-room wing opened in 1964. The inn dominates six thousand acres of land, maintains fourteen miles of highway and twenty miles of bridle trail, and has one of the finest golf courses in the East. In the winter the inn maintains one of the oldest and most popular ski slopes in the East. The resort is at the center of a community of 199 cottages, of which nearly all are privately owned by stockholders in the Buck Hill Falls Company. In the sixty-odd years since its founding the inn has grown into a colony with a summer population of 2500 cottagers, guests, and employees.

The Inn at Buck Hill Falls remained fairly primitive for quite a while. An early guest remembers that on the porch was a row of wooden pegs, each assigned to a cottager who had bought a forest lot. The pegs had a special function. After dark, when cottagers came to the inn for dinner, they carried windproof lanterns equipped with candles to light the way through the thickets that lined the paths to the inn. The lanterns hung on the pegs.

By 1923 the inn had 214 bedrooms. In the early extensions of the original inn all building was frame, but gradually the frame buildings were torn down and replaced. The last frame element of the older hotel was torn down in 1930 and replaced by a steel and concrete wing including an auditorium seating a thousand people. As the new units were built, the same building material was used. The wall surfaces were made of small boulders and broken native stone, all of which were found in local stream beds and nearby quarries. The result is remarkable and appropriate. Buck Hill Falls, with its rough slate-gray walls and gray roofs has an almost medieval look, like a Bavarian castle.

Guests at the Buck Hill Falls Inn usually enter through great stone main gates in the heart of the forest, wheel along a winding road for a quarter of a mile, and suddenly come to the main lodge itself, its stone walls vine-covered. Although the forest surrounds the inn, the immediate grounds are handsomely landscaped, with elegant small formal gardens here and there. Winding roads curve through the trees. The roads are flanked by the nearly two hundred cottages that make up the colony. Even though the cottages began as simply as the hotel, they too have changed over the years. Some are luxurious estates, many occupied year round. On one side of the hotel several roads merge to link several facilities. Nearby is a beautiful formal garden, a memorial to one of the gardeners. Beyond the formal garden are bowling greens, and bowling is a traditional diversion at Buck Hill Falls. Past these are the tennis courts, and beyond them a very big and handsome swimming pool set in a natural amphitheater with a bathhouse and sun terrace.

The golf course has twenty-seven holes spread over the mountain slopes. Walking trails meander through the several thousand forested acres within the inn's property, the most popular leading down a precipitous slope through the heart of Jenkins' Woods—a wild and fascinating remnant of the primeval forest that once clothed all of the mountain slopes. The woods are one of the few places where nature lovers can still find giant hemlock. Superb stands of rhododendron line the forest trail. Most of the important trees are marked with labels bearing their names. The woods are named for Howard M. Jenkins and his son Charles F. Jenkins, the founders of Buck Hill Falls Inn and the managers for many years.

Beyond Jenkins' Woods the forest trail breaks into a paved road that swings down a steep slope to end at Buck Hill Falls. The best-known cataract in the Poconos, the falls drop two hundred feet in a succession of steps through a primitive ravine. The dramatic quality of the falls varies with the flow of Buck Creek. When the volume of water is high, the falls are tremendous. They are easily viewed from two platforms built near the entrance gate. The pool formed at the bottom of the falls is one of the best places in the area for trout fishing.

Other facilities include a garage, parking lots, kennels for dogs in case guests happen to bring them, a dormitory for chauffeurs in case you travel with one, and the Camp Club, an informal school and recreation center for young people.

The inn's outdoor diversions are varied enough to suit every mood from porch sitting to golf, skiing, lawn bowling, fishing, swimming, carriage and horseback riding, hiking, and regional sight-seeing. The golf courses and ski runs are the most popular. The fairways become ski slopes in the winter. Golf began at the inn more than fifty years ago, when fairways were hacked out of the forest and climbed abrupt mountain slopes. For many years the course was famed for its ups and downs. However, it has been redesigned within recent years to accommodate golf carts and reduce climbing. The result is a spectacularly beautiful, superbly maintained twenty-seven-hole layout. Eighteen holes make up the two older courses, and add up to a 6665 yard course with a par 72. The newest nine holes, 2983 yards, have a par of 34. Some fairways run through dense forest with several greens set among clumps of white birches. The inn's golf season begins on April 15 and ends on November 15. Greens fees are $4 weekdays, $5 Saturdays, Sundays, and holidays.

From mid-November to early spring the course becomes transformed for skiing, bobsledding, and skating. A parking lot becomes a winter skating rink. Skiing slopes are established on the fairways of several golf holes. Snow-making machines ensure enough snow for full activity regardless of the weather. There are two ski lifts available.

Buck Hill Creek has limited but excellent trout fishing, which is done under state regulations requiring the usual permit and fees, creel limit, and minimum size of fish caught.

The relatively new swimming pool is surrounded by an extensive sun terrace and pool house with lockers. The area is next to the eight tennis courts and clubhouse.

Horseback riding is offered, and group rides are held daily. Riding horses are available at $2.50 per hour or can be engaged for the period of a guest's stay by advance arrangement.

The inn also maintains a well-stocked grocery and general store used by members of the cottage colony and lodge guests. There is also an extensive library with a trained librarian. There are two cocktail lounges at the resort. There also are an auditorium and a theater used for frequent concerts and lectures. The spacious public rooms on the main floor are graced with a remarkable collection of notable paintings, the result of an inn activity that began more than thirty years ago when a group called the Buck Hill Art Association began sponsoring frequent shows.

On the lower floors are meeting rooms used by business organizations and conventions. Playrooms on the lower level have facilities for billiards, table tennis, pool, shuffleboard, and television.

The Inn at Buck Hill Falls is on the American plan. The meals are traditionally American, with emphasis on unusual Pennsylvania Dutch dishes. Sometime luncheon picnics are held at scenic points reached by horseback or hiking.

The inn provides many activities for children and the younger guests. There is the Camp Club, with a trained staff of counselors. A program for children from two and a half to thirteen is held in a special building. There also are special sports and activities for older children.

The Inn at Buck Hill Falls, though pleasantly isolated in its setting, is easily reached by automobile. It also is accessible by bus and rail. It is 105 miles from New York City, 115 miles from Philadelphia, and 145 miles from Harrisburg, Pennsylvania. Boston is 340 miles away to the northeast, and Washington, D.C., is 240 miles to the southeast. From New York City the most popular route is a combination of U.S. 46 and Route 80 to the Delaware Water Gap Bridge, then Route 196 to East Stroudsburg and on that route to a junction with Route 191 to the inn gate. An alternate route from New York would be U.S. 22 to Clinton Corners, New Jersey, then Route 69 to Buttzville, and thereafter U.S. 46 to the Delaware Water Gap. From Philadelphia an easy route is the northeastern extension of the Pennsylvania Turnpike to the Pocono Interchange, then Route 940 to Mount Pocono and Route 196 to an intersection marked with a sign to the inn.

Rail service to the inn from New York is by the Erie-Lackawanna Railway from the terminal in Hoboken to Cresco, the nearest rail station to the inn where taxi service is available.

Bus service from Philadelphia is provided by Delaware Valley Transportation Company direct to the inn. The nearest commercial air service is to the combination Wilkes-Barre-Scranton airport at Avaco, thirty-eight miles from the inn, served by Allegheny Eastern Airlines and TWA. Allentown, forty-eight miles from the inn, has regular scheduled service at the tri-city airport of Allentown, Bethlehem, and Easton, served by TWA and United Air Lines. Private planes can land ten miles from the inn at the Mount Pocono airport, but arrangements for landing should be made in advance.

Guest rates at Buck Hill Falls vary with the season and the type and location of rooms. As noted above, all are on the American plan. Single-room rates start at $14 per day. Double-room rates, with meals for two persons, start at $28 per day, from June 12 to November 1. Single-room rates begin at $12 per day. Double-room rates for two people begin at $24 per day. The most luxurious rooms, including opulent suites, are in the new west wing, where a number of rooms have private terraces. In the new wing there are many public rooms available for meetings and conventions.

HIGH ABOVE CHOCOLATE TOWN

The Appalachian Mountains sweep through central Pennsylvania from the northeast to the southwest with precisely parallel ridges swinging in shallow arcs. They are not particularly habitable; forested slopes are steep and the valleys are narrow. The rock-strewn Susquehanna River slices through the range. Just before the river reaches Harrisburg, Pennsylvania's capital, it cuts through the easternmost ridge of the Appalachians, Blue Mountain. The eastern foothills of Blue Mountain and their valleys are a distinctive region known as the Pennsylvania Dutch country, extending east to Reading, south to Lancaster, and west to Harrisburg.

More than two hundred years ago this big triangle of rolling fertile land was a frontier—but not a hostile one. Its forest cover was easily removed, the soil was deep and rich, and it was accessible. In the first part of the eighteenth century settlers began to drift into this welcoming land over a web of forest trails and wagon roads from seaboard settlements. Mostly Germans escaping religious oppression in Switzerland and Germany, they called themselves "the plain people." Most of them belonged to a group called the Mennonites. They were Protestants —sober, industrious, and devout. They refused to bear arms or to take oaths. Rejecting most worldly concerns, they believed in simplicity of dress and habits. And they were superb farmers. They had been attracted to Philadelphia by the promise of religious freedom made by Quaker William Penn. Then they began to move west in ox-drawn wagons filled with farm tools. In a few decades the Mennonites had converted the frontier land east of the Susquehanna into one of the richest agricultural districts in the colonies. They built solid stone houses, put up great barns for their growing herds of fine cattle, and on the barns painted odd, decorative symbols. They developed colorful crafts, cooked savory dishes with strange names, and over the years their speech became a delightful and confusing combination of German and English.

The Mennonites are still in Pennsylvania, and still preserve their ancient ways, their distinctive dress, and habits. Some have grown rich and most are reasonably prosperous because of their productive fields. The Pennsylvania Dutch country lies on both sides of the Pennsylvania Turnpike for many miles. The smaller towns, with names like Ephrata, New Holland, Strasburg, and Paradise, are linked by pleasant country roads that separate the superbly cultivated fields and meadows.

One of the most improbable resort hotels in the United States—the Hotel Hershey—is in the northeast corner of the Pennsylvania Dutch country, at the crest of a hill between the Susquehanna River and the first range of mountains. There would seem to be little reason why the hotel should be there at all, to make it a resort that draws patronage from hundreds of miles away, for Hershey, the nearest town, seems like a prosperous country town and shopping center and not much more. But, as already noted, the answer is chocolate. When the wind blows from the south, a heavy fragrance pervades the air, its source a huge cluster of industrial buildings in the heart of town, the world's largest chocolate factory. It is so large that, if all the other chocolate factories in the world were put together, they would not even approach the size of the giant Hershey plant.

Chocolate built the town and the hotel. Their story is the story of Milton Hershey. He was born in 1857, of Mennonite stock, in the valley where the town and the hotel now stand. He died there, eighty-eight years later, leaving behind a remarkable achievement. The vast Hershey factory is part of it. So is the hilltop resort set among some of the most beautiful gardens in the East, surrounded by a noted golf course, and equipped with all the trappings of a successful modern resort. However, the town, factory, and resort are only a part of Hershey's achievement. Another is one of the finest schools in the country.

Milton Hershey's father, Henry, was a Mennonite, but not cast in the narrow, prohibitive mold so common among "the plain people." Full of worldly ideas, he lived on a farm but had little interest in farm work. He also had a genius for failure. He failed at speculating in oil, at farming, and at converting his land into a shrubbery and fruit-tree farm. He wanted his son Milton to escape the drudgery of farm life, and the son did escape by a curious route. He began with apprenticeship on the weekly newspaper *Der Waffenlose Waechter* (The Watchful Watcher). But he was not interested in printing and was fired for dropping his straw hat into the printing press with remarkable and disastrous results. The next step was the right one. Milton began learning an old and honored Mennonite craft—candymaking. He began in a Lancaster confectionery store where he soon discovered that he liked to make candy and was good at it. When he was nineteen and a fullfledged, candymaking journeyman, young Hershey decided that he wanted a candy store of his own. His aunt Mattie, the family financier, staked him to a store in 1876 in Philadelphia, a fortunate year, since Philadelphia was staging a centennial exposition. The store prospered and soon he was both a retailer and wholesaler. But he was a better candymaker than businessman and eventually was in financial trouble. The store failed.

Aunt Mattie again came to his rescue and in 1883, when he was twenty-six years old, she staked him to a new start in New York City. It prospered at first, as the Philadelphia store had done. He specialized in making caramels, which sold well. However, his poor business judgment led to a financial impasse and he had to sell out. He returned to the Pennsylvania Dutch country to start over again with the little money salvaged from New York. This time success was solid. In a few years Hershey caramels were known nationwide and he owned several factories. By the time Hershey was forty-four years old, he was a millionaire and had a check for a million dollars to prove it—proceeds of the sale of his caramel company to a rival candymaking group. He retired to travel and enjoy life.

At this point the Hershey destiny took a curious turn. Some years before, during a visit to the World's Fair, in Chicago, Hershey had been fascinated by a German machine for making chocolate, and he bought the machine and installed it in his Lancaster, Pennsylvania, factory. When he sold the caramel business, he kept the chocolate-making machinery and began to manufacture milk-chocolate coating for candy, and it was an instantaneous success. The demand was such that within two years of his "retirement" Hershey was back in the candy business again on a larger scale than before.

He decided that since he was starting over again he would pick a new setting, so he returned to the region of his birth and bought the old farm where he had lived as a boy. He decided to build a factory and a town for its workers around the farm. In 1904 he moved to the new town and factory with twenty employees, for whom he built a community center called Cocoa House. It is still there, but now an ultramodern version of a country hotel, the Cocoa Inn. Soon schools, civic buildings, athletic fields, playgrounds, parks, and hundreds of houses were built. Hershey became the company town to end all company towns. Almost everybody in the town worked for Hershey in one way or another, but practically no one hated the company. And why should they? The company gave them a way of life that their wages could not buy anywhere else.

In 1909, after Milton Hershey established his factory, he did an extraordinary thing. He transferred five hundred thousand shares of Hershey Chocolate Company common stock to create an endowment for a school for orphan boys, now called the Milton Hershey School. The plan attracted no special attention at the time the endowment was made, but four years later, when the Hershey Chocolate Company had grown to a giant, word of the endowment leaked out and created a snowstorm of headlines. The five hundred thousand shares of stock were estimated as worth sixty million dollars, making the school, which had about a hundred twenty boys, one of the richest in the world.

The 1933 Depression, which enveloped the rest of the country, scarcely touched the town. With the Government launching massive made-work programs, Milton Hershey launched his own program to fight the Depression. For years he had had a secret desire to build and run a fine hotel. He had picked the site years before—the highest hill north of the town.

When it became known that Hershey was going to build a big new hotel, unemployed carpenters, bricklayers, plumbers, electricians, and others swarmed to the town seeking work.

Hershey had very definite ideas about how the hotel should look. His notions about design were the result of buildings he had seen during his travels around the world. He admired many details of Spanish design—patios, fountains, glazed and colorful tile, and he directed that his vast hotel lobby should resemble a Spanish patio with a fountain in the center of the room and tile laid on the entire floor. It was built that way, and although it has been modified through the years, it still looks something like a Spanish patio. Hershey also stated that the dining room had to be huge and airy and look out on wide gardens. He specified that it should be an open room, without columns in the room itself. It appears that once during his travels he had been seated behind a dining-room pillar, and he had vowed that when he built his own hotel there would not be any pillars in the dining room for headwaiters to seat guests behind. The vast dining room was built according to Hershey's instructions, even though it involved unique engineering problems of supporting the roof by means other than interior columns. It exists now as a beautiful, semicircular open room with great windows on three sides revealing immaculately manicured gardens.

Visitors to the Hotel Hershey see it just about the way it was when completed during the Depression. The changes that have been made over the years are in details of décor and in recreational facilities. The main structure of the hotel stands proudly on its high hill, resembling a Spanish palace. The central section of the hotel opens on a wide sun terrace from which guests overlook the Hershey domain stretching miles to the south and including the town and the Hershey farms beyond. When the wind is right, guests can still sniff the faintly sweet aroma of cooking chocolate.

There are a hundred fifty guest rooms and suites, some with balconies and terraces. Over the years a good many facilities have been added that Hershey had not contemplated. A wide terrace at the rear of the hotel has been converted into a cocktail lounge. A nine-hole golf course has been built, part of thirty-six holes of golf available to guests on three different courses, all Hershey-owned and maintained. Cut in a hillside among a grove of pine trees behind the hotel is a handsome kidney-shaped swimming pool. The roof of the great dining room has been converted into a vast ballroom. Other meeting rooms have been built on the lower floors for conventions and business meetings.

Stunning rose gardens set on a slope below the hotel to the south can be easily seen. A group of guest cottages available for group and family use is west of the hotel.

Though the Hotel Hershey is open year round, the best seasons are spring, summer, and fall. Golf is very popular. The three golf courses at the hotel itself and in town are unique. The hotel course is nine holes and calls for skill and imagination in play. The Hershey Country Club eighteen-hole course is a championship course of 6928 yards, a par 73. It is tremendously long, with five holes over 500 yards and one of them almost 600. Built on rolling round, it is superbly maintained and has been the scene of some notable golf matches, including the P.G.A. championship. An unusual layout is the Juvenile Country Club Course, its nine holes designed just for children. For a long time the course was restricted to children only. Its longest hole is 440 yards; one is only 100 yards.

The new swimming pool is open from May 15 to October 1 and is available only to guests. There are excellent clay tennis courts, superbly maintained and free to guests. A new bowling-on-the-green court is increasingly popular, open to guests for a small playing fee. The hotel's stables are nearby, and horses are for hire to ride over scenic trails through the hills.

Though the general location of the Hotel Hershey would not appear to provide many sight-seeing opportunities, guests are surprised to discover that the opposite is true.

A tour of the chocolate factory is a must, giving guests full exposure to the processes by which the cacao bean of South America is converted into chocolate and cocoa.

One can also tour the Milton Hershey Junior-Senior High School, which is part of the extraordinary orphanage school begun by Milton Hershey. Twelve hundred boys of all ages through high school are enrolled. The school is scattered over twelve thousand acres, and the main high-school building is on a slope just below the hotel. Guests may also visit one or more of the family farms where the boys live in a comfortable and homelike atmosphere. The twelve hundred boys are selected from families that have lost one or more of their parents. The endowment established by Milton Hershey has grown so large that its income provides for most needs.

The handsome Community Center houses a well-equipped theater and books many Broadway shows. Hershey provides the spectator with many athletic attractions—professional and amateur—in a tremendous football stadium and sports arena with a year-round program of baseball, football, and ice hockey. The Hershey Bears are in the American Hockey League and have many home games. For the sight-seer, the Hershey Museum has one of the strangest collections of odds and ends ever assembled, from Alaskan totem poles to fine Stiegel glass. Much of the collection was assembled by Hershey, whose instincts never permitted him to resist buying an oddity.

One of the country's most notable sight-seeing attractions is an hour's drive to the southwest—the battlefield park and memorial of Gettysburg.

Every year at Hershey outstanding floral exhibits, staged at the hotel gardens, include a tulip festival and a rose show that draw flower lovers from every part of the country.

"Pennsylvania Dutch Days" are held in late summer. Bands, speakers, quilt-making and chair-caning contests, arts and crafts exhibits, and Pennsylvania Dutch food are featured.

Few important resorts are more accessible than the Hotel Hershey. It is within a few minutes' drive of a half-dozen converging highways leading in and out of Harrisburg, fifteen miles to the west. They include the Pennsylvania Turnpike; the express route of U.S. 22, leading to New York City; and U.S. 15, leading southwest to Gettysburg. Hershey itself is within a triangle formed by U.S. 422 and 322. The Harrisburg-York airport is fourteen miles away and serves several airlines. For the growing number of resort visitors who own their own planes the hotel has its own three-thousand-foot paved, all-weather airstrip long enough to handle conventional two-engine aircraft. The Pennsylvania Railroad goes through Harrisburg for those who wish train service. The hotel has a fleet of limousines that meet guests at the Pennsylvania Station in Harrisburg or the Harrisburg-York airport.

Hotel Hershey is one of the few resorts in the country that offer guests a choice between European and American plans. Although most guests elect the full American plan, some choose the European plan and pay only for meals eaten. American-plan rates start at $21 per day up for a single room; at $36 per day for a double room. Suites begin at $55 per day for double occupancy. Rates for the Hershey cottages, with family accommodations, are from $40 per day to $175 per week, and all cottages are fully equipped for light housekeeping.

Greens fees on the hotel's own course are $3.50 per day, $4 weekends and holidays. Electric-cart rentals are $4 for nine holes or less; caddie carts cost $1 per day. The Hershey Country Club eighteen-hole championship course can be played for greens fees of $5 per day, $6 weekends and holidays. Electric-cart rentals are $8 for eighteen holes. The hotel swimming pool, tennis courts, and shuffleboard courts are free to guests. Bowling on the green is $1 per person per game. Horses for riding on the hotel's own trails are $3.50 per hour with $5 per hour for lessons.

CHAPTER 8

HIGH MOUNTAINS OF
THE WEST

Mountains have been favored settings for resorts throughout the world. The original Shangri-La was in the mountains of Tibet. The reasons are obvious enough. Mountains offer isolation, which is something resorts need. And mountains offer scenic settings, often dramatically scenic ones, and they usually offer better climate than lowland areas. There are other advantages—clear lakes, swift, foaming rivers, and forest trails.

Resorts developed naturally in the Eastern mountains of North America. The first resorts in the mountains of Virginia grew almost casually from modest beginnings. New England's green and pleasant mountains are filled with resorts, some of which grew from mountain farms.

Thus it is not surprising that some of the great resorts of North America are in the high mountains of the West. But the Western mountains are quite different from those in the East. They are towering, craggy ramparts, with hundreds of crests rising more than two miles high. They cover thousands of square miles of forest wilderness. It took many years and cost hundreds of lives before men found safe ways to cross them. And nowhere in the vast and incredible mountains of the West today are there cities of any size. So it is not surprising that the establishment and building of great resorts in these heights took a lot of doing and cost a lot of money.

The great mountains of the far West are not one great unbroken system, but rather many ranges and subranges, each with its own name and character. The most familiar and famous are the Rockies, which begin in Alaska and extend three thousand miles southeast into New Mexico—a mountain belt five hundred miles wide. Two parts of the

Rockies are especially familiar: the Canadian section, which spreads over much of Alberta and British Columbia in Canada; and the central section, which consists of the Rampart Ranges of the Colorado Rockies. The Continental Divide—the ridgepole of North America—snakes through the entire range from northwest to southeast.

From the Rockies in Canada other great systems diverge through Washington, Oregon, and California, where one towering range is called the High Sierras, with crests higher and more inaccessible than those of any range south of Alaska.

The high mountains of the West were at first a barrier, but when this had been conquered and travel became possible, people began to regard the mountains as good places to visit. The conquering of them was done largely by the railroad men who laid their tracks, built trestles, tunnels, and bridges over and through the mountains in the greatest epic of land-conquering the world has ever known. But miners, who found treasure in the mountains, built the first towns there. As travel increased, the great Western railroads planned and built several resorts. One famous resort estate was the direct result of mining wealth.

Today there are six great resorts in the mountains of the West. Each is distinctive in setting and character; each has behind it a robust history of founding and development, with one exception.

Two of the resorts are in Canada, one is in Idaho, one is in Colorado, one is in California, and the sixth is in New Mexico.

The two resorts in Canada are near each other in a dramatically beautiful section of the Canadian Rockies. Both were established and are now owned and operated by the Canadian Pacific Railway, their stunning sites in the province of Alberta chosen almost as soon as the railroad had been completed in the mountains. The resorts are Chateau Lake Louise, facing what many call the most beautiful lake in the world, and forty miles away the Banff Springs Hotel, which also has a dramatic setting, established and named for a hot sulphur spring. After more than seventy-five years both resorts are now complete and luxurious resort estates.

Idaho is the setting for Sun Valley, in a corner of the United States within a remote cluster of slopes and peaks called the Sawtooth Mountains. The site of Sun Valley, celebrated as the finest ski resort in North America, was carefully selected by the Union Pacific Railroad about thirty years ago because it offered the best conditions for skiing in the West.

The Broadmoor, just outside Colorado Springs, Colorado, where the foothills of the Rockies merge with the Rampart Range, is a famous and luxurious mountain resort that owes its existence to a vast fortune made from mining. It was founded in 1918, when Spencer Penrose and his partner decided to use part of their huge mining fortune to build one of the finest and most fashionable resorts in the world.

The Feather River Inn is in the heart of the wild slopes of the High Sierras of California. The Feather River, one of the famous gold streams of California, surges through one of the most beautiful canyons in the country. The Feather River Inn, resembling a huge Swiss chalet, is close to the tracks of the Western Pacific Railroad. Conceived by the railroad as a way to lure passengers and patrons into the canyon, which has fine fishing and hunting, the inn was built fifty years ago during one of the great California land booms and now is the only important resort in the whole region.

Bishop's Lodge, the sixth resort in the high mountains of the West, is in northern New Mexico, in the wild heart of the Sangre de Cristo range, near Santa Fe. One of the smallest and most unusual resorts in North America, it is the only one in the Western mountains not founded and developed in the pattern of the others. Its name comes from a tiny wilderness chapel built as a private retreat for the famed cleric Archbishop Lamy of Santa Fe. Willa Cather wrote of him as the main character in one of her fine novels. The bishop's chapel, still used, is a central feature of the resort today, which offers a luxurious guest-ranch accommodation in a high mountain setting.

ALPINE OASES

The Canadian Rockies, which form the border between the provinces of Alberta and British Columbia, look the way most people think mountains ought to look. They have craggy crests, some of which rise to more than twelve thousand feet, and steep slopes are covered with some of the finest and most beautiful forests in the world. There are dozens of gemlike alpine lakes. The mountain valleys are narrow and almost always threaded by tumbling mountain streams. Many of the high slopes are blanketed with gleaming glaciers. The Canadian Rockies are sparsely inhabited, with but a few small villages and highways conspicuous by their scarcity. The Canadian Rockies are, in fact, as close to an unspoiled wilderness as a mountain area can be, a superb, majestic, tremendous wilderness with much of its wild splendor preserved within the limits of great Canadian national parks. Banff National Park, on the western side of Alberta, stretches from the province's high plains to the crests of the Rocky Mountain ranges and the Continental Divide, an awesomely scenic area spreading over 2564 square miles. It was established in 1885 to preserve some of the most spectacular scenery in the world.

The park was set aside for public use on the testimony of some hardy pioneers who then were surveying a route for the Canadian Pacific Railway, one of the great engineering achievements of all time. The railroad right of way runs through the wild mountains at the southern end of Banff National Park. From 1885 on, after the railroad was finished, the awesome splendor of the Canadian Rockies stopped being a legend and became a reality to an increasing stream of visitors.

The directors of the Canadian Pacific traveled the newly established routes through the Rockies and quickly realized that the unique scenery could make their railroad a greater and more prosperous one. They began building two remarkable resorts at two points in the Banff National Park area, east of the Continental Divide but within the heart of the mountains. In the seventy-five years of railroad ownership and operation, Chateau Lake Louise and Banff Springs Hotel have become among the most celebrated and popular resorts in the world. Chateau Lake Louise's extraordinary setting has been ranked among the world's ten great sights. Forty miles to the southeast, the much larger and more extensively equipped Banff Springs Hotel has a setting almost equal in magnificence. Both resorts are on the main east-west line of the Canadian Pacific Railway; they are also on the Trans-Canada Highway.

Although the two resorts are owned by the same organization and are within an hour's drive of each other, they are quite different in character.

CHATEAU LAKE LOUISE

A combination of curiosity and accident led to the discovery of Lake Louise, the incredibly beautiful glacial lake that gives Chateau Lake Louise its name and reason for being. In 1882 a pioneer mountain guide named Tom Wilson, who was a route surveyor for the Canadian Pacific, camped one summer night at a spot thirty-seven miles west of Banff. During the night Wilson was awakened by a distant rumbling that resembled thunder. He thought it might have been an avalanche, but his Indian companion had a more picturesque explanation—it was "the Great Spirit who speaks at the Lake of the Little Fishes." The next morning Wilson tried to discover the source of the noise. After a hike over immensely rugged and difficult terrain, he suddenly broke through the forest and gaped in amazement. A small mountain lake lay before him, in a narrow valley with tremendous snow-capped peaks rising around it. At the far end of the lake was an enormous glacier climbing in immaculate majesty. The color of the lake was a shimmering green. Wilson promptly named it Emerald Lake. His startling view of the lake is the same sight that greets every visitor to Chateau Lake Louise today.

Wilson promptly told his employers what he had found. Two years later the discovery was officially confirmed by a geological expedition that immediately changed the name to Lake Louise in honor of one of the daughters of Queen Victoria.

The Canadian Pacific Railway knew that the lake was a scenic bonanza. In 1890, eight years after Wilson's discovery, the railroad built a wooden chalet at the site. The chalet burned down two years later and was rebuilt. Part of the new one burned a few years later, and it was replaced with the present building, which is set in fifty-two acres of superbly landscaped grounds at the edge of the lake.

The lake is only a mile and a half long, three-quarters of a mile wide, about 275 feet deep, its surface at an altitude of 5680 feet. The extraordinary green color is caused by a combination of its depth and by minute fragments of glacial silt from the slowly creeping ice wall of Victoria Glacier. That vast river of ice slowly inching down the slope of Mount Victoria ranges from two hundred to five hundred feet in thickness. It is approximately six miles from Chateau Lake Louise to the crest of Mount Victoria, but four miles up the mountain slope a teahouse built on the eastern edge of the glacier gives guests a close view of the creeping ice river.

All around the lake mountains rise to crests from nine thousand to twelve thousand feet. Trails have been cut through the forest wilderness over their slopes, making dozens of lakes accessible. Guests start arriving at the end of the first week in June and continue until the first week in September. Most of them are from the United States, but the guest register includes visitors from every country, with a generous sprinkling of celebrities. Visitors have included Queen Elizabeth and Prince Philip of the United Kingdom, the Archbishop of Canterbury, the Lord Mayor of London, statesmen, leading politicians from almost every country of the world, Hollywood stars, and industrial tycoons. The Canadian Pacific has calculated that the average guest stays 1.8 days, which is probably the shortest average of any major resort. But, considering that the principal reason for their visit is to see one of the great spectacles of the world, it is long enough.

The Canadian Pacific has steadily enlarged its facilities and increased the number of activities at Chateau Lake Louise. The present establishment covers fifty lakeside acres and is complete, modern, and luxurious. Guest rooms are modern, public rooms are spacious, and nearly every room has a spectacular view. The grounds are superbly landscaped, with dozens of acres of flowers. More than a million poppy plants grow along the shore of the lake in brilliant orange, yellow, and white blooms. In front of the hotel is a huge, glass-walled swimming pool where the water temperature is maintained at seventy-two degrees. Chateau Lake Louise does not have a golf course—its only concession to golfers is a nine-hole putting green—but guests who want more golf go to the companion resort at Banff, where there is a championship course. The lake itself lures many guests, and for them there is a flotilla of canoes and rowboats at the boathouse. Horseback riding is very popular, with miles of forest trails available for it. For it, the hotel maintains a stable of sure-footed horses. Conducted rides are held at frequent intervals. Special trips range from a half day to a full day and from five to fifteen miles for a round trip. One of the most popular trails leads to Lake Agnes and the teahouse there. The same trail serves squads of hikers.

Although Chateau Lake Louise is not famed as a fishing resort, the upland lakes and streams nearby are well stocked with rainbow and cutthroat trout up to six or seven pounds. But Lake Louise has no fish in it.

The most popular of all diversions is mountain sight-seeing in glass-domed buses. There is a series of scheduled tours ranging from brief excursions of one or two hours to day-long trips, exhibiting some of the most superb mountain scenery in the world. The longest of the bus tours is to Jasper, Alberta, which is a hundred fifty miles to the northwest. On the way are the Columbia Ice Fields. During the summer months many guests ride up a mountain to the north of Lake Louise by the Whitehorn Sedan Lift, used for skiing but also maintained for summer sight-seeing. It carries riders two miles up a mountain slope in enclosed gondolas.

For the rugged and adventurous who want to sample mountain

climbing, the hotel is one of the best bases, and climbing opportunities are from easy to challenging. For the experienced alpinist, there are at least a dozen peaks within the view of the hotel to test rock-climbing skills. Trained guides and equipment can be arranged for by the hotel on advance notice.

The hotel's 386 rooms range from the comfortable to the luxurious. There are ten suites, each with two bedrooms and a sitting room. For ultimate luxury accommodation, the royal suite, on the first floor, will rank with the world's finest. It was occupied by Queen Elizabeth during her Canadian tour a few years ago. Some of the suites facing the lake have balconies.

The climate at Chateau Lake Louise is as alpine as its setting. The mile-high altitude ensures an average daytime temperature of about sixty-two degrees, which climbs to seventy or slightly higher in July and August. The air is brilliantly clear, the humidity is low, sunshine almost guaranteed, so the resort is a sanctuary for hay-fever sufferers.

Lake Louise has become an increasingly important winter resort. During that season the days are clear and frosty and the temperatures generally drop well below zero at night. Although the hotel itself is closed during the winter, there are lodges and motor inns for winter sports fans scattered along the highway near Lake Louise Village. Mount Whitehorn, to the north of Lake Louise Village, is equipped with a half-dozen tows that can accommodate up to fifteen hundred skiers at one time.

Chateau Lake Louise is easy to reach. All trains on the main line of the Canadian Pacific stop at Lake Louise Station, a short distance from the resort. The recent completion of the Trans-Canada Highway has made the resort accessible from east or west over one of the world's more scenic roads. Greyhound buses make regular stops at Lake Louise Village. Calgary, a city of nearly 300,000, is 120 miles to the east of the resort on the Canadian Pacific and the Trans-Canada. Edmonton, the capital of Alberta, with a population of 325,000, is 195 miles north of Calgary and easily accessible over fine new highways. From both Calgary and Lake Louise, main highways lead south to link with main U.S. highways in Washington, Idaho, and Montana. From Calgary, Canada Route 2 links with U.S. 89 at the Montana border. Canada Route 93, passing through Lake Louise, leads south to a junction with U.S. 95 at the border of Idaho, which in turn links to the west with U.S. 395 and 97, leading south into Nevada and California.

Accommodation rates at Chateau Lake Louise are on the European plan; room charges and meal charges are separate. Single-room rates vary from $16 to $19 per day, depending on location. Double-room rates are from $21 to $25 per day. Suites start at $50 per day for one or two persons. Table d'hôte meal rates start, for breakfast, at $1.75, for luncheon, at $2.50, and for dinner, at $5. Special rates include: transfers between the railway station and hotel, a distance of three miles, 75 cents per person; saddle-horse hire, $7.50 per person per day or $5.50 for half day, or $2.25 per hour.

BANFF SPRINGS HOTEL

Most travelers to Banff National Park stop at both Chateau Lake Louise and the Banff Springs Hotel, the latter southwest of Lake Louise. If one comes from the west, Lake Louise is reached first. For those who do so, it would seem that after the breath-taking setting of Lake Louise a stop at Banff Springs Hotel would be anticlimactic. But this is not so, since the setting of Banff Springs Hotel is highly dramatic in its own way.

Canadian Pacific engineers surveying the Banff area immediately realized that it was something special. They reported this to the railroad's officers, who lost no time in designating the valley as one where a resort would be developed.

The site of the hotel itself was selected in 1887 by Sir William Van Horne, president of the railroad. A five-story frame chalet was put up the next year. A townsite near the resort was also chosen and named. The name Banff was borrowed from a town in Scotland, birthplace of an early railroad director, since the valley vaguely resembled the craggy uplands of Scotland. Most visitors agree that it more closely resembles Switzerland. The valley extends ten miles from west to east, with three rivers flowing along its relatively level floor at an elevation of about 4600 feet. The Bow, the largest river, sweeps through the valley in great loops, linking several small and beautiful lakes. From the north a small river, the Cascade, comes into the valley to merge with the Bow, and from the south the Spray River joins the Bow River south of the present resort site. From the valley floor mountain slopes rise to peaks towering from seven thousand to ten thousand feet. Dozens of mountain streams tumble down the slopes, carrying glacial silt into the rivers to contribute to their extraordinary green color.

Sulphur Mountain rises steeply to the south of the hotel on the east side of the Spray. An early landmark, it gave the hotel its name when engineers surveying the site noticed steam coming from the mountain slope. Investigation revealed hot sulphur springs.

It was decided that the Banff Springs Hotel would be the largest and most splendid in the Canadian Pacific's entire chain. Officials chose a baronial style that suggested an ancient Scottish castle. Gray limestone, quarried from Mount Rundle, which rises just behind the hotel, was used as building material. The first massive unit of the great stone building was finished in 1913. Additional stone wings were added in 1927 and 1928. As the resort developed, it exceeded in size and magnificence anything ever dreamed of in Scotland. With its six hundred guest rooms, it certainly is the largest mountain-resort hotel in the world and may well be the most luxurious. With massive towers and pinnacles, it rises with impressive magnificence, dwarfed but not overwhelmed by the mountain slopes that rise around it.

But Banff Springs Hotel did not grow to its present size quickly, nor did the town of Banff, a sophisticated little city with a permanent population of 3500 and a summer population of over 15,000. The development took many years and a great deal of money. A photograph taken in 1905 of the main street of Banff shows a scattering of frame buildings on either side of a dusty, rutted dirt road. A horse and buggy are tied to a hitching rack in front of the general store, and there are more vacant lots than buildings. In 1905 the resort was little more than a frame chalet. It was another twenty years before it began to assume its present shape, and much of today's extensive resort, which spreads over almost four hundred acres, has been developed only recently. The latest development in the valley itself has been the completion of the Trans-Canada Highway, which gives Banff a fine east-west route linking it with roads leading south to the United States.

In the early days Banff was generally regarded as a spa because of the hot sulphur springs. Small resorts near the springs advertised miraculous cures as a result of the sulphur water baths.

But even in those early days the range of activity and diversion throughout the valley was growing steadily in variety. Fishing was a major sport in nearby lakes. The fame of Lake Minnewanka as a place where enormous trout lurked was beginning to grow. Automobiles were nonexistent and in fact were prohibited in the area. All visitors arrived on the Canadian Pacific, operating two trains a day. Today the railroad maintains a four-a-day transcontinental schedule, including the sleek new Canadian, one of the finest trains in Canada. The regular schedule is augmented in the summer by dozens of special trains carrying convention parties, educational tours, organized groups, many of them originating in the United States.

Thousands of visitors arrive by Greyhound bus. A considerable number of guests fly their own private planes and use the resort's own landing strip, two miles from town.

Most of the guest rooms in the Banff Springs Hotel command spectacular mountain views. There are thirty-three two-room and three-room suites. The royal suite has twenty rooms, probably making it the world's largest royal suite, and was used for the visit of King George VI and Queen Elizabeth in 1939. Most sitting rooms have fireplaces, and all rooms are spacious and modern. Most of the public rooms are enormous, decorated in feudal style. There are spacious vaulted halls, flag terraces, stone floors, refectory tables, ancient armor, carved furniture, and medieval tapestries. But the real life of Banff Springs Hotel is of course outdoors. The resort has everything except an ocean beach. The hotel grounds cover fifty-eight acres. A huge outdoor swimming pool set on a terrace just below the hotel building commands the best of many fine views. Another pool is indoors. Both pools are kept at a temperature of seventy-two degrees.

But the resort's most distinctive recreational accessory is one of the most beautiful and unusual golf courses in the world, a championship eighteen-hole course along the valley of the Bow River, a par 71, from 5977 yards to 6729 yards long, depending on which of the three sets of tees are used. Because the course is almost a mile above sea level, the rarefied air often adds up to fifty yards to the tee shots. The first hole requires a carry of at least fifty yards over the rushing waters of the Spray River. The eighth hole, called the Cauldron, requires a long carry over a lake. The most spectacular hole is the twelfth, or Papoose, a one-shot carry of 138 yards to the green. The waters of the Spray River are on three sides, and the green is set among towering pines.

The course has always presented special problems to its staff, since it is in a national park, where all game is protected. Players sometimes see a bear lumbering across their line of play. Coyotes have been known to pick up golf balls to take to their pups. A high fence around the course helps keep elk off the greens.

Fishing at Banff begins almost at the door of the resort. The three lakes are well stocked with trout—cutthroat, rainbow, eastern brook, and other varieties. There is even better fishing in the high alpine lakes that are easily reached from the hotel. Seven miles away is Lake Minnewanka, where huge lake trout weighing twenty pounds or more are taken by deep-water trolling with a copper-wire line. The resort provides boats, rods, reels, bait, and, if desired, guides.

Boating is also popular on the Bow River near the hotel and on nearby lakes, with launches hired by the hour or the day. Sight-seeing motor launches make frequent excursions on the Bow.

Trail riding and hiking are popular over the many miles of wooded mountain trails, which fan out in all directions from the hotel's corral, a few hundred yards from the main building. Horses can be rented for $2.50 per hour. There are organized riding groups with guides to accompany them. Banff offers mountain climbing and is in fact one of the great centers for this sport in the West. Its climbing school offers instruction in every type of alpine climbing, including rock and ice climbing.

Sight-seeing is almost continuous during the daylight hours of summer. Glass-topped buses use the resort as a terminal and are continuously leaving on short and long trips over the area. Two ski lifts operate during the summer months for sight-seeing purposes only. The Sulphur Mountain gondola lift goes up the slopes of that mountain, immediately south of the resort. The base station of the lift is about two miles from the town of Banff, from which the lift climbs several thousand feet to a terminal where there is a teahouse near the crest. The round trip costs $2. The Mount Norquay chair lift, north of the town of Banff, is an open ski lift and also offers sight-seeing. Passengers are carried to a teahouse terminal at a seven-thousand-foot crest, for $1.75.

Dining at Banff Springs Hotel is seldom formal. Menus are varied and abundant, specialties including roast beef, steak, and other meat dishes.

Banff and the Banff Springs Hotel have become increasingly accessible with the improvement of railroad service and the completion of new highways. A junction for both railways and highways is Calgary, eighty-two miles east of Banff on the Canadian Pacific and on the Trans-Canada Highway. As a result of the new highway, the resort is easily reached by automobiles from Pacific coast points of Canada and the United States. It is a little more than 550 miles from Banff to Vancouver, British Columbia, and about 150 miles from Banff to a highway leading south into the United States. The nearest scheduled airline service is at Calgary.

Banff Springs Hotel operates on the European plan, with rates varying with the location of rooms. Single-room rates on the Bow Valley

In the heart of the Canadian Rockies, Banff Springs Hotel, though huge in size, is toy-like among the mountains around it.

37. Those who use the pool and terrace of the Banff Springs Hotel have a stunning view of the mountain valley of the Bow River.

38. Terraced gardens filled with Iceland poppies and enhanced by a glass-enclosed swimming pool are between Chateau Lake Louise, in the Canadian Rockies, and the lake that gives the resort its name.

39. Glacier-fed Lake Louise has been called the most beautiful alpine lake in the world. One of the best views of it is from the lawn of Chateau Lake Louise.

40. In winter encircling hills protect the celebrated ski resort of Sun Valley, Idaho, from cold winds, and their slopes give the resort the finest skiing in the country.

41. Resembling a huge and luxurious Italian villa, the Broadmoor, in the foothills of the Rockies near Colorado Springs, is a resort estate of unique size and character.

42. Tall pines frame the fairways of the mountain valley golf course of the Feather River Inn, in California's High Sierras.

43. Trail riding is the most popular guest activity at the Bishop's Lodge, tucked away in the high mountains near Santa Fe, northern New Mexico.

side begin at $19; they start at $16 on the Sulphur Mountain side. Double-room rates on the Bow Valley side start at $24 and on the Sulphur Mountain side at $21. Suites run from $50 to $80, depending on location and size. All meal rates are table d'hôte: breakfast $1.75, luncheon $2.50, dinner $5. Transfer between the railway station and the hotel is 50 cents per person each way. Nominal rates are charged for horseback riding, fishing, boating, and golf.

"BEHOLD THE SUN COMING DOWN THE MOUNTAIN"

In the language of the buffalo-hunting Shoshone Indians, Idaho means "Behold the Sun Coming down the Mountain," a phrase that is uniquely appropriate for the resort of Sun Valley.

Among mountain groups of Idaho, all immensely rugged, heavily wooded, with steep slopes and narrow valleys, threaded by a web of streams, there are several clusters that have been given names, though all of the mountains are part of the vast Rocky Mountain system. The southernmost is the Sawtooth, where peaks rise to more than eleven thousand feet. From the heart of the Sawtooth the Salmon River cuts a scenic gorge before it swings to the west and joins Idaho's mighty Snake River. The Sawtooth Mountains, appropriately named from the many sharply peaked crests that thrust up among them, are among the most isolated of mountains, and until quite recently no highway led through them. But in the center of the Sawtooth ranges, miles from any community larger than a village, is a world-renowned resort—Sun Valley. One of the newest of North America, it is unusual in some ways, unique in a few. It is the premier ski resort of the United States, and one of the great ski resorts of the world, offering more and greater facility for winter sports than any other in this country. It is also a year-round resort with a full range of activities.

The development of Sun Valley was no accident. It was the result of a plan of Averell Harriman, chairman of the board of the Union Pacific Railroad at that time, 1936, and later Governor of New York. His father had built the railroad during the pioneering days of the Northwest. Harriman thought that the United States deserved a winter sports area comparable to the best ski resorts of Europe. Deciding to create one that would be accessible to his railroad, he sent scouts searching for the best site in Washington, Oregon, Nevada, California, Utah, Wyoming, and Colorado. The experts were looking for an area that would have powder snow and timber-free slopes. Investigation led to Sun Valley. It had all the things Union Pacific was looking for, and, in addition, it was protected by encircling mountains from winter winds.

Sun Valley opened in 1936 as a ski resort and began to draw skiers from everywhere. The late Ernest Hemingway was an early visitor who came back again and again and finally bought a home in Sun Valley. He is buried in the little cemetery at Ketchum, two miles away. Another celebrated visitor in Sun Valley's early days was the Shah of Iran. Harry Truman visited the lodge while president. The list of Hollywood stars who have been regular visitors is long. Governor Nelson Rockefeller was once a member of the Sun Valley Ski Club, and while in their teens, members of the Kennedy family skied at the valley.

The original guest accommodation at Sun Valley was the lodge, a luxurious hostel with 144 rooms, including many with balconies, or sun decks, and several suites that had living rooms with fireplaces. The lodge was built of poured concrete in molds faced with rough boards to provide a texture resembling that of timber. The illusion is so complete that guests today can still be seen testing the wall surfaces with their fingernails to make sure that they are not wooden. The lodge has a spacious and luxurious lounge where skiing guests gather on winter nights. An outdoor terrace opens from the lounge. In the basement are a game room and six bowling alleys.

As skiing developed into a national sport, other, less expensive facilities were added. The Challenger Inn, conceived by Harriman as a simple country inn like those found in the mountains of Switzerland, has 185 guest rooms and is built around a village square that resembles a setting in the Tyrol of Austria. The inn also has a post office, gift shop, service stores, sports shop, and a large self-service buffet that provides excellent meals at moderate prices.

Several attractive chalets built near the inn are quite popular with groups. The whole Sun Valley property today includes 4600 acres, with Sun Valley Village at its heart. The main skiing is done on Baldy Mountain, 9200 feet, in the Sawtooth National Forest. Part of the resort's property includes Dollar Mountain.

An enormous outdoor skating rink, the largest in the world, offers year-round skating. There are two glass-walled outdoor swimming pools —one near the lodge, the other close to the Challenger Inn. An opera house, children's playground, tennis courts, hospital, stables, and a new eighteen-hole golf course make up the rest of the resort.

Sun Valley has remained a pre-eminent winter resort, although it now draws thousands of summer visitors and has a full range of facilities for their diversion. In the winter skiing is the chief sport, though sleighing and ice skating are popular. On the slopes of Mount Baldy and Dollar Mountain, Sun Valley claims that it is possible to get more hours of skiing in per day than anywhere else in the world, with eight electric chair lifts to serve the skiers on Dollar. There are five lifts on Baldy. Beginners ski on a lower slope called Half-Dollar. Intermediate skiers use Dollar Mountain. Expert and intermediate skiers use Baldy, where the slopes and runs offer a wide variety of skiing. Two ski huts are on Baldy for lunch, one a picturesque chalet with a giant four-sided fireplace. Dollar Mountain, across the valley, also has a ski hut where lunch is served. Skating at Sun Valley goes on all day long and often far into the night, with other nighttime diversions including sleigh rides to Trail Creek Cabin, a mile and a half away.

The site of Sun Valley was chosen primarily because the snow, terrain, and climate promised nearly perfect skiing. Not long after the resort was established, it was discovered that the summer climate was also ideal, the air was crystal clear, and the six-thousand-foot elevation ensured invigorating, sunny days and cool nights. The winter season usually runs from December 20 to about April 6. The summer season includes July and August. The intermediate seasons of spring and fall are generally reserved for conventions.

Facilities for summer guests have gradually been expanded and now include many diversions. A recent development has been the building of an eighteen-hole golf course, a highly scenic par 71, 6227 yards, stretches along the valley to the northeast of the Challenger Inn. Trail Creek, the resort's well-stocked trout stream, wanders through the course, providing water hazards for golfers.

Sun Valley has four superb hard-surface tennis courts. Fishing is excellent in a network of trout streams. Silver Creek is one of the finest dry-fly streams in the country. The headwaters of the Salmon River, famed for large and hungry salmon, are forty miles away over good highways.

Sun Valley offers superb horseback riding, and a string of excellent saddle horses is maintained in the corral close to the Challenger Inn. Many miles of riding trails reach into the foothills in all directions. For veteran riders the resort will put guests in touch with guides for pack trips into the mountains. In the fall guides and horses can be arranged for big-game hunting.

For trap and skeet fans, the resort has one of the finest shooting layouts in the West. Competitive weekend tournaments are held for guests. In addition to trapshooting and skeet shooting, there is a pistol and rifle range. During the open hunting season in the fall, the resort provides guides for dove, partridge, grouse, and pheasant shooting in the foothills.

But the most remarkable of all summer diversions is the huge skating rink. There are instructors available for daily lessons. The huge rink, sheltered from the sun by a canopy, is a setting each Saturday night in July and August for an ice carnival.

Sun Valley is celebrated for its menu, which is mainly French. Summer dining at the lodge takes place on an open terrace. The inn provides a reasonably priced Continental buffet. At the Ram, a Tyrolean style restaurant in the Village, dishes of the Austrian mountains are featured. An occasional dining novelty is an outdoor barbecue at Trail Creek Cabin, sometimes followed by a moonlight dance.

The Stanley Basin Recreational Area is fifty miles north on U.S. 93. From the heart of it the Salmon River emerges, flowing north, closely skirted by U.S. 93, offering a dramatically scenic drive through the upper Salmon River Gorge. A natural curiosity called the Craters of the Moon National Monument, a hundred twenty miles to the southeast, is a weird and often grotesque landscape covering fifty-three thousand acres of mountain wilderness, created by lava flow from a volcanic eruption fifteen hundred years ago.

Sun Valley was once almost inaccessible, but now one can easily reach it by rail, air, or highway. The Union Pacific crosses southern Idaho, linking the larger centers of the Snake River Valley. The nearest station to the resort is at Shoshone, about fifty miles south of Sun Valley. Visitors are met there by Union Pacific bus.

The nearest airport, Hailey, twelve miles south of Sun Valley, is served by West Coast Airlines. A larger airport, with more frequent service, is at Twin Falls, eighty-five miles south of Sun Valley. Airport transfers between Twin Falls and Sun Valley cost $35 for the first passenger, $7.50 for each additional passenger. Between Hailey Airport and Sun Valley the transfer charge is $5 for the first passenger, $2.50 for each additional passenger.

More and more Sun Valley guests arrive in their own cars over U.S. 93, which passes through Ketchum two miles south of Sun Valley Village. To the south it joins U.S. 20 and 30 and Interstate 80N. Two hundred miles north of Sun Valley, U.S. 93 joins U.S. 10 at Missoula,

Montana; seventy-five miles farther north it meets U.S. 2, both of which lead into Washington and the Puget Sound area.

Rates at Sun Valley vary with the season. Winter rates are on the European plan. In the winter rates at the Sun Valley Lodge begin at $16 per day for single rooms, depending on type, and at $22 per day for double rooms. Double rooms with private balcony start at $30 per day. Suites for double occupancy start at $40 per day. Single rooms at the Challenger Inn start at $10 per day and double rooms at $15. There are a limited number of balcony rooms at the Challenger Inn; the rate of these is $2 per day more. Chalet dormitories offer accommodations at $3 per bed in rooms without running water, $3.50 per bed in rooms with running water. There are four beds in each room. Summer rates at the Sun Valley Lodge begin at $15 per day for single rooms; for double rooms $20 per day. Balcony rooms are $28 per day for two, and suites start at $38 per day. At the Challenger Inn summer rates start at $7 per day for single rooms and $11 for double rooms. Chalet dormitories in the summer are $2.50 per bed for rooms with running water and $2 per bed for rooms without running water. Meal rates in the various dining rooms are all à la carte. An approximate price range would be breakfast starting at 90 cents, lunch starting at $2, and dinner starting at $4.

Rates for various activities in winter include the following: ski instruction in groups or classes, $7 per day, $4.50 per half day; private ski lessons, $10 per hour, with $4 for each additional person using the same instructor; ski lift tickets, $6.50 per day or $35 per week; outdoor-ice-rink rates, $1 per session; ski rentals, $2 per day or $8 per week, with various types of additional ski equipment available for rent.

Rates for special summer activities include greens fees, $3 for nine holes, $5 for eighteen. Golf clubs may be rented for $2 per day. The outdoor ice-skating rink in summer charges $1 per session. The outdoor swimming pools, both summer and winter, are free. A recent change at the resort, announced in the fall of 1964, was the transfer of management from the Union Pacific to the Janss Corporation, with a promise of extensive development in the future.

IN PIKES PEAK'S SHADOW

Pikes Peak is the most celebrated mountain in the United States. It is not the highest—only 14,110 feet—for several neighboring peaks in the massive Front Range of the central Rockies are much higher. Nor is it the most beautiful or dramatic—others are more spectacular—but Pikes Peak is by far the best known.

Its fame started in 1806, when Lieutenant Zebulon Pike sighted its snow-crested summit from the prairies of Colorado and earned immortality by having the mountain named for him. For fifty years only map makers and geographers paid much attention to Pikes Peak. Then suddenly the flat-topped, snow-crested summit became a kind of national symbol. Wagons headed west across the plains with signs reading "Pikes Peak or Bust." The peak became a landmark with the discovery of gold near Denver, sixty miles to the north. Its frosted summit, looming above the western haze, was the first sign to prospectors that they were near the goal.

Prospectors swarmed over the Front Range thirty years after the discovery of gold near Denver. Some found gold, others found silver, and still others copper. Many made fortunes, many more went broke.

In 1891 gold was discovered on the western slope of Pikes Peak, one of the richest strikes in history. The Cripple Creek area quickly became a crowded mining camp with a population of nearly fifty thousand.

But in the meantime things had been happening on the eastern slope, where tumbled foothills merged with the eastward-stretching prairie. There, at an elevation of about five thousand feet, a settlement was founded in 1871 called Colorado Springs. The town owed its existence to climate—regarded as one of the best in the world and helpful to sufferers of tuberculosis. The settlement became widely celebrated and within a few years was called Little London because so many wealthy English people with tuberculosis went there to recover. Some of them built fine homes. Others took flyers in mining speculations based on the Cripple Creek gold strike and became so wealthy that the little town was known as the richest small community in the country.

In 1885 a German nobleman named Count James de Pourtales, who came to Colorado seeking adventure and fortune, was so impressed with Colorado Springs that he bought several thousand acres of land on the western edge of the town, and he established a residential community called Broadmoor. He built an artificial lake, landscaped and irrigated his property, laid out streets, and plotted lots for sale. In 1891 he built a casino overlooking the lake, designed to be elegant and spacious and to attract those of discriminating taste with money to gamble. He planned a fine hotel rivaling in elegance the best that Europe could boast. The count even persuaded the Colorado Springs Company to extend their streetcar line to the door of his casino, but his plans collapsed when the casino burned in 1897.

At about this time two young men from Philadelphia were lured to the region by the promise of mining wealth. One was Charles L. Tutt, the other Spencer Penrose. Penrose arrived in Colorado Springs in 1892 to visit Tutt. They decided to go into business together, with results that were to transform the Colorado Springs-Pikes Peak area. A year before Penrose's arrival Tutt had filed a claim on the C.O.D. mine, which proved to be unusually rich. Tutt and Penrose went into other mining projects, which made huge fortunes for each of them. They built a road to the crest of Pikes Peak, and it became one of the most remarkable highways in the world. They took over the ownership and operation of a cog railway on the peak and on nearby Manitou Mountain. After Charles Tutt died, in 1909, Penrose joined forces with his partner's son, Charles, Jr., and they began their most celebrated project, taking over the property of Count Pourtales, including his lake and casino property. They wanted to build one of the finest hotels in the world on the shore of the lake where the casino had stood. The new resort, named the Broadmoor, Italian Renaissance in style, was as lavish and luxurious as money could make it. Building materials were brought from all over the world, and craftsmen were imported from Europe to build the wonder of the West.

Around the hotel the partners established a three-thousand-acre playground including a golf course that was then, and still is, one of the best and most beautiful in the world. They added tennis courts. They stocked the wine cellar with the finest vintage wines and liqueurs. Master chefs were hired to plan a menu that was a gourmet's delight. The hotel opened in 1918, and the first name on the guest register was John D. Rockefeller, Jr., then touring the West. The Broadmoor, with four hundred fifty rooms and the combined Penrose and Tutt fortunes to develop it, quickly became renowned throughout the world.

The Broadmoor started with a celebrity guest list, and has had one ever since, but as the area of Colorado Springs grew in fame and population, the character of the guest list changed. Because Colorado Springs was chosen as the site of the North American Air Defense Command headquarters, more and more guests were top officers of the Air Force, high-ranking government officials, and military leaders from other nations. The trend toward military guests increased when Colorado Springs was selected as the site of the new United States Air Force

Academy, which opened in 1958. Broadmoor also has been used extensively for business meetings and conventions.

The main resort building, completed in 1918 and standing at the edge of the half-mile-long lake originally dug by Count Pourtales, is now the center of a cluster of buildings widely varied in type and function. Other buildings are across the lake and among the foothills that rise behind the resort property, with the grounds of the resort spreading over five thousand acres. In addition to the main hotel's 450 guest rooms, a 144-room annex was opened in 1961. The International Center was built, with an auditorium and theater seating 2400 and with banquet facilities for about 1600. Count Pourtales' second casino building was remodeled as a golf and swimming club, and nearby is a stadium big enough to stage a variety of outdoor athletic events. A full-fledged zoo six hundred feet up Cheyenne Mountain, a project developed originally by Spencer Penrose, is maintained by the Cheyenne Mountain Museum and Zoological Society. El Pomar Carriage House Museum is in front of the hotel; it exhibits horse-drawn vehicles dating from 1863.

On the original eighteen-hole golf course, designed by Donald Ross in 1919 at a cost of more than $200,000, the greens are famed for their visual deceptiveness: they look level but often slope surprisingly. Actually there is only one level green—the third—in the entire original eighteen holes. The golf courses, recently redesigned and extended to thirty-six holes by Robert Trent Jones, are set among the foothills of Cheyenne Mountain. The original eighteen holes are 6965 yards long. They spread over hills, are cut by canyons, water hazards, and other natural and contrived obstacles.

The resort's huge pear-shaped swimming pool is open during the summer months; another swimming pool, glass-enclosed, is on the hotel's lake terrace and is open every day of the year.

The Broadmoor riding stable is one of the largest and best equipped in the country, with miles of scenic foothill trails and mountain bridle paths. Luncheon rides and pack trips are arranged during the summer months, and guide service is available.

Ice skating goes on year round in the hotel's World Arena, the site of an annual ice revue held each August.

Winter sports have been expanded by the completion of Ski Broadmoor, with a double chair lift, a snow-making machine, and a ski school on Cheyenne Mountain.

The half-mile-long lake behind the hotel is big enough to permit water skiing in the summer, and, for the less daring, water cycles (for which Broadmoor is famous) and boats.

The annual Pikes Peak or Bust Rodeo is held in the hotel's stadium, also a setting for horse and dog shows. A miniature cog railway carries guests around the lake, along the edge of the golf course, and over a two-mile scenic route among the slopes of Cheyenne Mountain, and ends at the zoo, which houses over seven hundred animals. Broadmoor is one of the few resorts that stage international fashion shows. Leading French designers have flown their creations and models to the hotel for exhibits that have attracted national interest.

Dining facilities at the Broadmoor range from the elegant to the picturesque. One can dine at the roof-top Penrose Room, which fills the top floor of Broadmoor South. Or one can go to a steak fry, held once a week in Rotten Log Hollow, at nearby Fisher's Canyon. The Tropical Garden Room is built around a live-oak tree, with tables scattered among hundreds of growing plants and fresh flowers. Menu specialties are Continental and regional in type and include mountain trout caught within a few miles of the hotel, as well as fourteen varieties of fish flown fresh from France daily for the resort's famed bouillabaisse. Elaborate Continental buffets are served on Sundays during summer months. The Golden Bee, one of several cocktail lounges, is an authentic replica of an eighteenth-century English pub.

Guest rooms at the Broadmoor are very large. Suites with five and six rooms fill entire floors of the main building.

Although there are enough activities at the Broadmoor to keep anybody occupied, many guests take sight-seeing excursions in the mountain area nearby, where the most important mountain is, of course, Pikes Peak, a spectacular backdrop for the hotel. The summit can be reached by a highway that is open from May to October—a forty-mile round trip from Colorado Springs. The road itself actually climbs from a beginning base at 7309 feet to the 14,110-foot summit in a remarkable eighteen-mile section. Another way to reach the summit is by the famous cog railway, which starts at Manitou Springs, six miles west of Colorado Springs. The railway is open between May and October and makes two round trips daily, plus sunset trips July and August. The round-trip fare is $6, children $3. A combination of highway and cog-railway round trip is possible by taking a sight-seeing bus one way and the cog railway the other way.

A stunning short sight-seeing trip is by mountain highway up Cheyenne Mountain, the road twisting up the east face of the mountain twelve miles to the summit. Halfway to the summit is a memorial to Will Rogers, the Shrine of the Sun.

Many Broadmoor guests visit the striking campus of the United States Air Force Academy, which is ten miles north of the resort. The academy covers nearly eighteen thousand acres among the foothills of the Rampart Range.

The Garden of the Gods, just north of the Broadmoor grounds, is a scenic oddity that draws hundreds of thousands of sight-seers every year. A road winds among brilliantly colored rocks of fantastic shape. The area is open, free, dawn to sunset.

Denver is sixty miles to the north over an excellent highway. For lovers of rugged and beautiful mountain scenery, the 260,000-acre Rocky Mountain National Park has fifty-nine mountain peaks at twelve thousand feet or higher. Two-day circle tours through the park are available in Denver by the Rocky Mountain Motor Company.

Broadmoor is easily accessible year round by an excellent highway, by rail into Colorado Springs, over the Burlington, Rio Grande, Rock Island, and Santa Fe lines, and by air service to Peterson Field in Colorado Springs by Braniff, Continental, and Central airlines.

The Broadmoor operates on the European plan, with room and meal rates separate. Single rooms begin at $10 in the winter and spring (between October 1 and June 1), $15 in summer (from June 1 to October 1). Double-room rates start in the winter and spring at $12, at $20 in the summer. Parlor suites start in the winter and spring at $22.50 for one person, $27 for two, and in summer $40.

GOLD DUST AND FLOATING FEATHERS

More than two hundred years ago a group of Spanish explorers headed by a Captain Arguello was paddling its way up an unnamed river that joined a greater river, named the Sacramento. On their right were the towering ramparts of the High Sierras, which had never been penetrated. The river they were exploring was frothing and turbulent with melted snow. Captain Arguello, according to legend, noted that an unusually large number of feathers floated on the river's surface, presumably the feathers from great flocks of wild fowl. So he called the stream Río de las Plumas, or the River of the Feathers. It is hard to know now whether there actually were wild-fowl feathers floating on the river, or whether the frothing turbulence resembled them, but the name stuck, translated a hundred years later by prospectors into Feather River.

The main channel of the Feather River, parallel to the Sacramento, joins that river north of California's capital, Sacramento. Further north the river splits into three channels, the north, middle, and south forks. The middle and south forks rise into the Sierra and tumble through craggy, forested canyons. One of these is a deep, rugged gorge called the Feather River Canyon, famous for its scenic quality. But in early days it was also famous for gold. It was one of the great gold-discovery streams, and its waters and banks yielded millions in gold dust. Until 1913 dozens of gold dredges were operating near the junction of the middle and south forks. It is generally said that even today, if a well is dug near the river, it will yield enough gold dust to pay the cost of digging.

Prospectors paddled up the river and through the canyon in 1849 and found it wild and incredibly rugged country. It was also dramatically beautiful, with stands of pine, fir, and cedar, and a colorful variety of other plants and trees. The stream swarmed with trout. The miners left their mark on the land with trails and roads, with gold-mine tunnels, buildings, and fragments of flumes. The fish and the forest remain today, contributing scenic splendor and great fishing for visitors to the Feather River Canyon.

Those who visit the canyon today travel over a fine mountain highway or by rail. The train trip, one of the most celebrated scenic routes in the West, is made along tracks that play leapfrog with a highway, moving from one side of the canyon to the other. It is the main line of the Western Pacific Railway, which links San Francisco and Oakland with Salt Lake City, where passengers ride in Vista Dome cars of the California Zephyr.

Both the eastbound and westbound trains of the California Zephyr go through the spectacular gorge of the Feather River Canyon early in the morning, and though most passengers get up early enough to see the sight, some leave the train at a mountain hamlet called Portola, the nearest railroad stop to a remarkable mountain resort called the Feather River Inn, ten miles west of Portola on the edge of a village called Blairsden.

The Feather River Inn is set in six hundred acres of superbly forested mountain valley with the Feather River winding through its property. As resorts go, it isn't very old, the product of one of California's periodic land booms. In 1915 railways and promoters were staging campaigns to lure visitors to the Golden West. The operators of the Western Pacific thought they had something to offer. Before long a promoter named H. C. Leighton was persuaded to have a look at the Feather River Canyon. Leighton was president of the Interstate Company, which had news-vending concessions on the railroads as well as hotel operations in various parts of the country. Leighton quickly found a tract to his liking—about a thousand acres at an elevation of four thousand feet. The channel of the Feather River ran through it; towering pines rose above it; mountain crests surrounded it.

Leighton promptly hired a San Francisco architect. The early plans were modest and called for a two-story log lodge that would appeal to hunters and fishermen. As time went on, the heady air of the Sierra slopes began to inspire Leighton and the architect with grander ideas. Soon they were planning a large and luxurious resort. Its central lodge was made of timber and stone with high gables vaguely resembling a Swiss mountain inn. Chalets and cottages were built along a semicircle of walks and drives extending on either side of the lodge. There were guest rooms and assorted public rooms in the central lodge, and from eight to twelve bedrooms in each of the chalets on either side, giving the resort about 125 guest rooms.

Hundreds of guests began to arrive, not all hunters or fishermen. It was soon the largest and best-known resort among the northern mountains of California. The owners added a nine-hole golf course with fairways framed by towering pines, a par 36 course, 2880 yards. Guests were encouraged to try fishing in the fifty-two lakes and streams within fifteen miles of the resort grounds. A giant heated swimming pool was built within a terrace of lawns among high pines. A stable of horses was provided for jogging over mountain roads and trails in breakfast rides and trail rides. Hayrides and steak fries became standard activities. Ten years after its opening the entire resort was redesigned and rebuilt to accommodate guests coming from all parts of the country. Business organizations in California found that the secluded mountain setting and the resort's special facilities were ideal for meetings. A special auditorium was built and equipped with all the modern facilities of audition and demonstration.

The Feather River became famed in the West as a Shangri-La of unique charm tucked away in the heart of mountain forests. In 1957 the inn was purchased from the Interstate Company by Mr. and Mrs. Albert Favetto, who had years of experience in operating luxury resorts in Europe and South America. Their management of the Feather River

Inn has added many Continental dishes to the menu, particularly Italian, Swiss, and French.

Guests soon discover that the nearby area is quite historic. Practically within walking distance of the hotel is a remarkable wilderness mountain area called Plumas-Eureka State Park. It is a dramatically rugged mountain tract of five thousand acres, where intensive gold mining was carried on more than a hundred years ago. The park contains relics of the days of forty-niners, mining trails, mine tunnels, mill buildings, and a remarkable ghost town called Johnsville, where the state of California opened recently a gold-mining museum. During the gold-rush days it was reported that a gold nugget found in one of the nearby mines weighed fifty-five pounds and was worth thirty-three thousand dollars.

The best season for the Feather River Inn is the summer, when the air is dry and clear and daytime temperatures seldom rise above seventy-eight degrees. In the fall the mountain crests rising above the inn's valley are covered with snow. The resort opens on June 20 and closes on September 9. Planned activities are vigorous and varied. A sample of a recent week included these diversions and activities: a trail ride with a cowboy guide, a table-tennis contest, water-polo matches, a tennis tournament, a putting-green tournament, a breakfast ride with a mountain cookout, a swimming meet, a horseshoe tournament, a hayride and barbecue, a sight-seeing trail ride to the Feather River Canyon, a ladies' putting-green tournament, a shuffleboard contest, and a sunset ride. For those still on their feet after dinner there was dancing every night. The program was equally varied for children, their activities supervised by a junior hostess.

The Feather River Inn is under a modified American plan, which means that room, breakfast, and dinner are included in the rate. Under that plan single-room rates are from $19 to $26, depending on the type and location of room. Twin-bed rooms for two are $14.50 to $18 per person. Private-chalet rates (a living room, with fireplace, and two twin bedrooms, each with bath) are from $78 to $99 per day depending on the number of people involved. Children's rates are $6 per day up to six years, $8 per day from six to twelve years when children occupy a room with adults.

For guests wanting mountain sight-seeing, days of adventurous travel are possible over the slopes of the High Sierra to the east and beyond into the desert lands of Nevada. Lake Tahoe, less than an hour's drive away, is the center of a tremendous resort region of summer camps, small hotels, and winter ski facilities. One of the highest lakes in the country, with a surface elevation of about six thousand feet, Tahoe also is one of the most beautiful mountain lakes anywhere.

But for any visitor to the Feather River Inn the most beguiling sightseeing opportunity is exploring the Mother Lode country, which stretches south from the inn along the foothill slopes of the Sierra for more than a hundred miles. California Route 49—called the Mother Lode Highway—is the linking road of the gold country that reached old towns with odd and colorful names—some of which are ghost towns today and others still centers for mining.

The Feather River Inn is easily reached by highway. It is 238 miles from San Francisco over U.S. 40 and Alternate 40, or U.S. 40 and 89. It is 152 miles from Sacramento over U.S. 40 and 89, and fifty-six miles from Reno over U.S. 40 and 89. Greyhound Bus Lines maintains regular service from San Francisco, Sacramento, and Reno. The nearest plane connection for commercial flights is Reno, where the airport is served by United, Western, and Bonanza airlines. A field at Beckwourth, with an airstrip long enough to handle conventional two-motor aircraft, is fifteen miles from the inn. On advance notice the inn meets all passengers arriving by California Zephyr at Portola. Similarly the inn will meet guests arriving by air at Reno.

HIGH MOUNTAIN SANCTUARY

The highest mountains of the Southwest are the Sangre de Cristo. They are actually an extension of the Rockies into New Mexico. They are characterized by wild, rugged, and tumbled peaks and slopes. Among them Wheeler Peak, near Santa Fe, rises to 13,151 feet, the highest point in New Mexico. Dozens of other crests rise to 10,000 feet or more. Slopes are steep and heavily wooded, with superb stands of great trees. Here and there, cupped within steep slopes, are mountain lakes of great beauty, and from the heart of the mountains emerge two of the Southwest's most celebrated rivers—the Rio Grande and the Pecos.

The mountains were named for "the blood of Christ" more than three hundred years ago by a Franciscan padre who helped found the Spanish outpost called Santa Fe, the oldest capital in the United States and the most Spanish city in the country.

The site selected in 1609 was a fine one among the foothills. It had an elevation of about seven thousand feet, high above the valley of the

Rio Grande. Its altitude gave it a wonderful climate—clear, bright, pleasant, and very healthy. The settlement was to be the center of government for the vast province of New Mexico, where a Spanish governor would rule a wilderness empire. In keeping with its importance, it was saddled with an incredible name: La Villa Real de la Santa Fé de San Francisco, or the Royal City of the Holy Faith of Saint Francis. The first governor laid out a spacious walled city with a central plaza, a palace, and, of course, a church.

The tiny settlement did well. The Spanish priests who were members of the governor's staff began teaching the Pueblo Indians who had lived in the hills for hundreds of years. Although the settlement itself had little more than a handful of soldiers and nonmilitary residents, the Franciscan priests had built eleven churches and converted more than eleven thousand Indians by 1617. One of the churches, a sturdy and charming mission, is still there—the oldest church in the United States.

Though Santa Fe grew and prospered, and before long was the center of the Southwest, its development was not always tranquil. In their efforts to convert every Indian in the region, the priests evoked a bitter Indian revolt in 1680. The Spanish governor, his soldiers, and settlers were driven away. But they came back after twelve years, and for a century and a half kept control of their capital, which in time became a famous and sophisticated city. Rich Spanish planters and traders built handsome haciendas, and the governor's court was gay and brilliant.

But the Spanish court went out of business in 1846 when American troops marched into Santa Fe and took over the city from the government of Mexico.

Soon Santa Fe became the terminus for the Santa Fe Trail, bringing new wealth and new people into the city. Although the city stopped being officially Mexican, it continued to be Spanish in its culture and it also continued to be the most important center of the Roman Catholic faith in the Southwest.

Because of its religious importance the Church sent to Santa Fe one of its ablest clerics—Jean Baptiste Lamy, who reached Santa Fe in 1850, only a few years after the city had become part of the United States. He lived there for more than thirty years, his vast diocese one of the largest in the country. Father Lamy built a big cathedral in Santa Fe, the first Roman Catholic cathedral to be built in the Southwest, and was made a bishop a few years after his arrival, and about twenty years later an archbishop. He died in 1888 at the age of seventy-four. Years later

Willa Cather told Archbishop Lamy's story in a celebrated novel, *Death Comes for the Archbishop*.

One day, the story goes, the archbishop, while wandering among the green and fertile foothills of the Sangre de Cristo Mountains near Santa Fe, came upon a little valley where the Franciscan fathers, who had preceded him more than 200 years, had established a ranch and planted an orchard. The archbishop was entranced by the fertile valley, which reminded him of his native France. He bought the ranch with its ancient orchard as a retreat from the troubles and problems of his life in Santa Fe. He built a country home for himself and converted an ancient adobe house high on a hill into a tiny chapel with a vaulted ceiling and steeple, at the crest of which he put a copper cross. The glass windows were hand-painted to resemble stained glass. During the last years of his rich and fruitful life, Archbishop Lamy lived at his country ranch, meditating in his tiny private chapel. Following his death, the entire property was left to a Catholic order of the Sisters of Loretto. Later it was purchased by Joseph Pulitzer, the newspaper publisher, as a summer home for his daughters. To the ranch buildings Pulitzer added two substantial summer homes.

In 1918, James R. Thorpe, who had made a fortune in mining in Denver, discovered the property and bought it from the Pulitzer estate. He and his family have since converted it into one of the most pleasant resorts in the country, Bishop's Lodge, a thousand-acre resort estate spreading over mountain slopes and valleys. At the heart of the resort is the charming little chapel that the bishop built, carefully retained exactly as it was left by him.

In the forty-odd years that the Thorpe family has owned the property, they have changed the tiny religious retreat and ranch into a full-scale and thoroughly modern year-round resort. They have been careful to retain the flavor and architectural style of the original buildings and the distinctive Spanish design for which the Santa Fe region is famous. All of the resort buildings are designed in the adobe style. Furniture and décor also reflect the colorful Spanish and Mexican influence. A big swimming pool is set in a wide, sunny terrace. In a special wing a big auditorium, banquet hall, and special meeting rooms are designed for business meetings.

Excellent tennis courts, shuffleboard, and croquet courts are not far away, and set in the heart of the Sangre de Cristo Mountains is a nine-hole golf course. A stable of horses with cowboy guides is available to lead groups of guests on long rides over miles of scenic mountain trails.

Perhaps the popularity of trail riding as a resort activity at Bishop's Lodge is the reason its owners describe it as a ranch-resort, but the description is inadequate, for, although ranch activities such as trail riding and chuck-wagon cookouts are widely popular, so are other activities that have little to do with ranch life. Open the year round, Bishop's Lodge, during its season, from early fall until late spring, is a center for winter sports fans, with one of the finest mountain ski centers in the country only a few miles away, with a chair lift, rope tows, and all the accessories of winter sports activity.

Bishop's Lodge has accommodations for 125 guests in four separate beautifully appointed lodges. There are three dining rooms and two banquet rooms, also a special dining room for children under twelve, where special children's portions are served. Menu specialties are varied and colorful and tend to reflect the three hundred years of Spanish tradition. Occasionally a complete Spanish supper is provided. Cookouts served in traditional ranch style and steak fries on open grills are frequently held.

Guests have special privileges at the Santa Fe Country Club. Most guests join trail rides over a network of forest trails through the Santa Fe National Forest, which adjoins the resort property. Some take part in resort-sponsored pack trips, lasting for three or more days. For them the Lodge provides food, horses, camping equipment, and trained guides.

Guests quickly discover that the lodge is a convenient base for general sight-seeing. The most popular trip is to historic Santa Fe, a few minutes' drive away, one of the oldest and most picturesque cities in the country, where sights include the historic old plaza, once the terminus for the Santa Fe Trail. Facing the plaza is the old palace of the governors, which now houses the Museum of New Mexico, built in 1609. The oldest public building in the United States, it was the residence of a succession of Spanish and American governors for two hundred years. The Cathedral of St. Francis, the first Roman Catholic cathedral in the Southwest, which Bishop Lamy built, is nearby. Other remarkable churches in Santa Fe include the tiny San Miguel church, adjoining the city's oldest house and generally regarded as the oldest mission church in the country.

Santa Fe is probably the best place in the United States to see and appreciate the Southwestern Indians' distinctive crafts, exhibited in several museums and schools. Canyon Road, which grew from an ancient mountain trail, is now the center of Santa Fe's growing colony of artists and craftsmen.

Taos, seventy miles northeast of Bishop's Lodge, is one of the oldest and most charming cities in the country. There is the Taos Pueblo, a vast Indian apartment house, which is perhaps the oldest still-lived-in dwelling in the world, a striking example of the distinctive architecture developed by the Pueblo Indians.

The owners of Bishop's Lodge take special pride in their benign and invigorating climate. Summer temperatures are never hot, and winter temperatures—the altitude of nearly seven thousand feet notwithstanding—are seldom very cold. The percentage of daily sunshine ranges from about seventy to eighty, depending on the time of year.

Bishop's Lodge is quite accessible. Most guests arrive by automobile from Santa Fe, a hub of main express highways from all directions. The Santa Fe Railway serves Sante Fe. Frontier Airlines and Continental Airlines have scheduled service into the Santa Fe airport, where station wagons of the lodge meet planes and trains. Trans-World Airlines has service to Albuquerque, where cars can be rented for the fifty-mile trip to the lodge.

Guest rates at Bishop's Lodge are American plan (although meals in the dining room are available to unregistered guests on a per-meal basis). Rates vary slightly with the season. Lower seasonal rates are available between May 15 and June 15 and between September 15 and October 31. In those off-season periods single-room rates start at $14 per day. Double-room rates for two people begin at $24 and go up to about $34. Living-bedroom suites are available beginning at $28 per day for two and going up to about $44. The rates between June 15 and September 15 are somewhat higher. A single room begins at $16, double rooms for two at $32, and living-room suites at $36.

Steady riders can rent horses for $35 a week with the same horse and saddle reserved for their use. Occasional riders can rent a horse for $4 for a half day, $6 for a full day. Golf fees are $1.75 during weekdays, $3 weekends, with two courses available—the Santa Fe Country Club and the Los Alamos Golf Club. Rates for mountain pack trips are $20 per day, which includes food, horses, camping equipment, and guide.

CHAPTER 9

THE GREAT VALLEY AND
THE GREAT LAKES

South of the Great Lakes and west of the Alleghenies is one of the richest and most productive agricultural regions in the world. Such great states as Michigan, Ohio, Illinois, Wisconsin, Indiana, Kentucky, Missouri, and several more are within the area, the vast valley of one of the world's great river systems—the Mississippi and its huge tributaries. In addition to fine farms, it has great industrial centers—Chicago, Cleveland, Detroit, Cincinnati, Indianapolis, and St. Louis.

But this tremendous central region of the United States, so rich in many things, is poor in important resorts. There are a few resort communities here and there, particularly along the shores of the Great Lakes. But there are only two distinctive resort estates, both of which developed in special settings and from special circumstances.

The dearth of resorts in the great central valley is not difficult to explain. As a general rule, resorts have developed in accessible scenic settings that offered a distinct climatic advantage—in the mountains or along the seacoasts. However, the central valley has no mountains or ocean shore. The summer climate, except in the northern parts of Michigan and Wisconsin, is too often hot and humid.

The climatic exception of northern Michigan accounts for the establishment of one of the region's two resorts. It stands on a remarkable island between two of the Great Lakes—Michigan and Huron—in the Straits of Mackinac. With a historic and strategic location, the island was famous from the earliest days of exploration and settlement. It was known among the Indian tribes of the region as a place blessed by the gods, where the water was fresh and clear and the air gave strength and health.

During the nineteenth century, after steamers began to ply the lakes and railroads crept north through the forests, Southern plantation owners seeking escape from the summer heat discovered Mackinac and began to build summer homes. It became a resort center and an island sanctuary.

That was the beginning of the Grand Hotel at Mackinac Island, built during the resort boom in the late 1880's and designed to be the largest, finest, and most fashionable summer resort in the Midwest. For years it was just that, and in many ways it still is. The unique frame hotel with its high-pillared porch overlooks the Straits of Mackinac. The resort, reached only by boat, dominates the remarkable resort island. It is one of the few resorts in the country where guests never hear the sound of automobile traffic: there are no automobiles permitted on the island; only horse-drawn carriages are allowed. The Grand Hotel has grown and developed in seventy-five years through successive remodelings and extensions, until it offers guests modern and luxurious comfort in a setting of historic charm.

The Midwest's second resort estate began, like the Grand Hotel, as a favored gathering place of Indian tribes. Before the present state of Indiana was explored or settled, the whole southern part was covered with a dense forest. There one valley was a special rendezvous for Indians who had discovered that certain water was good to drink if they were sick. French settlers of the area discovered the spring years later, so it became known as French Lick. Later a doctor of dubious talents in healing, but a gifted promoter, acquired the spring and began to bottle and sell the water. He also built a spa nearby. Finally a consummate politician and business genius named Thomas Taggart bought the spring and built an exceptional resort.

For a generation the rambling and elegant hotel was a rendezvous for the wealth and society of the Midwest. But French Lick Springs Hotel suffered the blight of the depression years. It almost died. A few years ago the big Sheraton organization acquired the all but deserted hotel, spending a fortune to restore its late-Victorian elegance and adding modern comforts and facilities. Now the French Lick Sheraton—its historic spring still flowing and still smelling stoutly—draws guests from all over the Midwest.

"PRIMITIVE BOUQUET IN SEAS OF SWEET WATER"

Since earliest times islands have been special places of sanctuary and refuge, centers of resort and recreation. Among famous small islands a very special one is Mackinac Island, now almost completely a resort where a few permanent residents spend a brief, bustling summer keeping several hundred thousand visitors comfortably entertained. But Mackinac has deep roots that go back more than three hundred years. Then it was another kind of a resort—a favorite gathering place for Indian tribes where fighting was taboo and members of every tribe could gather in peace.

The climate was uniquely healthful. There weren't any swamps or mosquitoes, and the water was pure. The island was heavily wooded, rising abruptly from the waters of the lake to almost four hundred feet. The Indian name for the island was Michilimackinac, which meant "Great Turtle," because it looked like one from a distance.

Mackinac became important because of its location at the entrance to the strait that divides the upper and lower peninsulas of Michigan and links Lake Huron and Lake Michigan. The first European to recognize its strategic quality was Jean Nicolet, who paddled through the straits in 1634. French explorers, traders, priests, and soldiers who followed him also recognized its strategic importance.

The British, who had ousted the French from the wilderness region of the lakes, built a fort on the island in 1780, cannons dominating the strait between the two lakes. Mackinac was a strategic stronghold for more than thirty years, first for the British, then for the Americans. The fort now superbly restored, is a fascinating attraction for summer visitors.

Because Mackinac was the logical site for control of the enormously important fur trade of the northwestern wilderness, John Jacob Astor chose the island as the base for his American Fur Company. In 1820, his company accounted for more than three million dollars' worth of pelts cleared through the island base. Astor employed about two thousand fur buyers and four hundred clerks to count his skins and money.

About 1830 the fur traders moved west, and the island went into a temporary decline. But the reputation of Mackinac's pleasant climate began to spread. Mississippi Valley planters who had become wealthy from cotton began to journey north to the island in the summer. Some built palatial summer homes, but the Civil War played havoc with their fortunes and the Southern colony disappeared. It was followed by a group of rich Chicagoans for whom the island was a boat ride away up the length of Lake Michigan. They built cottages and summer mansions along the wooded bluffs that overlook the lake.

In 1881 a ferry service was established, making Mackinac accessible to railheads across the strait. It was the final event needed to turn Mackinac into a resort. In 1887 a group of lumber and railway interests combined to build what they called the "world's largest and finest summer hotel." At a dinner celebrating its opening Chauncey Depew gave the hotel a name. He called it the Grand Hotel. It is still called that and still claims to be the world's largest summer hotel.

The opening of the Grand Hotel drew celebrities from everywhere and gained national notice. Mackinac Island became the Newport of the Midwest, a sanctuary for the rich and socially elite, and a haven for hay-fever sufferers. Wealthy families built their Victorian "cottages" on the bluffs behind and above the hotel. The hotel's guest register resembled a Who's Who of celebrities.

Mackinac Island has changed little in the years since the Grand Hotel's flamboyant opening in the last quarter of the nineteenth century. The island has been spruced up, and facilities for recreation and comfort added, but the island looks as it did more than seventy-five years ago when it became the premier resort of the Midwest. Its status was guaranteed in 1895 when the state of Michigan declared Mackinac Island its first state park, thus protecting it against commercial exploitation.

The island is one of the few places remaining in the United States that have escaped the invasion of the automobile. It is three miles long, two miles wide, and is a remarkable geological oddity, scenically and historically, with a hard, close-grained limestone base that somehow resisted the grinding erosion of ice during the glacial period. So the island stands higher above the water than any other area around it. From its shore, completely encircled by a carriage road, steep cliffs rise to wooded bluffs. Except for relics preserved as historic sites, nothing remains on Mackinac related to its period of strategic military importance or commercial activity. Everything is geared toward the accommodation, comfort, and diversion of the thousands of visitors who come to it from all over the country every year. There are still summer homes at the crests of the bluffs, rambling mansions built more than sixty years ago.

There are more than a dozen resort hotels, in addition to the huge Grand Hotel, and many tourist homes. There are carriage tours to scenic and historic points, drive-it-yourself carriages, saddle horses, and hundreds of bicycles to rent. There is a large yacht harbor. There are two golf courses and a network of hiking trails.

But the Grand Hotel overwhelmingly dominates the island. In size, elegance, and facility it far surpasses any other resort accommodation. The original planners selected a commanding site, exactly one hundred feet above the level of Lake Michigan, so oriented that guests at night could see the lights of St. Ignace, on the tip of the northern peninsula of Michigan, as well as the lights of Mackinaw City, at the opposite side of the Straits of Mackinac. Across the wide façade, they built the world's longest porch—880 feet long—where the world's longest row of rocking chairs is almost always filled, with rockers regarding the expansive view: broad lawns and clumps of fragrant cedars sloping down to the lake, and beyond the lawn the strait with its ceaseless shuttle of ships.

When the hotel first opened, bathers trudged down to the lake shore to a row of bathhouses. Now they saunter down to a huge, serpentine swimming pool. There is a sunken garden, nearby, that is famed for the splendor of its floral exhibits. The view of the straits between St. Ignace and Mackinaw City also has changed. It now includes one of the world's longest suspension bridges, which links St. Ignace with Mackinaw City, one of the most beautiful bridges in the world.

The Grand Hotel has gone through a succession of ownerships and conditions. It has had its prosperous years and its bad years, depending on the changing times. Although it has been a good many years since it has been regarded as the only place in the Midwest to visit, its status has been steadily increasing recently because of the unique talents and energy of its present owner, W. Stewart Woodfill. Born in a small town in Indiana, he first visited Mackinac Island as a young man suffering from hay fever. He liked what he saw and what the island's climate did for his ailment, and he decided to stay. He talked his way into a job as a desk clerk at the Grand Hotel, in 1919. In a few years he was manager and had bought a substantial interest in the hotel. In the boom year of 1928 he sold his interest for a large profit. A few years later, when the hotel was in receivership because of the Depression, he bought back the entire property for a fraction of his original investment.

Woodfill has been the moving spirit in most developments at Mackinac Island ever since. He is the absolute master of everything that goes on in the hotel. He calls it his "little boardinghouse" and runs it with a flair for hospitality, public relations, and good hotel management. He keeps a sharp eye on the island to make sure that nothing goes on to impair its unique charms and special character. More than any one man, he was responsible for persuading the state of Michigan to build the superb bridge that links the two straits cities. He knew that once the bridge was built it would enormously increase the travel to Mackinac Island.

But he has been equally stubborn in making sure that the island was accessible only by boat and that no automobiles would ever be permitted to defile its charms with speed and sound. Consequently, if you want to go somewhere you walk, hire a bicycle, ride a horse, engage a carriage, or sail a boat. Some of the carriages are as old as the hotel itself. All of them are driven by uniformed coachmen. Guests are brought to the hotel from the steamer landing in one of the resort's opulent hacks. They then march up to the main entrance of the hotel over a long flight of steps covered with an enormously wide red carpet, a long-standing symbol of hospitality.

If you are allergic to horses but still want effortless sight-seeing, the Grand Hotel offers its guests a unique conveyance—a couchlike wicker chair built on a tricycle, pedaled by a uniformed hotel attendant.

In recent years the entire hotel has been remodeled and redecorated. The stuffiness of the Victorian décor has disappeared, to be replaced by modern furniture and fittings. The whole hotel is alive with color. There are three hundred guest rooms and suites. About the only evidence of its former character is a high-ceilinged spaciousness not usually found in modern design. The public rooms spread in a bewildering variety over the two lower floors, and they include everything from informal snack bars and intimate cocktail lounges to a huge ballroom and main dining room.

The hotel dominates five hundred acres of grounds that stretch from the lake shore back to the base of bluffs. Within the grounds are sweeping lawns and extensive formal gardens, a nine-hole golf course that is beautifully kept and that has a superb view of the lake from almost every point.

The most remarkable change in the Grand Hotel has been its patronage. There was a time when to be accepted during the summer season there was a status symbol assuring social success back home during the rest of the year.

This is no longer so and has not been so for many years. During the lean years of the Depression, Woodfill discovered new ways to fill empty guest rooms. They included conventions and business groups. Woodfill takes a personal hand in finding groups that like his "little boarding-house" and does everything possible to make sure that they have maximum comfort and service.

American families on vacation increasingly account for the summer business, both touring groups or as separate families, driving their cars to the bridgehead at St. Ignace or Mackinaw City and reaching the hotel by ferry. There are special rates for families.

For those who like to ride there is a stable full of horses and miles of wooded and lake-shore trails. There are hiking trails, and bicycling has a special charm, since it can be done without risk of accident from automobiles.

The island offers unique opportunities for sight-seers. The superb restoration of Fort Mackinac was largely the result of a vigorous campaign by Woodfill. For years he was upset by its shabby ruins, adjoining his hotel's grounds to the east. Through his personal efforts a restoration project was begun in 1958 with dramatic results. The fort has not only been restored, but in a sense it has been activated. Soldiers in authentic uniforms of the various periods of the fort's use march along its ramparts. Within the ancient buildings vivid dioramas tell the history of the fort. On a balcony adjoining one group of officers' quarters is a tea-room where visitors can relax with refreshments and a superb view of Mackinac town and harbor. The fort is easily reached on foot from the Grand Hotel.

Overlooking the harbor is an assortment of historic memorials to the early days when Mackinac Island was the heart of the wilderness fur trade. These include buildings associated with John Jacob Astor's American Fur Company and a reconstruction of an old store.

Many natural oddities are reached by easy trails—Arch Rock, Sugar Loaf, and Skull Cave. Arch Rock, which has been compared to Virginia's Natural Bridge, rises 146 feet above the lake level and has a span of fifty feet. Sugar Loaf is an isolated pinnacle that rises seventy-five feet.

Beyond the island itself other sight-seeing opportunities include a round-trip excursion by steamer to the east, passing through the cluster of summer resort islands called Les Cheneaux. Here several hundred islands hug the shores of Lake Huron and provide a moving panorama of an endless succession of channels, islands, resorts, and resort life. In Mackinaw City, which is a ferry ride from Mackinac, is the restoration of Fort Michilimackinac, the earliest fortification in the straits. It was the scene of the bloody massacre in 1763 that forced the British to move across the straits to Mackinac Island, where they built the stronger and more impregnable fort, the showpiece of the island today.

West of Mackinac Island, at the north end of the Straits of Mackinac Bridge, is historic St. Ignace, one of the earliest settlements in the northwestern wilderness. A fine highway goes north fifty miles to the extraordinary international community called Sault Sainte Marie, the third oldest community in the United States. It exists today as a service center for the great locks by which the waters of Lake Superior, tumbling over violent rapids to the lower level of Lake Huron, are made into a channel for steamers. The locks and channels are the busiest waterway in the world. The operation of the locks draws thousands of visitors during the summer months.

Although Mackinac Island is accessible only by boat, direct ferry terminals to the island are easily reached by automobile, bus, or airplane, and the island is a regular stop on a number of summer-excursion steamers operating through the Great Lakes. In one's own car, Mackinac will probably be approached through the lower peninsula of Michigan, using any one of a half-dozen main highways that converge at Mackinaw City, at which there are parking areas for cars. Ferry service directly to the island begins in mid-May and lasts until late September. One can also cross the bridge to St. Ignace and take a ferry from that point. Service from St. Ignace to Mackinac operates on approximately the same basis as the ferry from Mackinaw City.

Two airlines provide scheduled service in the summer to communities reasonably near the island. North Central Airlines maintains a terminal at Pellston, Michigan, from which limousine service operates to the Mackinaw City ferry dock at $2.50 per person. Trans-Canada Air Lines operates to Sault Sainte Marie, Ontario, from which chartered car or taxi service is available to the St. Ignace ferry dock.

The Grand Hotel is on full American plan, rates varying with the location of the room, its size and character. Twin-bed rooms on the lake-front side begin at $23 per day per person up; the same type of room on the interior side of the island begins at $20 per day. Studio rooms begin at $26 per day per person. Rates for children occupying the same room with their parents are $5 per day up to 5 years, $9 between six and eleven years, and $14 for twelve years and older. All guests are automatically charged a $1.50 fee for carriage and luggage service from the dock to the hotel. Fees for recreational activities and sight-seeing are: golf, $3 per person; bicycles, 60 cents per hour; swimming pool, $1; saddle horses, $4 per hour; tennis, $1 per hour; carriage tours of the island, $2.50. The Grand Hotel is open for normal patronage only in the summer season, from early June to late September. Reservations can be made for a slightly earlier or a later use for conventions and business groups.

PLUTO WATER AND POLITICS

Wild animals, mineral water, Indians, French settlers, and Midwest politics were involved in the establishment of the vast rambling resort dominating the village of French Lick.

The first pioneer settlers entered Indiana from the south and east and found dense hardwood forests covering steep-sloped hills. There were few lakes or rivers of consequence except the Ohio and, farther west, the Wabash. It seemed like a poor land for settlement, but the settlers were a stubborn and hardy breed. They cleared the forests and destroyed them, sometimes with community bonfires. Among the early settlers was a farmer named Thomas Lincoln, who crossed the Ohio from Kentucky and staked a claim to a patch of forest land. The land is still there, now part of a national memorial preserving the grave of Nancy Hanks Lincoln, the mother of Abraham Lincoln, who grew up in the southern Indiana forests.

But long before Thomas Lincoln settled in Indiana, another group of pioneers had come in from the south up the Mississippi, the Ohio, and the Wabash rivers, earliest of all the settlers in the Midwest. French in origin, they were intent on developing the rich fur trade of the forests. In southern Indiana they gave names to physical features, established trading centers, and built forts at such places as Vincennes and Terre Haute.

The French found a narrow valley where hot mineral springs gurgled from limestone clefts. Animals, so the legend went, licked the rocks and felt better. The Indians regarded the springs as important for health and declared the area neutral ground.

There the French built a small fort that was later named French Lick. The mineral spring, now one of the most famous natural springs in the world, is still called French Lick. After the land became a part of the United States, settlers began to trickle in, but few traveled to French Lick because the slopes were too steep for farming. So it was quite a few years after the settlement of Indiana until the mineral springs at French Lick attracted attention. In 1841 the therapy of the springs came to the attention of Dr. William A. Bowles, who had a flair for politics and promotion. He built the first hotel at French Lick, a wilderness spa that consisted of a primitive wooden building of peculiar design. But Bowles knew how to advertise and soon had guests coming from far and near in horse-drawn carriages and creaking farm wagons. They stayed at his hotel and bought jugs of his spring water to take home. The word spread that the water with the unpleasant odor was healthy. Dr. Bowles came up with an inspired name for his health-giver: Pluto Water. He built a bottling plant and sold the water far and wide.

During the Civil War, Dr. Bowles became a leader of a subversive group called the Knights of the Golden Circle. He was arrested and convicted of treason and his hotel venture collapsed.

Thirty years later the hotel and surrounding land came under the control of a remarkable man named Thomas Taggart. He rebuilt the hotel and restored its lost fame and glory and for a period of almost thirty years made it one of the really great resorts of the country.

The story of French Lick Springs Hotel's golden era is largely the story of Tom Taggart, who had a gift for people, politics, and business. He came to the United States shortly after the Civil War as a penniless immigrant boy from Ireland. He made his way to the developing frontier country of Indiana and began working in a saloon. Soon he owned the saloon and became involved in politics, a game he played with such skill that before long he was mayor of Indianapolis. He became a power in Democratic politics, first in Indiana, then in the nation. At the height of his career he was one of the most powerful political leaders of the country—Democratic national chairman and, for a few years, United States senator.

In 1891 Tom Taggart and a few friends put together a company to buy the French Lick property. It seemed a foolish thing to do. French Lick Springs turned out to be one of the most profitable investments of the era, and Pluto Water became famous throughout the world.

It was no accident that Tom Taggart turned the shabby wilderness hotel of Dr. Bowles into a sophisticated spa of world-wide renown. It took imagination, money, hard work, and time. He built an elegant new hotel that was the wonder of its day, seven stories high, and it had mechanical marvels called elevators. It had hundreds of guest rooms, and its spacious public rooms were decorated with sedate elegance. It covered twenty-five acres of floor space and stood in the middle of more than four thousand acres of wooded and superbly manicured grounds.

Taggart took other steps to add to the prosperity of his property. The Monor railroad ran from Chicago to Louisville on a right of way near French Lick. Taggart persuaded the railroad to run spur lines into the resort, with a special station and parking tracks. Soon rich and fashionable guests began flocking to French Lick. Several passenger trains passed through its station in a day, and at times a dozen palatial private cars were parked on the French Lick siding.

Tom Taggart knew that, to maintain the procession of patrons who could afford his rates, he needed more than a fine hotel, a wilderness setting, and a good golf course. His resort needed what nearly all the great spas of Europe had—a casino. Gambling in Indiana was illegal and Taggart had no intention of trying to involve gambling directly with his own name, which was beginning to be known as that of a shrewd and successful political leader. In 1904 a luxurious gambling house called Brown's was built directly across the street from the hotel. It is still there today. Most of its windows are boarded up and the old building is dilapidated and shabby. In its heyday Brown's was both elegant and busy. It was so busy, in fact, that getting in after dinner sometimes took a bit of doing. It offered all the conventional gambling devices, with dice games leading the list. Stakes ran high. Old-timers remember Brown's during the peak of its golden era when winnings or losses of fifty thousand dollars in a single night per person were fairly common.

It was never clearly known who owned Brown's, and never established that there was anyone named Brown. Regardless of who owned the casino, it operated quietly and successfully. Although gambling was illegal, it was clearly understood that any sheriff of Orange County who bothered the patrons would find himself back on the farm. The taxes paid by Brown's and the French Lick Springs Hotel went a long way toward paying county bills.

Taggart did one more thing. He quietly made the hotel an unofficial gathering place for political leaders. In 1904 he became the national chairman of the Democratic party, a position that he held with skill and success for many years. It is probably true that many of the decisions made by the party during the next twenty years were made at French Lick. Taggart had a special genius for public relations. His relations with newspapermen were at a level of good will and understanding that almost always ensured a favorable press.

When Taggart died in 1929, the golden hue of his resort was beginning to tarnish. It was no longer *the* place to go and few millionaires could still afford private railroad cars. The era of opulence was passing. French Lick still ran successfully, but its profits diminished year by year, and as the income level of guests diminished, so did the rewards of Brown's casino. When Taggart died, French Lick went into a decline. The *coup de grâce* came in 1949, when public outcry against gambling forced Brown's to close. Although French Lick didn't close as a hotel, it might well have done so. Its illustrious public rooms became shabby and disordered. Losses became astronomical. It was controlled by a succession of owners over a number of years until the Sheraton chain became the operating owners in 1955. They promptly allocated several million dollars to renovate and modernize the extraordinary building.

The job looked hopeless. The vast rambling structure that Taggart had developed over the years was little more than a shell. It needed almost everything that modern hotel management and operation could give it. It was obvious that mere modernization, air-conditioning, and a fancy swimming pool would not be enough. The hotel needed a completely new orientation toward patronage. This had to be developed while the renovation of the great sprawling building proceeded. The Sheraton sales experts went searching for guests. And found them in two areas: comfortably off or moderately well-to-do American families, and corporations.

Nowadays French Lick is crowded. Business-convention planners find that the isolated seclusion of French Lick makes their meetings more successful. And special family rates make a visit to French Lick a sensible investment of holiday time, with something to do for everyone of all ages.

The main structure and wooded grounds of French Lick are about as Taggart left them. The last wing, which he built in 1924, is still the most recently added part of the main hotel. Outside its windows Pluto still presides over the Grecian temple that houses the historic spring, still flowing at a rate of about ninety gallons per minute, at a constant temperature of fifty-five degrees. Most guests sample the spring water, but very few drink it.

Opposite the main entrance of the hotel is a huge swimming pool set in a wide sun terrace. Nearby is an extraordinary kidney-shaped swimming pool equipped for year-round use, with a plastic dome rising forty feet. There are areas for tennis, badminton, croquet, table tennis, horseshoe pitching, softball, and archery. Two golf courses beguile both the amateur and the expert. A flat but well-maintained valley course of eighteen holes permits the duffer to play to his heart's content. The hill course is three miles away, spreading over ridges above wooded slopes, and it is a championship course.

The Continental elegance of the public rooms has been restored and in many ways improved. More than twenty-five rooms have been set aside for group meetings. The vast main dining room, once one of the largest and handsomest formal dining rooms in the country, has been divided so that hundreds of family guests can be dining in one part while a chairman of a board inspires delegates on the other side.

Guest rooms at French Lick were always famed for being spacious and high-ceilinged. They now are all air-conditioned, an essential improvement, since summers in southern Indiana can be hot. Antique plumbing has been replaced.

The mineral-bath section of Taggart's day is still there. Although not as popular as it was in the Taggart era, it is still used by more than fifteen thousand patrons a year.

French Lick's far-ranging facilities for fun, recreation, and diversion are available to all guests. Crowning a nearby hill is a complete skeet-shooting and trapshooting range with clubhouse, instructor, and guns and shells for rent. A rambling old stable houses dozens of horses for guests who want to canter along the miles of forest trails.

Carriages are for hire and in an hour or two of trotting will take guests over miles of quiet country roads. A miniature train operates at intervals over several miles of narrow-gauge track through the resort grounds to the nearby town of West Baden.

During the Taggart era French Lick Springs was famous for its dining room. Meals were superb and abundant, featuring Southern cooking. At dinner waiters provided impeccable service with a flair. Room service was a celebrated tradition, with selected waiters carrying loaded trays balanced on their heads.

The real sight-seeing rewards at French Lick are a bit afield. East and south of the town Paoli, nine miles to the northeast, is an extraordinary forest tract, a unique remnant of the primeval forest that once covered the whole area. It is now protected by the U. S. Forest Service.

Another exhibit of pioneer days is Spring Mill State Park. It is about twenty miles to the north outside the town of Mitchell. Spring Mill is a completely reconstructed pioneer village with an operating gristmill, shops, houses, and craft centers, rebuilt just as they existed during the first half of the nineteenth century, when Spring Mill was a flourishing stop on a stage route.

The most rewarding tour of the region is fifty miles to the southwest. One of the sights is St. Meinrad's Abbey, an extraordinary group of religious buildings founded in 1857 and maintained by a teaching and working Roman Catholic order. The abbey church is regarded as one of the best examples of pure Romanesque design in the United States. About ten miles away is the village of Santa Claus, which exists because of its name. More than a million pieces of mail are passed through its post office each Christmas season to get its distinctive frank. The little village draws a steady stream of visitors who find a gigantic statue of Santa Claus and a fairy village.

About five miles down the road is a national shrine preserving a fragment of the farm cleared from the wilderness by Thomas Lincoln. The foundations of the Lincoln cabin are within the tract. Nearby, within an iron fence, is the grave of Nancy Hanks Lincoln, who died there in 1818.

French Lick is easily accessible by highway from various cities. Indianapolis is 110 miles to the north; Louisville is sixty miles to the southeast. The nearest small cities that have regular rail service are Mitchell and Orleans. Arriving by air, visitors will probably fly to either Indianapolis or Louisville, and then rent a car. For those who own or charter planes a modern airport with a 4400-foot paved runway has been completed not far from the hotel.

French Lick operates on the American plan. Single-room rates start at $18 per day; twin or double-room rates start at $30 per day per couple. During the off season, between mid-November and mid-March, there are special rates for families, with arrangements for children under fourteen, who are guests without room charge. There are special rates for various activities. An unusual feature not common among resorts is that most of the sports facilities are free, including golf, tennis, swimming, archery, shuffleboard, badminton, softball, volleyball, horseshoes, and table tennis. Skeet shooting or trapshooting is $4 per round for twenty-five shots. Golf clubs can be rented for $2. Golf-course caddies charge $2 for nine holes, $4 for eighteen holes, or $6 for carrying double. You can hire a horse for $2.50 an hour, take a surrey ride for $1, or ride the miniature train for $1, with children on each half price.

44. The high pillared façade of Mackinac Island's Grand Hotel conceals the longest front porch in the world—880 feet.

45. A mineral spring deep in the heart of the southern Indiana hills accounts for the fame and success of huge French Lick-Sheraton, home of Pluto Water.

46. On the edge of wilderness and the shore of a lovely mountain lake, the Harrison Hotel in British Columbia commands a stunning prospect.

47. For dramatic scenic beauty few resorts can match the setting of Del Monte Lodge, on Monterey Peninsula, in California, where a typical prospect is the lone cypress at Midway Point.

48. The lodge offers guests six eighteen-hole golf courses, including the famed Pebble Beach course, its renowned seventh green on the sea.

49. Remarkable in size, design, and setting, huge, rambling Hotel Del Coronado, near San Diego, California, is the oldest and most celebrated resort in this southern region.

50. Aqua-bikes built for two let guests at the Del Coronado resort go scooting over a private lagoon near its quaint Victorian boathouse.

CHAPTER 10

THE WESTERN SHORE

The Pacific coast of the United States and Canada is one of the most dramatic meetings of land and sea in the world. To the north, great fiord-like arms of the ocean slice between towering, snow-crested mountain slopes. To the south, just beyond the U.S.-Canadian border, is one of the world's largest and most beautiful harbors—Puget Sound. From the entrance to that great bay the Pacific shore stretches southeast more than twelve hundred miles, flanking three Western states—Washington, Oregon, and California, with a dramatic and sometimes awe-inspiring shore. Towering headlands rise hundreds of feet above surging surf and here and there are beaches of shining sand.

There are few natural harbors below Puget Sound. One is San Francisco Bay. Another, almost at the Mexican border, is San Diego Bay.

The Western shore has big and handsome cities: Vancouver and Victoria in Canada's British Columbia, Seattle in Washington, Portland in Oregon, and, in California, San Francisco, Los Angeles, and San Diego. But curiously, there are relatively few resorts. Only three along this highly scenic coast qualify as true resort estates, one in Canada and two in California.

This dearth of important resorts is due to several reasons. One, clearly, is the lack of natural harbors. And, too, the Pacific states have been developed relatively recently, and only within the last sixty years or so have there been large centers of population from which resorts might draw patronage. A third reason is that for a long time access to the coast itself was difficult. Few railroad lines led to the shore; main highways were inland, beyond the mountains.

The Canadian resort got its start from a boating accident that led to the location of a hot mineral springs nearby. In time, this wilderness watering place became a luxurious resort estate on the shores of Harrison Lake, surrounded by wilderness and snow-capped mountains.

At about the same time a land-development company had taken over remarkable Monterey Peninsula, south of San Francisco, a forested tract of about six hundred acres which thrust into the Pacific from the old Spanish settlement of Monterey. The plan was to develop a residential community on the peninsula that would appeal to the rich and discriminating homeowners. That ambitious project led to the Del Monte Lodge, one of the most beautiful resort estates in the world.

The third resort on the Western shore developed during a land boom in the San Diego area, where two Midwestern promoters conceived the idea of taking over a sandy island in San Diego inhabited exclusively by rabbits. They would dispossess the rabbits and build a tremendous hotel surrounded by a new community of homes called Del Coronado. The sale of the lots for the homes would pay for everything, including the resort.

When the resort was finally built, it turned out to be the most extraordinary hotel in the West—a huge, shingled building of remarkable design. The Del Coronado, one of the few great wooden hotels that didn't burn down, passed through a succession of ownerships and was recently restored to its former Victorian elegance. Equipped with all possible accessories for comfort and convenience, it is now a resort estate of unique character in one of the world's best climates.

LAND OF THE SASQUATCH

Southwestern British Columbia is a tangle of rugged, forested mountains, channels, alpine lakes, and rivers surging through craggy gorges. It is one of the most spectacular primitive wilderness areas in the world —dramatically scenic and almost unpopulated. It is also a region that legend says is the home of a mysterious monster called the Sasquatch, the North American counterpart of Asia's Abominable Snowman.

Trappers and hunters in the area swear that they have had fleeting glimpses of a gigantic creature covered with hair. One hunter claims to have found an enormous footprint that could have been made only by the Sasquatch. The particular area where the footprint was found is near one of the most enchanting alpine lakes of North America, Harrison Lake, a narrow, forty-six-mile lake starting about five miles north of the spectacular canyons of the Fraser River.

From the lake's shores, mountain slopes rise abruptly to crests of more than seven thousand feet. The southern end is about a hundred fifty miles from Seattle and eighty miles from the Canadian metropolis of Vancouver. The lake itself leads north into the heart of an untamed, unpopulated, and, in many ways, unexplored primitive wilderness. The only settlement on it is at the southern end—Harrison Hot Springs, a village of a few hundred inhabitants. There, overlooking the lake is the wonderful resort that owes its existence to a boating accident.

The story of the Harrison Hotel began in 1846 with the discovery of Harrison Lake by Hudson's Bay explorers seeking a new route to the Pacific coast. Two years later, when gold was discovered in British Columbia, hundreds of prospectors began to struggle into the wild mountain region. They soon discovered that traveling up Harrison Lake toward the gold fields was easier than following the treacherous channel of the Fraser River. While following this route a miner fell from a boat and was astonished to find the water warm, a fact duly reported. Investigation led to the discovery of mineral hot springs at the southern end of the lake. They were named St. Alice's Well, after one of the daughters of a governor of British Columbia. About twenty-five years later, an enterprising promoter took over the hot springs and built the St. Alice Hotel. It was an immediate success, drawing a steady stream of visitors and vacationers from the growing communities that fringed the coastal area to the west. The St. Alice Hotel eventually burned down, to be rebuilt in 1926 as the Harrison Hotel. It has been growing in size, reputation, and facilities ever since. It is now a superbly equipped resort estate with grounds spreading over seven hundred lakeshore acres, many guest rooms commanding a stunning view of the lake against its backdrop of distant, snow-topped peaks. But there is nothing rustic about the appointments of the Harrison Hotel. Most visitors agree that it resembles one of the fine Swiss-lake resorts, owing to its direction by a European-born and Swiss-trained resort and hotel expert, Max Nargil. It would be difficult to find a language in which some member of the hotel staff of nearly two hundred is not fluent. Dining rooms, menus, service, and settings are truly Continental.

The hotel now has two hundred guest rooms and suites, including guest bungalows scattered over the extensive grounds. A new wing with forty-six rooms and suites has been added recently. Public rooms have a restrained but colorful elegance. The striking Copper Room is a supper club with nightly dancing, where everything in the room, including the piano, is copper-plated. There are a number of public rooms for business meetings and conventions.

In the lobby is a duty-free store where guests purchase imported commodities at substantial savings. Two mineral pools with hot sulphur and potash water, piped from the hot springs, are under the jurisdiction of a health department, supervised by registered therapeutic operators. On the immediate grounds of the resort are tennis and badminton courts, a heated fresh-water swimming pool, areas for croquet playing and horseshoe pitching. A boat dock nearby has a flotilla of small craft for guest use. A fully equipped stable has horses for riding over more than eight miles of mountain bridle trails. Golf can be played on a dramatically scenic nine-hole course, a par 36, two miles south of the hotel.

The Harrison Hotel is one of the few resorts in the country that are civilized bases for big-game hunting. The mountains to the north are famed for grizzly, brown, and black bear, moose, deer, and mountain goat. The hotel will arrange licensed guides and help provide transportation to the best hunting areas, as well as for fishing on the lake or on the mountain streams that feed into it. The catch is usually trout, which grow to giant sizes.

Most guests at the hotel usually make a sight-seeing safari on the lake in one of the hotel's special launches, which offer comfortable, close-in views of one of the country's most notable wilderness areas. Another popular sight-seeing trip from the hotel is by automobile along Canada's new transcontinental highway, which for many miles follows the course of the Fraser River through rugged Hell's Gate Canyon. A novelty along the way is the intricate ladder network used to help salmon travel upstream on the Fraser River.

As a result of a mild climate, the Harrison Hotel is open year round, with a series of special events during the year, climaxed by an old English Christmas during the holidays.

Dining at the Harrison is varied. The main dining room features Continental cooking, while the Copper Room leans toward American dishes.

From Seattle the Harrison Hotel is less than a four-hour drive on freeways. It is less than a two-hour drive from downtown Vancouver on one of the most scenic roads in the country. Motorists coming from the East can meet the Trans-Canada Highway at many points east of the hotel.

The Canadian Pacific Railway and the Canadian National Railways have regular station stops near the hotel at Agassiz, five miles away, and taxi service is available to the hotel door. Rail travelers from the United States can take the Great Northern Railway to Vancouver and transfer there to either the Canadian National or Canadian Pacific.

The hotel has its own 2200-foot landing strip, which is adequate for most light and executive aircraft. Harrison Lake is often used for float planes, and there is a landing ramp on the lake. Several major airlines provide regular scheduled service into Vancouver, where air-charter service to the resort is available.

Rates at the Harrison vary with the season and type of accommodation. All rates are European plan—rooms only. During the main season, May 18 to September 15, single-room rates start at $11 per day, and double-room rates at $14. In the new luxury wing single rooms start at $21, and double rooms at $24. Suites vary from $27 to $80 per day, depending on size and location. The off-season rates, from September 16 to May 17, begin at $8 per day for a single room, $10 per day for a double room, and single rooms in the new luxury wing start at $15 and double rooms at $19. Suites in the off-season start at $20 per day and go up to $65. Rates for meals are highly flexible, depending on the dining room selected and menu desired. Rates for boat rental range from $3.50 per hour for a small outboard skiff to $6 for larger boats. Nominal fees are charged for use of the golf course, for rental of various types of sports equipment, and the hire of horses by the hour or day.

DEL MONTE'S ENCHANTED SHORE

Enchantment invests the Monterey Peninsula and with gentle magic converts an association of land and sea into a region of special felicity. But there is little on the map of California to suggest the virtues of the peninsula. It juts into the sea between two famous bays—Monterey on the north and Carmel on the south. Along its base highways swarm with the traffic of a rich agricultural district and link a chain of booming towns and cities. San Francisco is 125 miles to the north; Los Angeles 350 miles to the south. None of this suggests why the Monterey Peninsula is a very special place. The reasons lie in a beguiling quality that transforms the land. The saintly Father Serra must have felt it when, in 1770, he picked the peninsula as a center for his chain of missions along the California coast. His military and civil associates must have felt it when they selected Monterey as the place from which California was to be governed for many years.

The magic of Monterey is hard to describe. Part of it is topographic: the square shape of the peninsula thrusts into the sea. Rugged hills break down to the shore of dark cliffs and tumbled rocks against which the sea shatters into leaping spray. Foils for this marine violence are quiet crescent coves fringed by fine white beaches. The sand is so fine, in fact, that one of the odd commercial enterprises of the area is selling the sand all over the world for special purposes.

Part of the magic of Monterey is climate, never hot, never cold, and silver morning fogs drift in from the sea, followed by a sun so clear and sparkling that the sea turns as blue as the Mediterranean.

Part of Monterey's magic is botanic: thousands of acres of virgin forest cover the hills. Fringing the shore are groves of the rarest tree in North America—the twisted and beautiful Monterey cypress. The odd and wonderful shapes of this extraordinary tree form a background for almost everything that happens there.

Finally, part of the magic is the gentle hand of history, which, unlike history in other places, has not done violence to the land, but instead has contrived to maintain a pleasing balance. It was a Spanish hand, at first, that gave the peninsula a lovely old mission and California's most distinctive type of architecture, the Monterey house.

Over the years three quite different communities have grown up on the fringe of the peninsula, each with its special charm. Monterey, California's most historic town, and Pacific Grove, famed for its butterflies and marine gardens, are at the base of the peninsula facing Monterey Bay. The third town, facing the peninsula across Carmel Bay, is the informal resort community of Carmel, long the home of artists and writers, built around one of California's most cherished historic relics —Carmel Mission, where Father Serra lived and is buried.

Much of what Monterey is today is the result of the enlightenment of a great company, Del Monte Properties, which since 1919 has jealously guarded the land and its dramatic beauty. It owns Del Monte Forest, which fills most of the peninsula, company-maintained access roads that lace the forest, including the famed Seventeen Mile Drive, which skirts the shore, offering one of the most beautiful scenic drives in the world. Perhaps its greatest single achievement has been the building of golf courses, spectacular to see, challenging to play, including the most famous single golf course in the country—Pebble Beach.

The core of the company domain is Del Monte Lodge, its grounds spreading along the south shore of the peninsula. The central building of the lodge overlooks Carmel Bay and the Pebble Beach Course, which stretches thousands of yards along the shore, coming to a spectacular climax with its eighteenth hole directly in front of the central lodge building. Diners sitting close to the window of the main dining room can almost peer into the cup on the eighteenth green.

Nothing about the design of the lodge, with its many linked buildings, clashes with the almost theatrical beauty of the setting: the forests behind, the perfectly manicured fairways and greens of the golf course in front, edging the shore above surging surf.

Del Monte Lodge was built in 1919 and was first planned only as a modest haven for golfers playing the Pebble Beach Course. The main resort, Del Monte Hotel, was miles away on the crest of a hill overlooking the town of Monterey. The hotel, a vast neo-Spanish building of almost baronial splendor, had been built in 1880 by the Pacific Improvement Company. For fifty years Del Monte Hotel was the last word in gilded opulence and provided guests with unmatched luxury.

During World War II the Navy leased the hotel as a preflight school, and after the war used it as a Navy postgraduate school for officers. The Del Monte managers were left with their land but no resort. So they turned to the modest lodge overlooking Pebble Beach and began to develop and extend it.

Del Monte Lodge today is one of the great resorts of the world and one of the most famous, familiar to millions who have caught glimpses of its setting through televised golf tournaments held at Pebble Beach. It is not big as resorts go. There are only 110 guest rooms, most of them in wings stretching out from the main building. Many of the rooms have private terraces or balconies. All of the rooms are spacious and maintained with a casual charm, with the accent on comfort, including wood-burning fireplaces.

The public rooms of the lodge include a spacious lounge, an adjoining library, a card room, a meeting room, a taproom decorated with photographs of famous golfers, and a tremendous dining room of distinctive charm, deriving much of its attractiveness from a wall of glass along one side overlooking the golf course.

Although Del Monte Lodge is famous for golf, it has long since ceased to be exclusively a golfing center. If a guest doesn't know the difference between a putter and a divot, he can still have a fine time at Del Monte. The lodge has its own yacht harbor and dock adjoining the

Beach Club. Sailing is continuous and, weather permitting, there usually is a regatta every week.

If you like to ride, Del Monte offers about as attractive a setting for doing it as one could ask, with extensive stables within easy walking distance. Horses are trained to both English and Western saddles. Instruction is available. One's own horse can be stabled. The hundred miles of bridle trails through the forest and along the shore are as scenically rewarding as bridle trails can be. The resort sponsors many riding events during the year, including hunts, point-to-point races, hunter trials. For several years it has been the setting for the Olympic Three-Day International Equestrian Event.

For hunters and gun fanciers there is the Pebble Beach Gun Club on a beautiful site among sand dunes overlooking the ocean. Facilities for trapshooting and skeet shooting are available. There are five championship tennis courts, a staff of professionals, and many exhibitions and tournaments during the year. There is a big heated pool near the Beach Club.

Sooner or later, however, the focus of interest comes back to golf. The concentration on the game began fifty years ago, when the Pebble Beach Course was laid out. It has grown with the years, both on the Pebble Beach Course itself and on the other championship courses nearby. The spectacularly set Cypress Point Golf Course, the Dunes Course, the new Shore Course, of the Monterey Peninsula Country Club, the Del Monte Golf Course. A new course spectacularly set among high dunes to be called Spyglass Hill Course is being built by Robert Trent Jones. It is expected to be ready for play in the fall of 1965. All are championship eighteen-hole courses, superbly maintained. Thanks to the flanking sea and the general setting of the area, they are among the most beautiful golf courses in the world. From a golfing standpoint they are regarded as among the most challenging and, by the same token, the most rewarding. Several holes at Pebble Beach and nearby Cypress Point have been chosen by famous golfers for inclusion in a mythical all-American golf course. These include the eighth and the eighteenth at Pebble Beach and the fifteenth and sixteenth at Cypress Point, where the tee shot must carry a 210-yard stretch of ocean. A similar ocean hole at Pebble Beach is the seventh, where the roar of surging surf, often above the level of the green, is a unique psychological hazard.

Since its opening, almost fifty years ago, Pebble Beach has been the annual setting for the California Amateur Golf Championship, which sometimes draws more than a thousand entries. Pebble Beach has been the setting for the U. S. Golf Association Amateur Championships on three occasions. Each January, Pebble Beach is the site of the Bing Crosby National Pro-Amateur Championship.

Dining at Del Monte occurs in several locations. The dining room of the pleasant and colorful Beach Club, near the boat harbor and dock, is informal and is open for lunch. Most guests prefer the spacious main dining room, with its stunning view of Carmel Bay and the golf course beyond the window. Del Monte menus are varied and abundant. If anything unusual about them can be singled out, it is that only the highest quality produce is used. Most of the fresh vegetables and greens come from the area east of the resort that calls itself the "salad bowl of the world." Other Del Monte specialties are seafoods taken from California's offshore waters. (Del Monte's chef contends that he cooks better abalone steak than any other chef in California.) Buffet dinners are held in the main dining room every Thursday. Some guests who might otherwise leave on Thursday stay over for the buffet; residents of the neighborhood flock in to sample it.

Many guests discover that Del Monte's unique location makes it a good base for sight-seeing jaunts. Historic Monterey, a few miles to the northeast, became the capital of the province of California in 1775, remaining so for more than seventy years. Fortunately for the visitor, Monterey is well aware of its historic past. Winding through the town is a unique guidance device called the Path of History, painted in the middle of the street and linking more than forty sites, each one carefully labeled. Among them is the Presidio of Monterey, a military reservation older than any other in California. It began as a Spanish garrison and now is the Army's remarkable Language School.

North of the Presidio is the residential town of Pacific Grove, with a fine public beach and a distinctive marine garden that can be viewed from glass-bottomed boats. The famous butterfly trees are north of the town at a roosting place where tens of thousands of monarch butterflies stay between November and March.

Carmel, in the opposite direction from Monterey, was established in 1904 as a vacation haven for artists and writers, and it has stoutly resisted attempts to turn it into a conventional city. There are no house numbers, nor is there mail delivery, and many streets are without sidewalks. It has a fine public beach and a pleasant scenic drive flanking the shore. Carmel Mission, just south of the city proper, was the second of Father Serra's twenty-one missions and was founded in 1770. It was

Father Serra's home through most of his life, and his grave is its most revered shrine.

Just below the mission is one of the most sensational scenic drives in the country, the Carmel-San Simeon Highway, called the Big Sur Road. It offers guests at Del Monte Lodge a long day's round trip to San Simeon State Park, where the opulent Hearst castle, San Simeon, is set in sixteen hundred acres of hilltop estate.

Del Monte offers a long list of special services. There are instructors available on an hourly or a daily basis for golf, riding, tennis, shooting, or swimming. On advance notice guests are met at the Monterey Airport or at the railroad stations in nearby towns.

The resort is very easy to reach, as any map will reveal. It is 125 miles south of San Francisco and about 350 north of Los Angeles. California's U.S. 101 goes through Salinas, which is sixteen miles away. The Southern Pacific Railway has connections at both Monterey and Salinas. United Air Lines and Pacific Airlines have scheduled flights into Monterey Airport, which also has facilities for the servicing of private planes.

Guest rates at Del Monte Lodge are full American plan. Rates vary with location and type of room from a minimum of $21 per day, for a single, to about $40 per day, for a double, and a sitting-room suite with a fireplace for $60. There are special rates for several separate cottages, each large enough for a group. The President's House has seven double rooms, each with bath and sitting room. Rates for special services include greens fees for golf all day, $10 for guests. Caddie fees are $5 per bag; caddie carts, $6 weekdays, $8 weekends. Riding is $3.50 per hour weekdays, $4 per hour weekends and holidays. Tennis courts are free for guests and are restricted to guests.

HOTEL DEL CORONADO, SAN DIEGO BAY

History does not record the thoughts of Juan Cabrillo when, one warm September day in 1542, he found by accident the almost hidden mouth of a great bay and sailed in with his tiny Spanish vessel. Cabrillo was a Portuguese working for Spain, which was rapidly extending its possessions in the vast new world that Columbus had discovered fifty years before. Cabrillo goes down in history as the man who discovered California and claimed it for Spain. The bay he found was the vast safe harbor of San Diego—a bay of curious shape, about fifteen miles long and two miles wide, created by two overlapping fingers of land.

One of the fingers, a promontory that rises several hundred feet above the surf of the Pacific, has at its crest a tiny national monument that commemorates Cabrillo's discovery. This rugged high land that forms the western flank of San Diego Bay is Point Loma. Cabrillo supposedly tied up his tiny ship at a point of land in the harbor entrance called Ballast Point. The second finger of land extends north almost from the border of Mexico to create the southern half of San Diego Harbor. While Point Loma on the west is high and rock-ribbed, the peninsula to the east is low, flat, and sandy.

The end of the eastern peninsula bulges into a thumb of land about three miles across; the stem extends south some ten miles in a narrow, sandy strip, called the Silver Strand, only a few hundred feet wide. It is almost certain that Cabrillo sent boats ashore on the Silver Strand, since it was the home until recently of a vast colony of frolicsome rabbits. Doubtless Cabrillo's crew clubbed enough rabbits to stock his diminished larder for weeks to come.

It was long after Cabrillo's discovery that anyone bothered about San Diego Bay and the land around it. Then, in 1769, Spain sent an expedition into California. A mission and a settlement on the east shore of the bay were established and named San Diego. The mission was the first of many to be built by the Spaniards in California. The settlement of San Diego became the great city of San Diego, the oldest city in California. But it took a long time to grow, and for more than a hundred years the rabbits were the sole residents of the Silver Strand.

By 1880, when San Diego had grown into a delightful small city with a few thousand people and distinctive Spanish charm, the first of many land booms that were to sweep California began. One day in 1884 two promoters rowed across San Diego Bay. They had their eyes on a brush-covered peninsula—the bulge of land at the northern end of the Silver Strand—Coronado. They found it swarming with rabbits. On one side the peninsula had the surf of the Pacific pounding on golden beaches; on the other the quiet waters of San Diego Bay and the little town itself. One of the promoters was a Hoosier named E. S. Babcock. The other, H. L. Story, was from Chicago. Babcock was a man of imagination and action. He saw the brush-covered peninsula as the base for the largest real estate development in the West. It would grow around a vast new resort hotel—opulent, elegant, and distinctive.

Babcock's enthusiasm was infectious. In 1885 he and Story formed a syndicate and bought 4185 acres at the north end of the Coronado Peninsula, and the next year they began to sell land in lots and build a resort. In a two-year frenzy of planning and building they displaced the rabbits and established Coronado as a new community built around the Hotel Del Coronado.

The crews worked night and day. Babcock hired an architect who had a flair for Victorian elegance. He designed the hotel as a vast Victorian pile, made almost entirely of wood. Redwood was shipped from Southern California and cut and fitted on the spot. Mahogany for bars was brought in by ship around the Cape. Babcock began selling his real estate by promotional stunts that made the average medicine man look modest. Balloon ascensions drew huge crowds to the site. Advertisements were displayed throughout the country. Inducements to purchase thousand-dollar Coronado lots included such lures as free water for one year and a hundred twenty single-trip tickets on the ferry connecting Coronado with San Diego. By the time the hotel was ready to open in 1888, most of the lots had been sold and Coronado was beginning to take on the aspects of a real city.

Babcock may have practiced chicanery in selling real estate, but he spared no expense in the design or building of his hotel. It had four hundred guest rooms, with vast and numerous public rooms. The hotel was built in a rectangle with balconied inside rooms overlooking a huge patio. A profusion of gables and towers rose above the roof. The hotel's most remarkable feature was the incredible Crown Room, the main dining room, which overlooked the bay and the ocean. The room was oval in shape, 155 feet long, 62 feet wide, and 32 feet high, the ceiling of beamed wood vaulting.

Nearly every guest room had a wall safe and a fireplace with cherry mantel. Among the hotel's features was electric lighting in every room, supplied by the largest incandescent-lighting plant outside of the city of New York. Thomas Edison made a trip to the West Coast to help set up the system. Soon the hotel's guest register was a roster of rich and famous from far and wide. Leading the list were two California railroad tycoons who had arrived in their private cars, which were parked on the hotel's own railroad siding. For many years the only parking problem was created by private railroad cars.

Although Babcock was a shrewd promoter, he was a poor businessman. Soon after the gala opening in 1888 he was in trouble. The land boom that brought him a fortune from the sale of lots collapsed. He had used the real estate money to complete the hotel, and there was little left to maintain, equip, or operate it.

Though the hotel was a mecca for lovers of the outdoors and a base for hunting, fishing, yachting, golf, and tennis, it lacked social graces. Women who arrived with trunks full of pretty clothes often took them away unpacked. Then one event occurred and changed everything. Bad weather drove the luxurious yacht *Lurline* into the safe anchorage of Glorietta Bay, opposite the hotel. The yacht's owner was John Spreckels, who with his brother Adolph decided to wait out the storm at the Hotel Del Coronado. Babcock was on hand to greet them, and before long Spreckels lent Babcock $100,000. He later bought Babcock out entirely, taking over the hotel.

The vast sugar fortune of Spreckels provided the money needed to equip the hotel properly. Under Spreckels' ownership the Coronado ushered in a golden era of elegant opulence. It became a glittering playground, one of the leading resorts of the world. Spreckels added thick red carpets, deep divans, and dining-room menus to please a gourmet.

A Japanese tea garden was built on the grounds, and a golf course was designed. On Christmas Eve of 1904 the hotel exhibited the world's first electrically lighted outdoor Christmas tree, and in 1906 it introduced polo. By 1911 its polo team included titled English members as well as local players. In 1906 the hotel sponsored a sensational automobile race from Los Angeles to San Diego, a distance of about a hundred miles, covered by intrepid drivers in two frantic days. In 1907, the hotel introduced water polo. The next few years were crowded with a variety of contests and events: clay-pigeon tournaments, golfing events, polo matches, and pony races. Archery became popular in 1909, and in 1912 the hotel sponsored a two-day aviation meet, exhibiting eight airplanes in the air at once.

The guest register was star-studded with names of celebrities from every rank and region. President Benjamin Harrison visited the hotel in 1891. But no celebrity visit topped the glamour and acclaim surrounding that of the Prince of Wales in 1920, photographed at the hotel entrance in his uniform of a high-ranking British naval officer.

The Spreckels era and ownership lasted into the early twenties. From that time until a few years ago the big hotel passed through successive ownerships. It had lost the luxurious elegance of the Spreckels period. Many of its unique and valuable Victorian fittings disappeared and were replaced by shabby accessories. The Coronado had trouble staying open during the Depression.

Then, a few years ago, the hotel was bought by a syndicate from San Diego headed by John Alessio and his brothers Angelo, Frank, Russell, and Tony. They began a program of renovation and restoration designed to remove the clutter and shabbiness of succeeding decades and restore the atmosphere of the elegant 1880's. The program took several years and cost a great deal. The result is an extraordinary blend of elegance and modern conveniences, such as air-conditioning. The long front porch, beloved by the rocking-chair brigade, has been replaced by a spacious promenade adjoining a patio. The hotel's delightful open elevator was considered too rare a treasure to be improved upon, so, encased in a beautifully designed grille, it has been retained. The Crown Room was left unchanged. At the rear of the main lobby a sixty-foot wall of glass now reveals the full-acre patio around which the hotel was built.

A bleak arcade was turned into a luxurious Victorian cocktail lounge. An enormous swimming pool, set within several acres of sun terrace and encircling cabañas, was added. An enormous parking lot replaced the polo field and railroad siding. The original boathouse has become a rendezvous for guests interested in sailing, water skiing, and deep-sea fishing. Other facilities include fine tennis courts and an eighteen-hole, 6450-yard golf course. New interior facilities include a health spa, with exercise rooms and steam baths, and a gay dining room called the Luau Room, which serves Polynesian food and drinks. A modern-day outdoor accessory never dreamed of in the old days is a landing field for helicopters.

Like most successful resorts, the Coronado has abandoned hope of recruiting patrons who arrive in yachts and private railroad cars. It seeks American families who travel in their own cars. For the children of these families there are special facilities, including a children's swimming pool, a playground, and a merry-go-round. A second type of patronage is the business convention, for which the hotel now has many meeting rooms. Recently a group of California businessmen acquired the hotel and have placed it under the management of Western International Hotels.

For visitors, the Coronado is a good sight-seeing base. The Cabrillo National Monument, at the crest of Point Loma, is a thirty-minute drive around San Diego Harbor. On the way many stop to explore Mission Bay Park, one of the most unusual marine parks in the country, with more than four thousand acres of lagoon and waterways. In San Diego itself is the 1400-acre Balboa Park, one of the great city parks of the world, with, among other things, one of the best city zoos in the United States. Old Town, part of San Diego, where the first mission and presidio stood, is easily explored on foot and has charming old Spanish buildings and picturesque restaurants serving authentic Spanish and Mexican dishes.

At the north edge of San Diego is the Mission San Diego de Alcala, established in 1769. Farther north is the luxurious residential community of La Jolla, with notable beaches, excellent restaurants, and the Scripps Institution of Oceanography.

It is an easy day's round trip from San Diego to Mount Palomar, rising 6126 feet and crowned by the Mount Palomar Observatory.

Many guests at the Coronado spend at least a day visiting Mexico, to the south, and the border city of Tijuana, famous for its race track and its Mexican shops.

North of San Diego is Del Mar, the only horse-racing track in the area, and near it the celebrated inn at Rancho Santa Fe. Golfing guests of the Coronado have their choice of at least a half-dozen courses in the area.

The Coronado is one of the most accessible resorts in the country, only a few minutes' taxi and ferry ride from downtown San Diego, terminus for main-line service of the Santa Fe Railway, as well as for several airlines providing scheduled service to San Diego's Lindbergh Field.

The Coronado operates on the European plan: charges for accommodations and meals are separate. Rates for the hotel's four hundred rooms and suites start at $12 per day for a single room and at $15 per day for a double room. Dining is available in five different rooms varying, in size, appointments, and price, from the extraordinary Crown Room and the Luau Room to the informal coffee shop with its associated outdoor dining terrace.

Charges for other activities include $2 per day for greens fees except on Saturdays, Sundays, and holidays, when the fee is $3. Caddie hire and electric-cart rentals are additional. The hotel's boathouse rents all types of craft for sailing, water skiing, and deep-sea fishing by the hour or by the day. There are no seasonal changes in the rates at the Coronado.

CHAPTER 11

DESERT OASES

A fascinating phenomenon has been the recent transformation of the desert in Arizona, Southern California, and Nevada from a very hot and very dry land of little promise into one of the most remarkable resort regions in the world, dotted with oasis resort estates and several resort communities. Most of the transformation has occurred within fifty years, a very large part within the last twenty. New and better highways have made moving around in the desert easy and comfortable, and air-conditioning made it possible to temper the blazing heat. Many people discovered that the desert climate could be delightful and that the extreme dryness and clarity of the air made it healthy as well. In a relatively few years the Southwest has become one of *the* places to go in the winter.

Streams of visitors to the Southwest have turned two sleepy towns in Arizona into the fastest-growing cities in the country. In Southern California a once desolate tract of desert was transformed into opulent Palm Springs, an oasis favored by Hollywood stars and vacationing ex-presidents, with more swimming pools per capita than any other community in the world. In the southern tip of Nevada, Las Vegas has become the most glittering gambling mecca in the world.

Although Palm Springs and Las Vegas are remarkable resort communities, the true resort estates of the Southwest desert are in or near two cities, Phoenix and Tucson, where there are four resort estates of a stature and character worthy of being called great. One is on the suburban edge of Tucson, two are in the suburbs of Phoenix, and the fourth is in a small city southeast of Phoenix. Two of the resorts were the result of the dreams and ambitions of women. These four grew from the special devotion of their founders to the strangeness, color, and beauty of the desert.

ARIZONA'S FIRST RESORT

Twenty miles southeast of Phoenix, in the small but prosperous city of Chandler, the business district is built around a beautifully land-scaped central park, an area that many cities would consider a waste of valuable real estate. In the heart of this district is the entrance to the San Marcos Hotel and Country Club. The entrance is deceptive and suggests nothing of the resort's character—an estate that covers more than three hundred acres. The first modern resort to develop in the Arizona desert, San Marcos is the end product of the dream of a re-markable pioneer.

Dr. A. J. Chandler came to the Arizona Territory in 1887 at the request of the Government. For years Texas cattlemen had been driv-ing half-starved cattle out of their state into the adjoining areas of New Mexico and Arizona in search of better range land. Dr. Chandler's as-signment was to stop the practice. He did so by requiring the physical inspection of every steer discovered crossing the Arizona border. While developing his embargo on Texas cattle, Dr. Chandler became fasci-nated with the desert's beauty and climate. He purchased eighteen thousand acres of desert land extending along the banks of the Gila River, drilled wells that produced abundant water for irrigation, and began to develop the area for citrus fruit and other crops. He also founded an ostrich farm that became one of the largest in the country, and he went into banking and newspaper publishing. In 1910, having begun the community that now bears his name, he began the construc-tion of a resort that he proposed to make the core of a resort community. Frank Lloyd Wright, who had a home fifteen miles to the northwest, was persuaded to design the village and resort. The San Marcos Hotel and Country Club today is the only resort that Frank Lloyd Wright planned and supervised during construction.

The San Marcos opened for business in 1912. Wright had adapted Spanish colonial architecture, so appropriate to the desert. The main building faced the city park, with the lush and superbly gardened grounds of the resort stretching behind it. Bungalows were scattered over the grounds. The resort could accommodate eighty-eight guests, a capacity that soon proved inadequate.

The whole region began to boom in a few years, became an urban center and a control point for the tremendous development of desert lands and irrigation projects which has been going on ever since. Chandler grew slowly, but the small resort, with its sun-drenched setting and beautiful grounds, became increasingly popular. In 1929 the original eight bungalows were increased to twenty-eight, giving the resort room for 275 guests. A full-scale eighteen-hole golf course was built. Each successive decade has seen additional growth.

Chandler lost control of his properties in the 1920's. They were acquired by an insurance company that in turn sold everything to a Cincinnati industrialist who engaged John H. Quarty, a man of wide experience in running big hotels and resorts. In 1961, Quarty became the sole owner of the resort, which then had 156 guest rooms and suites, an eighteen-hole golf course, tennis courts, shuffleboard, horseback riding, and a luxurious swimming pool. A multimillion-dollar art collection graced the walls of the spacious public rooms. The golf course, completely redesigned, now has twenty-one bent-grass greens, sand traps, and two lakes have been added. A new type of guest accommodation —fifty lanai suites—was added in 1962, bringing the capacity of the hotel to over four hundred guests. The entire hotel has been redecorated and refurnished. The elegance of the colonial Spanish period is accented by a notable collection of old masters hung in the lobby and the dining room.

All lanai suites are equipped for light cooking and dining. Each has a small bar, dressing room, large patio, and is air-conditioned. Lanai guests have all privileges available to other guests of the San Marcos. In addition to the main eighteen-hole course, which is 6775 yards long, and a par 72, there are two practice fairways and an eighteen-hole putting green. Adjoining the course is a modern clubhouse with complete facilities, including a dining room and cocktail lounge.

An unusually large heated swimming pool is within the main grounds. The resort has excellent facilities for business meetings and groups of all kinds.

Most of the San Marcos's guests spend time exploring the immediate area of desert and mountains, where the most notable sight, a few miles away, is the prehistoric Indian ruin Casa Grande National Monument. About sixty miles east of Chandler is the old mining town of Globe, famous for both silver and copper mining, where visitors can explore operating copper mines. The Department of the Interior maintains a museum near Globe in connection with the Southwestern Archaeological Center. One of the finest collections of rare trees, shrubs, and flowers is in a remarkable exhibit twenty-five miles west of Globe.

It is possible to take scenic mountain drives from Globe that will lead past Roosevelt Lake and Dam, the largest and most famous of several dams and reservoirs that control the vast irrigation development of the whole valley to the west.

Phoenix offers many diversions, including horse racing, dog racing, and a number of good golf courses where San Marcos guests may play. Most guests spend a half day or so immediately north of Chandler on the eastern edge of Phoenix browsing through Scottsdale, a community that combines aspects and facilities of Fifth Avenue and a frontier town of the Far West.

The San Marcos Hotel is easily accessible by highway, air, or train. Interstate 10, linking Tucson with Phoenix, 100 miles to the southeast, runs west of Chandler. Coming from the east is the multilane express highway of U.S. 60 and 80, leading across Arizona from New Mexico to the east and extending west across the desert into California. From Phoenix, Interstate 17 leads north to Flagstaff, where it joins another main east-west route, Interstate 40.

Rail and air routes to Chandler all converge on Phoenix, fifteen miles to the northwest, where hotel cars will meet guests on advance notice. Rental cars are also available at the airport. Phoenix's Sky Harbor Municipal Airport is on the southeast part of the city, less than fifteen miles from Chandler and the resort. It is served by American, Continental, Delta, Bonanza, Frontier, Trans World and Western airlines. Both the Rock Island and Southern Pacific have rail service into Chandler, and the Santa Fe maintains service to Phoenix.

Rates at the San Marcos are full American plan. The resort is open for the winter season only, from October to May. Rates, applying to all rooms except those in the lanais, start at $22 per day for one person and $42 for two. Suites start at $70 per day for two. Rates in the lanais are on the European plan and include no meals. For two people the lanai rates in the early and late season are $14 per day, $28 per day in the high season. Transient meal rates in the dining room are $2 for breakfast, $3 for luncheon, $6 for dinner. Greens fees for the golf course are $5 daily.

VALLEY OF THE SUN

When Arizona became a state in 1912 and the raw settlement of Phoenix was selected as its capital, the town had only a little more than ten thousand people. About twelve miles northeast of the little city was a bare and craggy red sandstone mountain that local residents had given a name suggested by its shape, Camelback. As mountains go, it wasn't very important, for it rose only seventeen hundred feet above the level of the desert. It actually was an eroded butte—a gaunt and naked twin-humped pile of rock, the two humps accounting for the name. A few miles north was another mountain with an equally curious name —Mummy. The valley between, supporting luxuriant desert growth, came to be known as Paradise Valley. As Phoenix began to grow, the area around Camelback Mountain and in Paradise Valley became popular for desert outings, trail rides, and picnics, and the sort of robust diversions that dwellers in the Southwest desert enjoyed. The area was far enough from Phoenix to be pleasantly isolated, yet near enough to reach in a couple of hours by horseback or a few minutes by automobile.

Then Phoenix began to grow. The construction of Roosevelt Dam, sixty miles to the east, controlled water for irrigation of the Salt River, which flowed through Phoenix. The dam provided enough water to irrigate several thousand acres. In a few years other dams were added and before long Phoenix was a booming little city. Irrigated fields near the city produced such abundant crops that many people began to get rich from the profits of cultivation. It was soon predicted that Phoenix would have a population of a hundred thousand people, though such predictions were generally dismissed as chamber-of-commerce enthusiasm. The city began to take on some of the trappings of wealth and leisure; resorts began to spring up nearby and attract winter guests who found the desert pleasant from October to May.

With all this development, little happened to Camelback Mountain and the Paradise Valley area except that the residents of Phoenix continued to go there for desert outings. Then in 1936 something happened that was to make the valley one of the most celebrated suburban regions in the country, and Camelback the most famous mountain in Arizona. The event was the establishment of a small resort in Paradise Valley. Its proprietor was a young Scot by the name of Jack Stewart, who had graduated from the University of North Dakota and had come to Phoenix to work on a newspaper in 1930. He also worked as a press agent at local resorts near Phoenix. Stewart saw how resorts were operated and he decided he wanted to run one, and in fulfilling that ambition soon met a young architect from Evanston, Illinois, named Edwin Loomis Bowes. He broached his idea to Bowes, who agreed to make some plans, though neither of them had money. Then Stewart met another Midwest migrant in Phoenix—John Cromwell Lincoln, an inventive genius, an industrialist, and a pioneer in electrical engineering, who had founded the Lincoln Electric Company in Cleveland and had made a fortune from its success. At sixty-six he had come to Phoenix to find a pleasant winter climate. Arizona—and Phoenix—impressed him and he soon found himself owning a power plant, a gold mine, a citrus grove, and a five-hundred-acre patch of desert, between Camelback and Mummy mountains. It was an almost valueless wilderness tract that Lincoln had picked up for a few dollars an acre. The land spread over much of what was known as Paradise Valley.

Stewart showed Lincoln the plans that Bowes had drawn. Lincoln liked Stewart and was impressed with the plans, which projected a new concept in desert resorts.

At the time, the traditional resort did everything possible to eliminate the desert. It usually was developed by clearing a patch of desert growth from the land, transplanting to it luxurious green lawns, palm trees, and exotic gardens with an impressive Spanish hacienda in the center. The Loomis plan retained the desert and accented it with supplemental plantings. The plan proposed to house guests in villas, scattered over a stretch of desert and linked by winding walks and drives. The main building, flanked by sunny patios, would contain only dining room, kitchen, and lounges. Bowes proposed to be faithful to designs and materials that had characterized Southwestern life from the days of Spanish and Indian cultures. He planned to use native adobe bricks in buildings in the pueblo style, exterior walls to be tinted with warm tones that would blend into the true colors of the desert. In short, Bowes proposed a resort that would fit the desert, be closely related to the area where it stood and to the mountains around it in form, color, and feeling.

Bowes's concept was revolutionary, but it pleased Lincoln and so did Jack Stewart's plan for operating it. He agreed to finance the resort under an unusual deal that required Stewart to put up part of the capital but permitted him to acquire ownership by repaying the money advanced by Lincoln through the profits of the resort, a deal that would work only if the resort were a success. Construction began at once on the land that Lincoln owned in Paradise Valley, using the name that Jack Stewart had selected—Camelback Inn.

The inn opened in mid-December of 1936 with accommodations for seventy-seven guests. Its desert grounds were isolated in the heart of

Paradise Valley, with only a few scattered homes, ranches, and a couple of schools within ten miles. In the earliest days there was no swimming pool or bar or golf course. Charming small villas were scattered over the desert, linked to a central lodge, designed with heavy beamed ceilings in a main lounge and dining room, with colorful touches of décor derived from Indian symbols of the Navajo and Hopi tribes. The resort was so isolated that it was not unusual in the early years for a guest to saddle a horse in the corral and within a few minutes' ride "jump a coyote or two."

Camelback Inn has become part of one of the most remarkable regional developments in the history of the country. Phoenix has grown from a city of less than a hundred thousand people twenty-five years ago to a booming metropolis of more than half a million. The area of Paradise Valley around the resort has become the center of an opulent suburban development, with luxurious villas set in emerald lawns climbing the lower slopes of Camelback and Mummy mountains. Camelback Inn is practically the only patch of desert remaining in the area. Stewart has been true to the original concept that a desert resort should be in the desert and make the most of what it has to offer.

The concept of individual villas has been retained, some equivalent in size and character to big luxury suites in the average resort. The facilities of the main lodge have been extended, and a spacious dining room and an immaculate new kitchen have been added. On the roof of the main lodge, several luxurious suites called presidential penthouses have been built. In front of the lodge an extensive patch of desert has been converted into an enormous sun patio with a huge swimming pool in the center of it. The pool area, set with palms, is glass-enclosed. Along the poolside is a handsome air-conditioned building called the Cholla, which has a dance floor, bar, and facilities for casual meals. The newest building of all, the Peace Pipe, has an assortment of meeting rooms and facilities designed to serve business organizations.

Camelback Inn now spreads over 268 acres, where the desert has been modified by subtle and inspired landscaping by the head gardener, Jack Geimer, who has kept the desert character but adapted it to the growth of other things in one of the most remarkable feats of landscaping in the Southwest. Beds of native cactus are bright with flowers, small patches of brilliant lawn are spotted throughout the grounds, and the areas around the guest villas are planted with desert shrubs, date palms, orange, lemon, and grapefruit trees. There are unusual and often startling associations of plants and flowers. Thus the green shafts of a desert paloverde rise from a sea of coral nasturtiums. A huge cactus called the ocotillo will grow out of a wide circle of Shasta daisies. Outside the main entrance to the central lodge a tremendous saguaro cactus grows beside a big bed of roses. Jack Geimer has not only retained the typical desert plants; he has nurtured and developed them so superbly that many are bigger and better than the desert ever produced by itself.

One of the most important changes in Camelback Inn is the Paradise Valley Country Club Golf Course, west of the inn. One reason for its convenient location is that of the golf course's 250 acres 180 originally belonged to Camelback Inn. In transferring the land to the country club, Stewart made a deal that gives Camelback guests free access to play the club course. A championship eighteen-hole course, 6654 yards long, it is superbly maintained and set on a slope between Marshmallow Hill and Mummy Mountain. The fairways are green all year, thanks to an underground sprinkler system, an unusual condition among desert courses.

Along with its physical growth in the last twenty-five years, Camelback Inn has extended the range of guest activities. For those who enjoy riding there are breakfast rides, noon picnics, and all-day rides, and fifty horses are kept ready for use in the inn's corral. Three excellent tennis courts are available, as well as shuffleboard, and of course the huge swimming pool with its wide flanking patios. Although Camelback Inn makes no pretense of being a spa, it has recently added facilities for health and weight control which combine diet, exercise, steam baths, beauty treatments, gym classes, and mechanical exercisers.

The inn provides extensive facilities for young people through a recreational and schooling program called Hopalong College, with an almost dawn-to-dark series of events that include cookouts, athletic contests, desert rides, and at the end a graduation complete with diploma, probably the only college where you can work toward a degree by learning roping.

Jack Stewart has made a fetish of his dining room. His success has been so notable that Camelback Inn is well known for the quality and character of its dining. It has been accomplished by three things: a modern and efficient kitchen, the best cooks Stewart could find, and the use of only the best foodstuffs. An average dinner menu may reflect a complete cross-section of American dining, including such dishes as Colorado mountain trout, Florida pompano, New England chicken pie, fresh Arizona vegetables, and dozens of samples of fine regional American cooking. A poolside buffet is held each day for guests who prefer to stay outdoors and dine at tables within the glass-enclosed pool area. Once a week there is a desert steak fry on Mummy Mountain. Desert breakfast rides with cowboys doing the cooking in chuck-wagon style are frequent events.

Most Camelback Inn guests are content to bask in the desert sun, play golf, ride horses, and spend their time sampling all the facilities and diversions that the resort provides. Some guests, however, make safaris into and around Phoenix. Less than an hour's drive to the south is a curious relic of prehistoric days called Casa Grande, now a national monument. It is a four-story apartment building made of mud, probably the chief structure in a group of Indian villages six hundred years ago. The mining town of Globe is an easy drive to the east deep within the mountains that frame the Salt River Valley. Southwest of Globe is a curious prehistoric ruin called Besh-Ba-Go-Wah, an Indian pueblo believed to have been inhabited in the thirteenth century.

Between Globe and Phoenix on U.S. 70 is the Southwest Arboretum. From Globe it is possible to return to Phoenix by a fascinating mountain drive called the Apache Trail, which leads past a chain of lakes created by dams in the mountains, including Roosevelt Dam, completed in 1911 and named for President Theodore Roosevelt. A lake behind it stretches thirty miles. Tonto National Monument, with its ancient cliff dwellings, is nearby.

Almost every guest discovers and explores Scottsdale, which is almost at the doorstep of the inn. It began as a planned community that would exhibit and preserve aspects of a typical pioneer Western town. But in recent years Scottsdale has developed into a sophisticated suburban community more typical of Hollywood or Miami Beach.

A few miles northeast of Camelback Inn is the historic house designed and built by Frank Lloyd Wright—Taliesin West—the distinguished architect's desert home, now maintained as a school from November to May.

Camelback Inn is easy to reach by automobile, air, or train. Main highways converge on Phoenix. From downtown Phoenix city streets lead eleven miles northeast to the gates of the inn. El Paso is a 350-mile drive to the east. The California border to the west is about 150 miles over Interstate 10 and about 175 miles over U.S. 80 and Interstate 8. Las Vegas is 240 miles to the northwest over U.S. 70. The Mexican border town of Nogales is approximately 150 miles southeast over Interstate 10 and Interstate 19. Phoenix's new airport is on the south side of the city and is served by American, Trans World, Western, Continental, Bonanza, and Frontier airlines. Excellent and frequent rail service through Phoenix is maintained by the Santa Fe, Southern Pacific, and Rock Island railroads.

Guest rates at the Camelback Inn are on the American plan and vary with the type of accommodations and time of year. From October through December 20, minimum rates are $21 per person per day, with two people occupying a room. For the same period single-room rates are $30 per day, all American plan, although European-plan rates are also available at this time. High-season rates apply from February 1 to April 10, when the minimum rate is $27.50 per person per day, with two occupying a room. During the high season only American plan rates apply.

The inn provides an unusually large number of free services and activities. These include the use of tennis courts, swimming pool, poolside luncheons, programs for children, movies once a week, use of all facilities such as table tennis, shuffleboard, horseshoe, putting and pitch-and-putt golf courses, and free golf privileges at Paradise Valley Country Club except for normal greens fees. The fee for the hired horses for desert rides is nominal and includes the free services of cowboy guides on organized rides.

AN ARTIST'S PARADISE

Arizona's Grand Canyon, a gifted artist's love of the desert, and a Mexican family's need for cash were the ingredients that account for the small but sophisticated luxury resort called Paradise Inn.

Nearly fifty years ago a talented artist from Illinois, Mrs. Jessie Benton Evans, was commissioned to do a series of paintings of the Grand Canyon of Arizona. She began her assignment in 1916. But the Grand Canyon gets cold in the winter, so Mrs. Evans looked for a warmer place to finish the paintings. An alluring desert scene in a Santa Fe travel folder led her to the small city of Phoenix.

There Mrs. Evans discovered Paradise Valley, east of the city, dominated by a craggy mountain named Camelback. The desert fascinated her. She moved from Phoenix to the village of Scottsdale, just south of Camelback Mountain and she went into the desert daily to paint, often setting up her easel at the base of Camelback. A Mexican family lived near her favorite spot in a tiny adobe house built with their own hands. They were trying to homestead forty acres of desert but were having a difficult time. The mother took in washing—including the painter's—to help.

Mrs. Evans had returned to Chicago and one day she received a letter from the Mexican mother saying that the family wanted to leave the desert and desperately needed money. She offered to sell the forty-acre homestead tract for five hundred dollars. Although similar tracts of land could be bought for as little as fifty cents an acre, Mrs. Evans sent the five hundred dollars and became the owner of a forty-acre patch of desert with an adobe house in the middle of it.

Desert lovers say that once you have lived in the desert you always return. Mrs. Evans did return, time and again, living in Scottsdale and painting at her favorite desert spot at the base of Camelback. She finally concluded that she might as well live in the desert and began to transform the primitive little adobe house into a proper home and studio. The conversion was extraordinary. Visitors to Paradise Inn today, seeing the charming and distinctive villa that Mrs. Evans achieved, are amazed to learn that it started with an adobe hut.

Mrs. Evans had lived for many years in Italy, and she loved that sunny, ancient land. She began to convert the Mexican adobe hut into a spacious Italian villa with the help of her son, Robert, an architect. Using only local labor, she added room after room and set the whole villa in a charming garden area, where green lawns were edged with slender cypresses. There was a sunken garden with ancient stone fountain, benches, and wrought-iron gates from Italy.

All the rooms of the house were large, high-ceilinged, with thick adobe walls to temper high summer heat, with the colorful accents of Italian and Spanish tiles for floors and fireplace mantels.

In time Mrs. Evans became a personage and numbered acquaintances by the hundreds who called her Madame. Many close friends often came to visit her. To accommodate them, she added a wing to her villa, approaching the threshold of resort operation without actually planning to do so. She built Jokoke Inn, a kind of tearoom. Her son decided to move his family to Paradise Valley and took over the tearoom and converted it into an inn.

In the early forties the stage was set to turn the villa into a small, luxurious desert resort, actual work beginning on Paradise Inn in 1945. The plan for the new resort was to preserve the character of the desert and the charm of the locale. It would be accomplished by putting most guests in villas scattered over many acres. Mrs. Evans's villa stood at the southwest corner of the development. Larger villas of adobe were nearby. The rest of the resort stretched toward the mountain, climbing up its southern slopes and covering hundreds of desert acres.

A main lodge with dining room and lounges was built near the center of the resort. Such fringe benefits of desert life as a big swimming pool and sun patio, putting green, tennis courts, and shuffleboard were added. A big stable and corral were built at the extreme southeast corner of the property, and about twenty smaller brick villas spread over an area north of the central lodge.

Designs and colors were kept in harmony with the desert setting. Most guest villas were equipped with private patios or sun terraces, many with open fireplaces. Mrs. Evans died shortly after the resort opened in the late forties, but her son completed the development of the inn.

Paradise Inn has grown since its opening, but everything that Mrs. Evans planned and built is still there. The original villa is the winter residence of the manager of the resort, no longer owned by the Evans family, but by Alsonett Hotels, owned by C. H. Alberding.

An unusual recent change by the present owners is a championship eighteen-hole golf course built in a circle around the resort so that no matter which villa you occupy you can step onto the course and begin playing. The course is regarded as one of the best in the Southwest and offers a variety of play. The lower nine, along the south side of the resort, has rolling fairways, but the upper nine, built among foothills, has varied slopes. On one hole there is a fountain in the middle of the fairway.

On one side of the swimming pool area is an open cocktail lounge, used for poolside buffet luncheons and twilight cocktail parties. Adjoining the pool area are a putting green, several tennis courts, shuffleboard, and a croquet court. A recently added facility is a meeting hall seating five hundred people, for conventions and social functions. At the south end of the resort grounds are the stables, where daily desert rides and chuck-wagon breakfast safaris begin, supervised by veteran cowboys.

Dining at Paradise Inn is varied and eventful, the menus a blending of New England dishes and Continental specialties. A popular dining event is a weekly steak fry held high on the slopes of Camelback Mountain, while dinners at the inn are staged with informal elegance in several candlelit dining areas.

The sight-seeing opportunities are identical with those available to the guests at nearby Camelback Inn.

Paradise Inn is as accessible as Camelback. Express highways converge on Phoenix from all directions. Guests will be met at rail and airline terminals in Phoenix on advance notice. Airlines and railways serving the Phoenix area are listed in the preceding section on Camelback Inn.

Paradise Inn is a winter and spring resort, operated entirely on the American plan. There are two seasons. A low-rate season begins early in December and extends to January 20; single rooms start at $18 per day, double rooms at $28 per day. The high-rate season begins January 20 and extends until the closing of the resort on May 1. Single-room rates begin at $28 per day, double-room rates at $38. Rates for a third person in a room regardless of the season are $12 per day. Rates for children under six years of age occupying rooms with their parents are $8 per day; children from six to twelve, $10. Greens fees on the golf course are $3 per day weekdays, $4 Saturday and Sunday.

GREEN JEWEL OF THE DESERT

Among a growing army of desert enthusiasts there are many who regard the vast sun-drenched area of southern Arizona and northern Mexico as the most interesting and beautiful desert in the world. Geologists call it the Sonora Desert. A region spreading over several thousand square miles, it has extraordinary variety and is vividly colorful. Along its eastern edge mountains rise to more than nine thousand feet, and the rest of its surface is broken by low, rugged ranges, their upper slopes forested with pine, the lower slopes and valleys covered with a fascinating variety of desert plants, including the most spectacular cactus of the west, the giant saguaro, and dozens of other fascinating desert growers.

But except for ranches, working cattle ranches, and desert guest ranches, very few people live in the desert itself, and there are no towns of consequence and no cities of any size, with one exception, which is the spectacular, booming desert metropolis of Tucson, the second largest city in Arizona and one of the oldest cities of the Southwest. Tucson dominates one of the few rivers of the desert region, the Santa Cruz, on the eastern edge of the desert about seventy-five miles north of the Mexican border. Tucson now has a population of almost three hundred thousand people.

It began almost two hundred years ago as a thriving Indian settlement of nearly fifteen thousand industrious Pima Indians who lived in a large village called Stjukshon, on the west bank of the river. In time the name was corrupted to Tucson. It was supposed to mean "Dark Spring" —the spring was north of the village and now is part of a city park. The Indians successfully practiced irrigation, and had fertile patches along the river stretching to the present border of Mexico. In 1690 a Jesuit priest named Father Kino, who came to the valley to convert the Indians to Christianity, succeeded so well that shortly after 1690 he built a great mission church, San Xavier, which stands today. But the town of Tucson didn't amount to much for a long time. In 1860 it had less than a thousand people and was a scraggling village built around a Mexican fort. The Southern Pacific extended its tracks through Tucson in 1880. And after that it began to dawn on visitors that the climate of Tucson—dry, bright, and clear—had special virtues. Soon Tucson became a health center and remained one until World War II, when it was a training center for the Army and Navy. At the end of World War II, Tucson began to grow, and it has been booming ever since.

But it was World War I that started the chain of events resulting in the Arizona Inn, a luxurious, small, distinctive resort with many unique features. The inn is the direct result of a rehabilitation project for disabled World War I veterans, begun by General J. C. Greenway, who had been a member of General Pershing's staff. When the War was over, Greenway turned up in Tucson, then a quiet city of several thousand people, where he established the Arizona Hut to give employment and instructions in crafts to partially disabled veterans. The craftsmen made fine furniture, but it was hard to sell, and gradually the furniture piled up in a warehouse. Then General Greenway died, and his wife, Isabella, took over the rehabilitation project. She discovered the warehouse crammed with furniture and decided that if the furniture couldn't be sold it could be used in a hotel. So she started a small, handsomely appointed desert inn north of the city in a patch of Arizona desert.

Mrs. Greenway had definite ideas of what a small desert resort inn should be, and she had the taste and resources to carry through her ideas. In keeping with the tradition that the Southwest was a land of wide open spaces, she made all the rooms large and uncluttered, with unusually large closets. She insisted that most rooms should have their own patios. For architecture, she chose a combination of Spanish, Mexican, and Indian styles compatible with the desert. All of the exterior walls were painted pink; windows, shutters, and doors blue, and throughout the rooms the handsome, solid furniture made by the veterans was distributed.

On the walls Mrs. Greenway hung selections from several remarkable collections of prints and paintings she had been making for many years. She devised landscaping that kept the strange and beautiful desert plants growing happily among beds of flowers and shrubs from other regions.

When the inn opened in 1930, it was a tiny but stunning example of a luxurious desert resort, and though it has grown substantially since its opening more than thirty years ago, it is still small and distinctive. As the years passed, Tucson began to grow, spreading out in all directions. In a few years the Arizona Inn, which was far outside the limits of the city when it was opened, began to be surrounded by a spreading residential area. To preserve its character and guarantee its isolation, Mrs. Greenway built a wall around the entire resort, enclosing about twelve acres, or the equivalent of four city blocks. The Arizona Inn today is probably the only walled resort in this country.

Mrs. Greenway had many friends in Army circles. An early guest was her husband's former associate, General Pershing. In 1934, four years after the opening, Mrs. Greenway was elected as a congresswoman from Arizona. She served for three years in Congress and widely extended her acquaintants in Washington and New York. It resulted in a steady stream of distinguished guests at the Arizona Inn, including Mr. and Mrs. John D. Rockefeller, Jr., the Tom Watsons, the Hartley Dodges, and many others.

In the beginning a principal activity was horseback riding in the desert. The stables, originally built across the road from the inn, have since been moved to the fringes of Tucson, but riding is still popular with guests. Although the inn does not maintain its own golf course, within easy driving distance there are eight notable courses available to guests. Tennis courts have been added, but the most popular addition has been an unusually handsome swimming pool and flanking patio, the setting for a daily buffet luncheon. The chef, born in Greece and trained in Switzerland and France, keeps his menus varied and abundant but typically American. Regional specialties are frequent dishes. Maine lobsters, Idaho trout, Texas pheasant are among them, but the inn also is famous for Mexican and Southwestern recipes.

An early guest was Lowell Thomas, who helped found a ski club on the top of Mount Lemmon, a few miles north of Tucson. It provides inn guests today with a unique winter skiing facility.

Guests at the Arizona Inn spend part of their visits exploring the immediate area. One of the most remarkable sights, twelve miles west of Tucson, is the Arizona-Sonora Desert Museum, within the thirty-thousand-acre Tucson Mountain Park. The museum displays the finest exhibits of desert life in the world. Nearby is Old Tucson Village, Hollywood-built desert setting of a typical Western town of 1860. The most superb display of cactus anywhere is fifteen miles east of Tucson, the Saguaro National Monument, a giant cactus forest with hundreds of towering saguaros, some of which are fifty feet high and two hundred years old.

Southwest of Tucson is the striking Spanish mission San Xavier del Bac, built about 1692 and regarded as one of the finest examples of Spanish Renaissance architecture in the country. Twenty-five miles south of Tucson is Tumacacori National Monument, where the ruins of pioneer Spanish days in Arizona are preserved. Tubac, the oldest European settlement in Arizona and once a walled town, is now partially restored as a picturesque center for an artist colony. Nogales is sixty-seven miles south of Tucson at the end of the same road that leads to Tubac. Across the border is Nogales-Sonora, a distinctive and typically Mexican city crowded with shops and restaurants.

The pioneer city of Tombstone, once a center of lurid life, is an easy drive from Tucson. Tombstone, a bloody town during the frontier days, now draws thousands of visitors to see its relics of the Wild West.

Tucson is easy to reach by air, highway, or rail. But once guests reach Tucson they may have a little difficulty in locating the resort. The actual address is 2200 East Elm Street, in the center of a prosperous residential district where zoning laws prohibit the use of advertising signs. A small and inconspicuous sign directs guests to the inn itself. Most guests locate it by its American flag, which is raised on a high flagpole every morning and lowered each evening.

Guests arriving by train or plane should have no concern about finding the inn. They will be met at the airport or station on advance notice. For guests planning to drive, many main highways converge on Tucson. From the east there are two main routes: Interstate 10 through El Paso, skirting the southern edge of New Mexico and Arizona; farther north, Interstate 40 through Albuquerque and Flagstaff and then highly scenic U.S. 17 goes from Flagstaff south through Phoenix. Interstate 10 leads into Tucson from the northwest.

From the north U.S. 89 leads south from Utah into Flagstaff, where Interstate 17 and Interstate 10 out of Phoenix lead into Tucson. Another route from the northwest is U.S. 93 and Arizona 93 through Las Vegas to Phoenix, thence Interstate 10 to Tucson. From the west and California two main routes cross the desert to Tucson. In the south Interstate 8, through Yuma, links with Interstate 10 just south of Phoenix.

Tucson is served by Trans World, American, Frontier, and Continental airlines. Its municipal airport is on the southern edge of the city about twelve miles south of the inn. Guests arriving by railroad come in over main lines of the Southern Pacific, with a terminal in the heart of the city about three miles south of the inn.

The Arizona Inn is open for the winter season only, November 1 until May 1.

Rates are all on the American plan and vary seasonally and with the type of room selected. The high-rate period is January to March, when a single room begins at $28 per day, and double rates at $38 per day for two. Guest rooms with sun terrace or porch start at $42; rooms with fireplace and sun terrace at $46; some guest rooms with a glassed sunroom in addition to bedroom start at $48. Lower rates are available in November, December, and April, when a single room starts at $26 per day, and double rooms at $36. The rate for a third person in a double room is $14. In addition to regular guest accommodations in the inn proper, there are several complete homes within the twelve acres of grounds leased to people who bring their own servants. Each has its own lawn and garden with private patio. Guests leasing the houses can have them either on house plan or on American plan, the latter including all meals and service.

51. Most important place for sun-loving guests at Camelback Inn, near Phoenix, Arizona, is the big pool and sun patio, edged with desert palms.

52. First resort in Arizona, still one of the finest resort estates in the Southwest desert, is San Marcos Hotel, at Chandler, near Phoenix.

53. Like a great castle, the luxurious Manoir Richelieu, rising above the bluffs of the lordly St. Lawrence River, offers facilities of the finest resort estates.

54. Poolside loungers at the Manoir Richelieu enjoy opportunities both visual and audible: at the pool music is played, and the terrace commands a superb view of the St. Lawrence, occasionally including a ship of the Canada Steamship Lines, which owns the resort.

55. Pink Jeeps and dozens of mountain-slope villas, many with private pool, are unusual and delightful features of Las Brisas resort in Acapulco, Mexico.

56. Just outside Acapulco, on one of the world's finest ocean beaches, is the opulent Pierre Marques Hotel, flanked by a luxurious pool and terrace.

57. Fortín de las Flores, in eastern Mexico, is famed for a distinctive resort, Hotel Ruiz Galindo, its gardenia-filled swimming pool one of the most celebrated in Mexico.

CHAPTER 12

CANADA'S GREAT RIVER
AND ATLANTIC SHORE

Canada's great river is the mighty St. Lawrence, a majestic channel of more than seven hundred miles linking the Great Lakes with the sea. More than four hundred years ago it became a gateway to the New World, then successively a route of discovery, exploration, and settlement. Canada's finest and largest cities—Quebec and Montreal—grew on its banks.

But the St. Lawrence is more than a convenient and strategic river. It is a beautiful one. Its shores, framed by wooded bluffs, offer commanding sites for great dwellings or great resorts. So it is not surprising that there is a great resort standing high above the ramparts of the St. Lawrence on its northern shore at a place called Murray Bay. Towering above the wide river in turreted splendor like a vast French château is the Manoir Richelieu.

Another important resort in eastern Canada commands a shore setting quite different from the impressive site of the Manoir Richelieu. It fills a point of land thrusting into a remarkable arm of the sea called Passamaquoddy Bay, famed for the greatest rise and fall of ocean tides on the North American Continent. The resort is the Algonquin Hotel, which resembles a huge Tudor manor house of England. The hotel adjoins a village of great charm with a delightful name, St. Andrews-by-the-Sea, which in turn suggests a facility of which the Algonquin is very proud: one of the most distinctive golf courses in Canada, not unlike the great seaside course in Scotland from which the village takes its name.

RAMPARTS OF THE ST. LAWRENCE

The majestic St. Lawrence carries the waters of the Great Lakes from the eastern end of Lake Ontario northeast to the sea. Its upper end, near the Great Lakes, is a dramatically picturesque channel foaming with rapids, filled with islands, and called the Thousand Islands region, which is shared by Canada and the United States. Below that the St. Lawrence becomes a Canadian river, passing Montreal and then Quebec. Below Quebec, the St. Lawrence is tidal, gradually widening until at its mouth it is ninety miles wide—a vast estuary that is the gateway to a continent.

One of the first to pass through this gateway was the French explorer Jacques Cartier, who discovered the great river in 1535. He sailed up it for many miles and claimed the region for France. Seventy-five years later Samuel de Champlain followed Cartier's trip up the river, traveling several hundred miles inland from the sea, and where the river narrowed to a mere fifteen miles stopped to replenish his supplies. Because of low tide his boats were stranded for a time on a bank where a small river entered the St. Lawrence. Champlain, doubtless because of the accident called the bay Malle Baye, or "Bad Bay." The name—slightly altered over the years—still designates the bay on the maps of Quebec.

Just west of the bay, rising in architectural grandeur above the St. Lawrence, is one of the most splendid resorts in the world, the historic Manoir Richelieu, named for the French cardinal and statesman. The great hotel resembles a gigantic medieval château out of a French novel. Its official address is Murray Bay, ninety miles northeast of Quebec and two hundred fifty miles northeast of Montreal.

The first hotel on the site began in 1872, when a Montreal businessman named John Chamard leased the site and built a small, elegant hotel called the Lorne House, in honor of the Marquis of Lorne, who had married Queen Victoria's fourth daughter, Princess Louise. The fame of the small resort spread; its setting was superb and the food memorable. It soon began to attract patronage, not only from the great Canadian cities, but from the United States. William Howard Taft visited Murray Bay in 1892, when he was Solicitor General of the United States, and he was so delighted that he purchased a summer home nearby that he and his family were to occupy during summer seasons for many years to come.

In 1900 the property was purchased by the Richelieu and Ontario Navigation Company, which built a five-story wooden resort hotel with three hundred guest rooms and named it the Manoir Richelieu. The new resort was immediately popular and drew fashionable and wealthy patrons from Canada and the United States. Almost all of the guests arrived by ship on vessels of the company, which in 1913 was consolidated with other lines to form the Canada Steamship Lines. Soon the Manoir Richelieu became known as the "Newport of the North."

During the night of September 12, 1928, the big wooden hotel burned to the ground.

The directors of the Canada Steamship Lines took decisive action: they voted to replace the burned hotel with an even finer hotel that would be fireproof. Plans for it—completed and accepted within a few weeks—called for a tremendous building of Norman design, with towers and turrets proudly crowning the bluffs of the St. Lawrence behind a terraced flagstone promenade. Work on the great new hotel began and continued in one of the most extraordinary building sagas in the history of North America.

It was decided that the new hotel must be ready for occupancy the next summer. This required building it during the bitterly cold winter, so a tremendous protective wooden shell was built to permit the construction work to continue. Within the shell a thousand men swarmed over the rising structure, setting steel beams and pouring concrete. Great charcoal fires burned continuously to keep the cement and the men from freezing. The accomplishment seems almost miraculous when one realizes that material and labor had to be transported hundreds of miles in the winter.

The new Manoir Richelieu opened its doors to guests on June 15, 1929. It was a tremendous building, on one of the most superb sites imaginable. The new fireproof resort had walls more than two and a half feet thick. It was 427 feet long, 52 feet wide, and had 300 guest rooms and suites and some of the most beautiful public rooms in any resort in the world. The general atmosphere was one of French baronial splendor, suggesting a great estate of the Loire River.

The owners decorated the rooms with a collection of art reportedly worth more than $1,500,000. The tremendous, 200-foot-long dining room was hung with a collection of Audubon prints worth more than

$200,000. There are more than 3000 prints and paintings exhibited throughout the hotel today.

Additional facilities are now part of the original building and its grounds since its reopening in 1929. The resort's immediate grounds now cover four hundred acres, extending along crests of bluffs a hundred feet above the river and down to the river. East of the main building is the casino, the setting for dancing and favorite place for large meetings. In front of the casino is a huge swimming pool flanking a sun terrace, protected by transparent walls from the wind but permitting a superb view of the river. Each morning, because an orchestra plays at the pool, guests swim to lilting melodies. In front of the main resort building are a beautifully maintained croquet court and lawn-bowling courts. On the west side of the resort building is an adventurous eighteen-hole putting green. Behind the main building, in the forest, is the stable, where excellent riding horses are available for the miles of forest trails leading from the stable.

An eighteen-hole golf course filling the west end of the resort property is one of the spectacularly beautiful courses in Canada and widely regarded as one of the best in North America. The course, designed to take maximum advantage of the immensely rugged setting, spreads out on a ledge called The Ridge and extends down toward the river. It is so rugged that at two holes an electric lift and inclined railway carry players from lower slopes to the tees. The various levels of the course make it technically challenging to the most skillful of golfers. The course has been redesigned since its opening in 1927, when former President William Howard Taft initiated play by hitting the first ball. The big clubhouse in the center of the course is a fine copy of an old seignioral manor house.

The Manoir Richelieu maintains a fishing camp about forty-five miles away in a wilderness area, with thirty-two lakes within easy distance of the camp itself. Cabins, boats, guides, and tackle (fly-fishing only) are available to guests.

The great dining room is decorated in off-white and green, perfect color foil for Audubon prints on the walls. As many as 750 guests have dined at a single sitting. The cooking and menus are Continental.

The resort maintains a variety of specialty shops, including a handicraft shop exhibiting Canadian craft items, a gift shop, and a fur shop. There are four cocktail lounges. In addition to guest accommodations in the main building, there are six cottages, each with six bedrooms, three baths, and a spacious living room with fireplace, designed to handle at least eight guests. The cottages have full hotel service.

Though most guests at the Manoir Richelieu spend almost all their time at the resort itself, for those curious about the nearby area, the hotel provides special sight-seeing services with horse-drawn carriages.

Most guests reach the Manoir Richelieu on the big vessels of the Canada Steamship Lines, which operates regular summer service down the St. Lawrence. Passengers booked for Murray Bay can board the steamers at either Quebec or Montreal. The steamship company arranges special combination steamship and hotel rates, which vary with the accommodation.

The resort also can be reached by rail, car, or air. Trains leave Montreal at midmorning and arrive at Murray Bay in the late afternoon on a daily schedule in the summer. Route 15 leads northeast from Quebec along the north bank of the St. Lawrence River. The distance is about ninety miles. At St. Simeon, Route 15 connects with a ferry to the south bank, where roads lead south into Maine. A new airport at Murray Bay makes regular air service possible by scheduled flights of Trans Canada Airline to Montreal or Quebec, then Quebecair to the Murray Bay field during summer months. Private float planes can land on Lake St. Agnes, which is eight miles away.

The Manoir Richelieu is open from June until September. Rates are based on full American plan and vary with the type and location of the room occupied. Single rates start at $21 per day; double-room rates start at $42 per day. Additional fees for various activities include greens fees for the golf course, $3 per day; fishing guide, $10 per day; transportation to the fishing lodge, $10 per person, round trip. Use of the lodge is free. Hire of a horse-drawn carriage is $3 per hour or $5 for two hours.

LOW TIDE, GOLF AND LOBSTERS

One of the most jawbreaking names in the atlas is applied to an arm of the sea that separates the state of Maine from the province of New Brunswick in Canada. Passamaquoddy, an irregular bay that is an extension of the larger Bay of Fundy, is famous for four things: extraordinary tides that climb and drop as much as twenty-five feet every twelve hours; a big offshore island by the name of Campobello; an unusual resort named the Algonquin, with the finest golf course in Eastern Canada; and a profusion of lobsters.

At one time Campobello Island was frequently in the headlines because Franklin Delano Roosevelt maintained a summer home there.

The Algonquin and the lobsters have attained regional fame for different reasons: the hotel for its setting and notable golf course, and the lobsters for their succulence. Also, the largest lobster pound in the world is near the quaint village of St. Andrews-by-the-Sea.

The Algonquin Hotel, dominating a slender finger of land in Passamaquoddy Bay, is owned by the Canadian Pacific Railway. Its setting is superb and commands a view of the entire bay. It resembles an outsize Tudor mansion with many gables and half-timbered walls. The Algonquin is famed for its golf course, which was designed by Scottish experts and resembles the most famous of all golf courses—St. Andrews-by-the-Sea in Scotland, for which the nearby village is named.

The charming old village was founded in 1784 by United Empire Loyalists from Maine whose continued residence in the United States had become uncomfortable. They moved across the channel dividing Maine from New Brunswick and selected a jutting point of land as a site for a new settlement. Several families brought their houses with them from Castine, Maine, knocked down and ready to reassemble. The settlement, one of the first in the province of New Brunswick, grew and prospered. During the War of 1812 the residents built five blockhouses, complete with earthen ramparts and bristling with cannon. The cannon never fired a shot, but one of the blockhouses is still there. St. Andrews was a brisk and busy seaport in the nineteenth century, when sailing vessels from all over the world received and discharged cargo. Although it ceased to be a port of importance with the decline of sailing vessels, it began to develop a fishing industry—chiefly sardines and herring.

Shortly after the turn of the century a syndicate of Boston land developers spotted the narrow promontory where the resort now stands. They discovered that the summer climate was delightful and virtually free from the pollens that plagued hay-fever sufferers, and built a resort hotel on the site in 1907. Eight years later the Canadian Pacific acquired the property and converted it to its present size and character.

Since that time the Algonquin has become a fine resort estate with many facilities and diversions, but the emphasis is on golf. The main hotel building can accommodate 350 people in 234 guest rooms and suites. It has a commanding setting overlooking the bay, in the midst of acres of handsomely landscaped grounds. It is within a few minutes' walk of St. Andrews-by-the-Sea, where an unusual number of pleasant and distinctive small shops offer guests a bonus in shopping opportunity.

The Algonquin has a bathing beach and swimming cove called Katy's Cove, where the normal rise and fall of the tides is controlled to provide a two-hundred-acre tidal lake with a constant water level and temperature. The cove is only a few minutes' walk from the hotel through pine-woods. There are dressing rooms, cabañas, a tearoom for lunch and snacks, and the usual beach accessories such as diving rafts and floats.

The Algonquin's golf course includes a remarkable championship eighteen-hole course and a highly challenging nine-hole course. From the championship tees the long course plays 6314 yards, a par 71, thirteen holes near or within sight of Passamaquoddy Bay, and the green of the fifth hole is directly above the sea. Small greens, skillfully sculptured, challenge the most expert putters. The nine-hole course has been described as a "nine-hole monster with tight fairways, postage-stamp greens, and foot-high rough that eats up balls."

The Algonquin, one of the best fishing bases in the East, offers easy access to a tremendous variety of fishing. The hotel will arrange for or maintains itself the facilities to engage in every kind of fishing. A half hour from the hotel deep-sea fishing parties in Passamaquoddy Bay generally bring back haddock, cod, pollack, and smelt. In the nearby hinterland of New Brunswick, virtually untouched lakes, streams, and pools offer landlocked salmon and speckled trout. One of the best known and most attractive fishing lakes nearby is Chamcook Lake, where the mirrorlike water yields togue and lake trout from deep-water trolling. Nearby waters swarm with black bass, sea salmon, and rainbow trout. The hotel provides its own boats, guide service, and, if need be, tackle and bait for guests.

In addition to golf, bathing, and fishing, the Algonquin has the usual array of lesser sports activities, including tennis, bowling on the green, and shuffleboard. The hotel's pleasant dining room is justly famous for the variety and quality of seafood offered, particularly lobster and locally caught salmon, as well as other seafood dishes.

Most Algonquin guests spend some time shopping and sight-seeing in St. Andrews-by-the-Sea, buying English dinnerware, Scottish cashmeres and woolens. The unique sight-seeing novelty a few miles from the village is Conley's Lobster Pound, the largest in the world, with a capacity for a million pounds of live lobster. Also nearby is the world's largest sardine packer. Fascinating weirs are maintained in a nearby channel, containing millions of slithering, silvery tiny herring, to be converted into sardines in the company's packing plant.

The Algonquin and St. Andrews-by-the-Sea are not difficult to reach by automobile, rail, or air. St. John, New Brunswick, sixty-five miles to the northeast, has a big commercial airport with scheduled flights from Montreal, Toronto, New York, and Boston. The resort is easily reached by highway from all major cities in the northeastern part of the United States and in Eastern Canada. The most direct route from New England is historic U.S. 1 along the coast to Calais, in northern Maine, then Canadian Route 1 to St. Andrews. The resort is 385 miles from Boston, 625 miles from New York, 450 miles from Montreal.

For railway travelers the Canadian Pacific provides service to St. John. The Algonquin is open during the summer only—early June to September 4. Rates are full American plan. Single-room rates start at $17 per day, double rooms at $15 per day per person. Golf fees on the eighteen-hole professional course are $3.50 per day. No charge is made for playing the nine-hole practice course.

13

MEXICO: TROPICAL SHORES,

MOUNTAIN RAVINES,

TROPICAL FLOWERS

The dusty desert land below the two-thousand-mile U.S.-Mexico border gives no suggestion that any unusual resorts will be found in the region that stretches in drab monotony to the south. But the Mexico that most visitors see when they cross the Rio Grande, or pass through the customs gates at Nogales or Tijuana, suggests little of the true character of Mexico. The border is shabby, remote, and neglected. The rest of Mexico is a country that in contrast, color, and variety is one of the most remarkable regions in the world.

The main body of Mexico is shaped like a slightly bent triangle, its base to the north against the United States. Oceans converge on either side of the triangle toward the apex, a narrow isthmus. If the desert of the north may be called Mexico's back yard, it is not too inaccurate to call the coastal plains on either side of the triangle Mexico's front yards. They were the gates through which the country was discovered, conquered, and developed. Within a frame of northern desert, southern jungle, the Pacific in the east, and the Gulf of Mexico on the west, Mexico is an astonishing land. Towering mountain ranges enclose a highland plateau with one of the world's best climates. Steep slopes drop toward tropic seas and narrow coastal plains. The contrast between the two coastal plains is great. The shore on the west is desertlike, the mountains arid, but the coastal plain on the east is luxuriantly verdant and tropical, flowering in riotous profusion. The mountains of Mexico are mostly hostile and bleak. Here and there are exceptions—an occasional valley, green and beautiful, or a wide canyon the walls of which are covered with tropical trees and the canyon floor flooded with gushing springs and clear-flowing streams.

There are resorts in this vast mosaic of color, but they are sharply different from those found in other parts of the world. The first resorts in Mexico grew from complex and ornate ancient civilizations that disappeared long ago. The first was established about the ninth century on the peninsula of Yucatán. Within a community (now a mass of incredible ruins) called Uxmal, certain buildings and the great city were preserved for the use and pleasure of priests and nobles of the Mayan court.

Though there may be some doubts whether Uxmal was actually a resort, there is no doubt at all about another resort in Mexico—Xochimilco. It is still there and still a place of pleasure and escape for thousands. It is still called Xochimilco, but most who visit it today know it as the "floating gardens," a place to spend a gay and tuneful afternoon, cruising in a flower-decked boat to the strumming of guitars.

In the days of the Aztecs it was a true resort where the nobles of the court had handsome homes fronting canals cut through a floral wilderness. Fulfilling the definition of a resort, the Aztec amphibious flower garden represented wealth and leisure, it had a setting, and it was accessible. It was close to Lake Texcoco, the site of the great Aztec capital. Xochimilco flourished as a resort during the fifteenth and sixteenth centuries, at the height of the Aztec rule. For more than a hundred years the Aztec rulers and their courtiers enjoyed the resort. Then suddenly the Aztec Empire was engulfed in disaster. In 1519 a remarkable adventurer named Hernando Cortez landed on the east coast of Mexico, burned his fleet of ships to make going back impossible, and headed west into the mountains with about five hundred men, sixteen horses, and ten brass cannon. Four months later he and his men had climbed to the high central plain and were guests of the Aztec emperor at his fabulous city around the shores of Lake Texcoco. Within two years he had destroyed the Aztec Empire and killed the emperor and most of his nobles. His weapons were craft, deceit, ingenuity, superstition, luck, ambition, murder, torture, and an occasional contest of arms. Cortez destroyed almost everything the Aztecs had built.

The Spanish rulers of Mexico had little need for or interest in resorts. Their interest was in exploiting the land, to dig treasure from the mountains and ship gold and silver back to Spain. The mines were worked with Indian slave labor, while the Spanish rulers of Mexico lived as if they were in Spain. They built Spanish-type cities and ornate churches, and owned vast haciendas in the country. During the more than three hundred years of Spanish rule, no true resorts were developed. Good settings for them were inaccessible, and travel in Mexico was difficult and hazardous. There was wealth enough, but it was held and used by a small, widely dispersed class. There was probably leisure enough, but little inclination to use it in ways that made resorts likely to develop.

Mexico became its own master. It established first a republic, then it was an empire, and then a republic again. But the same factors that made resorts improbable during the long Spanish era continued to prevail, and a new one was added—political and economic chaos, lasting well into this century.

About fifty years ago things began to change in Mexico. The Government became reasonably stable. Railroads and then highways improved. Perhaps most importantly, Mexico was "discovered." Several million visitors a year descended on Mexico from the U.S. and Canada, first by train, lately by automobile and plane. So now again there are resorts in Mexico, more and more each year. Many of them are quite small and modest and take advantage of a spectacular shore setting, an upland lake, or a mountain valley. A few have been developed from old Spanish haciendas; some have been built to provide resort facilities for visitors who seek to explore the ancient Mayan ruins. Two small resorts offer luxurious modern facilities in a setting of lush tropical splendor for visitors to Yucatán. One of these, the Hacienda Uxmal, offers luxury and comfort to those who may want to poke around among the ruins of Mexico's first resort.

Once remote fishing centers, such as Guaymas and Mazatlán, first discovered by sports fishermen along the west coast of Mexico, have become resort communities with luxury hotels. A classic and dramatic example is Puerto Vallarta, which, as recently as a few years ago, was an almost inaccessible fishing village, two hundred miles west of Guadalajara. It had a dusty main street flanking a superb bay, a cluster of shabby houses, and two small, primitive inns. Then Puerto Vallarta was discovered by the California movie colony. *Night of the Iguana* was filmed there. Now it is being rapidly converted into a major resort community. It is reached by air from Guadalajara and boasts a smart new 160-room resort hotel, fully air-conditioned, with a private beach and boat dock, salt-water pool, tropical patio, and cocktail lounge— the conventional trappings of a luxury resort.

Mexico has developed suddenly as a resort region with a growing cluster of resorts of importance in exotic and unusual settings. There are dozens of resorts and a few truly notable and distinctive ones. Some reached by fine new highways are in the mountains and offer superb climate in rugged forest settings. Others are near the ocean on either coast. One of these is the mountain spa of San José Purua. It is dramatically built within a canyon deep in the heart of a semitropical forest. Another resort is on the east coast not far from where Cortez landed, in one of the most tropical regions in the world. Colorfully Spanish in aspect and character, it is famed for its swimming pool filled with floating gardenias.

But there are complete and important resort communities in Mexico. One that will rank among the most important resort cities in the world is Acapulco, on Mexico's west coast, a day's drive or an hour's flight from Mexico City.

In the material that follows, Acapulco, with all its color and flamboyance, is described as a resort community as a whole, with two of its most distinguished and unusual resorts—each clearly qualified to rank among the great resorts of North America—described in detail.

"THE RICHEST SILKS OF FAR CATHAY"

The quotation above is taken from one of the stories of Bret Harte, in which he described the landing of a Spanish galleon in Mexico that had crossed the Pacific. The ship, loaded with treasures of the Orient, was due to land at Acapulco, the most important Mexican west-coast port. Acapulco was a rich and booming port for a hundred fifty years. Spanish treasure ships sailing east over the Pacific used it as their first and most important port of call. From Acapulco the Spanish conquered the Philippine Islands and sent expeditions north to explore and colonize what is now California. But the richness and fame of the port made Acapulco prey for Dutch and British sea rovers. Pacific traffic slowed down by the end of the seventeenth century, and Acapulco was no longer important. It went to sleep and it did not wake for more than two hundred years.

The year of awakening was 1928, when a new highway from Mexico City to the bay of Acapulco was completed. Scheduled air service was inaugurated a few years later. President Alemán began to carry out a precise plan. He knew that the ancient little city of Acapulco had a superb setting and a fine climate. He proposed to make it a

Mexican Riviera, a resort city ranking with the great ones of the world. He succeeded.

In a remarkably short time Acapulco became the talk of the world, and the place to be basking in. A forest of hotels, large and small, modest, elegant, and luxurious, rose along the bay, crowded the crest of hills, and perched on cliff tops. A fine bay-front boulevard was built, night clubs sprang up, the bay filled with pleasure craft, and the beaches flanking the bay and ocean became crowded with tourists. Alemán's plan succeeded beyond his wildest dreams; it succeeded so well, in fact, that as a resort Acapulco almost stopped being an exclusive and luxurious community. But here and there in Acapulco are important and distinctive resorts established in settings that guarantee isolation.

The first glimpse of Acapulco is breath-taking. The great blue bay is rimmed with steeply sloping mountains. The older, more congested part of the resort crowds a rugged peninsula that forms the western flank of the bay. The peninsula is jammed with hotels of every type, which rise tier on tier above the water. There are more than a hundred resort hotels in Acapulco today, some quite new, none more than twenty-five years old.

Three hotels important enough to be mentioned because of setting, facility, or outstanding character are on the western peninsula. The Hotel Coleta is the largest in Acapulco and usually teems with business. It was one of the first big hotels in Acapulco and thus acquired one of the best settings and one of the few good ocean beaches.

The Hotel Prado-Americus does not have a beach, but it has a superb view and abundant charm and makes the most of colorful Spanish and Mexican traditions. The luxurious Hotel Club de Pesca is also on the peninsula. Its facilities range from a night club to aqualung accessories.

The most celebrated of all Acapulco resorts, El Mirador, owes its fame to a remarkable setting. It is built on a cliff top west of the old town, overlooking the surging open sea. From perches near its cocktail terrace and dining room, Mexican boys dive into a fifteen-foot-wide pool. They drop 135 feet in Acapulco's most renowned show.

The Acapulco Hilton and the slightly older El Presidente—both sleek and expensive—are east of the old town, close to the bay. The most remarkable resorts in Acapulco are not in the city at all, but on its eastern fringe. One overlooks the bay from the east; the other is eleven miles east of the city. Both qualify as great resorts.

PINK JEEPS AND PRIVATE POOLS

No one who has seen Las Brisas (The Breezes) will ever forget it. No resort approaches it in conception and character. Soon after Acapulco began to get important, a syndicate of wealthy American and Mexican businessmen decided to build a luxurious club for themselves and their friends. But the Acapulco terrain tends to be perpendicular rather than horizontal. There are few level areas, and the few there are had already been taken over as sites for soaring hotel towers. However, on the east side of the bay there was an undeveloped mountain slope that dropped from a crest of about a thousand feet to a patch of shore. No conventional builder would have thought it possible to put a resort on that mountainside. Fortunately the syndicate found an unconventional builder who proposed a startling idea: convert the entire slope into a remarkable new kind of resort with a hundred or more private villas. They would be placed so that each commanded an unobstructed view of the bay and the city and each could catch its share of the prevailing breezes. The idea of a personal and private resort was revolutionary. It also involved fantastically expensive and unusual problems of engineering. But the group had money and went ahead. It took a lot of money and a long time to finish Las Brisas, but the final result is fantastic. There are 151 private villas jutting from the side of the mountain. Each is adroitly placed so that no occupant is aware of other villas above, below, or on either side. Each villa has a private terrace commanding a superb view of Acapulco Bay. Most of the villas have either private swimming pools or share a pool with an adjoining villa.

The public facilities of Las Brisas are as unusual as the guest accommodations. A cocktail lounge and dining room are at the crest of the mountain. Along the shore are two huge salt-water pools flanked by a wide, tropically landscaped terrace.

Las Brisas has a fleet of about a hundred pink Jeeps, available to guests at nominal rates. They provide transportation up and down the slope over the roads that link the villas. Sometimes the Jeeps are organized in cross-country safaris, when groups of guests travel to see native fishing villages or discover remote ocean coves along the coast.

Las Brisas started as a club but didn't stay one long. Within a couple of years after completion it was being operated as a full-scale resort hotel. Las Brisas dining is casual, colorful, offered with flair and style. Breakfasts are packed in special containers and are placed outside each villa door in the morning. Lunch—supplemented by a motorized bar—is a huge buffet with an array of Mexican and Continental dishes served at the Beach Club. Lavish dinners are served in the mountaintop dining room.

Guest rates at Las Brisas vary with type of accommodation and season. The high-rate season, when the climate is at its best, is from mid-December through mid-April. Lower rates are charged in the off season, which is from mid-April to mid-December. Rates range from a low for a villa without swimming pool to the utmost in luxury—a spacious, several-bedroom mountaintop villa, the Casa Encantada. In between are rates for a villa with private pool or a villa with a pool shared by a neighboring villa. Rate modifications are also based on family groups and special honeymoon rates. Las Brisas makes quite a thing of honeymoons and offers free champagne and free use of a pink Jeep to newlyweds.

The minimum off-season rate for a villa without pool is $16 per day for two. The lowest rate for a shared pool is $24 per day for two, off season. High-season rates start at $28 per day for two. Rates include a Continental breakfast, a daily basket of tropical fruit. They do not include lunch and dinner.

OCEAN BEACH AND TROPICAL JUNGLE

The second Acapulco resort that ranks among the great is Pierre Marques. Where the setting of Las Brisas is almost vertical, the elegant and renowned Pierre Marques is horizontal. It covers several hundred acres of tropical shore flanking one of the world's finest surf beaches. Guests look out over tropical grounds and the open sea.

Pierre Marques was built by J. Paul Getty, one of the richest men in the world. Getty was visiting Mexico in 1940 and was taken to Acapulco to see the beginning resort community. One day a local resident took him on a long trip through the back country and finally down to the shore southeast of Acapulco. The rough country road followed a narrow bay called Puerto de Marquez. One arm of the bay was a slender peninsula on the seaward side of which was one of the world's finest beaches—twenty miles of wide golden sand and surf. Getty decided that the beach would make a superb setting for a great resort. He bought it and hundreds of acres of adjoining land, which was tropical wilderness.

After the war Getty began to plan and develop his luxurious resort.

The conversion of the wide surf beach with its fringe of jungle took time and money. When the Pierre Marques opened in 1957, the jungle had been transformed into a superb tropical park with wide green lawns, clusters of palms, hedges of sea grape, and flamboyant beds of flowers. The wide beach had been combed and curried. A huge swimming pool and tennis courts were behind the beach. The resort buildings were low and wide-eaved, and each guest room had a private terrace.

The Pierre Marques was an immediate success. It became renowned as a distinguished resort that offered greater seclusion than any other resort in the Acapulco area. Its guest list began to glitter. It included President Dwight D. Eisenhower, who visited Mexico in 1959.

After a few years the resort was expanded by the addition of the five-story Pacific Wing, so that guest rooms now number more than two hundred.

The Pierre Marques, self-contained and self-sufficient, has its own water-purification plant and its own heating and electric plants. The several hundred acres of grounds that surround it are much greater in area than those of any other resort in the region, and the facilities for diversion it offers exceed those of any nearby resort. Instructors give lessons in skin diving, water skiing, or surf casting. Lawn games include tennis, table tennis, shuffleboard, and a golf driving range. Public rooms are numerous and handsomely appointed. Dining areas, both indoors and out, offer a rich variety of Continental and Mexican dishes. There is a gift shop, and for sight-seeing a fleet of Jeeps.

Rates are either modified American plan, with breakfast and dinner, or the European plan, with no meals. During the high-rate, or winter, season, December 20 through April 20, modified American plan starts at $32 per day for a single room with terrace and goes up to $75 per day for a de-luxe bungalow. Under the European plan single-room rates start at $24 per day; double-room rates begin at $28 per day (the double-room rate for modified American plan starts at $44).

The deep-sea fishing in Acapulco ranks among the best in the world, and charter boats are available at the public docks or at the resorts themselves. Most visitors eventually watch the diving boys at Hotel El Mirador. Other nighttime diversions include dinner shows at various night clubs.

Travelers can get to Acapulco by any one of three methods of travel.

One is by automobile from Mexico City over Route 95, a fine and a frequently scenic road. The drive can be made easily in less than a day. Most who take it, however, stop for a few hours at the charming mountain city of Taco. Several nonstop flights a day leave for Acapulco from Mexico City. The jets cover the distance in less than an hour. The third method is by ship. An occasional cruise ship arrives from California ports, and an increasing number of private yachts visit Acapulco.

SWIMMING AMONG GARDENIAS

About 475 miles northeast of Acapulco is a strip of Caribbean coast ninety miles wide completely different from Acapulco. It is blanketed in a lush tropical jungle where bananas are a commercial crop and orchids and gardenias grow wild in overwhelming profusion.

From the coast at Vera Cruz, the oldest highway in Mexico leads west and north to Mexico City, following the approximate route of Cortez.

Humidity and temperature diminish as the highway climbs. At about three thousand feet the climate stops being humid and assumes a benign softness. In that pleasant zone there is a village with a curious name—Fortín de las Flores (Little Fort of the Flowers). The "fort" is because the village was the site of a Spanish outpost. The "flowers" part is self-evident. Orchids, camellias, gardenias, groves of orange trees, and dozens of others blanket the community with a heady fragrance. At Fortín de las Flores there is an extraordinary resort—the Hotel Ruiz Galindo.

Its story has Horatio Alger aspects reminiscent of those that resulted in the Hershey Hotel in Pennsylvania: poor boy makes fortune and returns home to spend it. In the early years of Mexico's modern era Antonio Ruiz Galindo left his shabby home in the all but forgotten village of Fortín to make his fortune. He became one of the top industrialists of Mexico. He returned to Fortín to build a remarkable resort and spruce up his native village.

When the hotel was built, it included a very large and handsome swimming pool set within a tiled Spanish patio. Galindo filled the pool with thousands of fresh-cut gardenias that floated on its surface like patches of wavering snow and were replenished daily. In almost no time at all the resort was famous because of its pool, and it has remained celebrated ever since. A bonus is a stunning view of Mount Orizaba, 18,600 feet high and Mexico's highest peak.

Though the gardenia-filled swimming pool has made the resort widely known, it is only one of many pleasant features. The resort has about a hundred fifty guest rooms, most of which have balconies overlooking the pool.

The guest rooms and most public rooms of the Hotel Ruiz Galindo are colorfully Spanish in the best tradition. The gardens that surround it are the most beautiful anywhere. There is a bowling alley in the hotel and a small theater for motion pictures. A nine-hole golf course makes up for its lack of challenge with the floral beauty of its setting. Dining at the Ruiz Galindo is under full American plan. The dishes are typical of Spanish and Mexican cooking. As might be expected, tropical fruit is served at every meal.

Rates are fairly moderate. They start at about $18 per day for a single room, and about $30 per day for two; they go up to about $40 for a de-luxe suite.

The most exciting way to reach Fortín de las Flores is by car, over a route from the east that is one of the most exciting and spectacularly scenic drives in the world. It is 84 miles from Vera Cruz to Fortín, and 215 miles from Mexico City. The route from Vera Cruz is through lowland tropical jungle and plantations, but on the route west from Fortín to Mexico City the road begins to climb with a sensational series of hairpin turns and switchbacks that climb more than two thousand feet in less than five miles of travel. The road leads over a pass eight thousand feet high to Mexico's high central plateau. Views are spectacular, and the tricky, touch-and-go driving usually leaves travelers breathless.

Generally speaking, the mountains of Mexico are impressive to see from a distance but are usually inhospitable. With a few exceptions mountain valleys do not lend themselves to pleasant living. One of the exceptions is about 115 miles west of Mexico City, just off Mexico's famed Route 15, where there is a mountain-set resort of remarkable character, a canyon Shangri-La.

The most densely settled section of central Mexico is the region between Mexico City and Guadalajara, which is 270 miles to the northwest and linked to Mexico City by Route 15. It is a fascinating road to travel, full of scenic surprises and historic old towns. About five miles west of a colorful old village called Zitacuaro, a side road drops steeply into a pine-filled canyon with plunging waterfalls and tumbling mountain streams. After a few miles the pines give way to tropical vegetation. The canyon walls widen and the road emerges into a jewel-like valley almost filled with dozens of red-tile-roofed buildings. This is the extensive establishment of San José Purua, a remarkable resort that is also one of Mexico's few spas.

San José Purua, one of the largest resorts in Mexico, has more than 250 guest rooms accommodating more than 500 guests. It was established in the early 1940's after the improvement of Route 15 made access to it reasonably safe and comfortable; its site was in part dictated by the existence of mineral springs that give the resort its status as a spa.

But the mineral springs are only one of San José Purua's special features. Another is climate, which at 4400 feet is delightfully tropical without being hot, the air balmy by day and brisk in the evening. The resort is built on a series of terraces in the canyon, with long wings rambling up and down a central area where mountain streams have been controlled to make four great pools. The hotel buildings are so designed that most guest rooms have balconies overlooking either the central pool area or the rising mountain slopes. Public rooms include an assortment of lounges, five cocktail bars, and several dining areas where the menus are famed for their variety and huge portions.

San José Purua is a self-contained resort estate. Activities and facilities include horseback riding over mountain trails, golf-putting greens, bowling alleys, table tennis, shuffleboard, and a colorful night club with an orchestra and weekend shows.

The area around the resort offers a variety of sight-seeing opportunity. It is in the heart of the picturesque Tarascan Indian country. Lake Pátzcuaro—famed for its butterfly boats—is within easy driving distance. The nearby town of Pátzcuaro is one of the most colorful and distinctive of Mexico's old cities. Toluca—renowned Mexico's largest mining and ranching center—is an hour's drive away. The resort will make arrangements for sight-seeing for guests who lack their own transportation.

Guest rates at San José Purua are based on the full American plan, starting at $25 per day for a double room. Single-room rates start at about $15 per day. The resort has no high- or low-season in rates, since there is little variation in climate.

It is virtually impossible to reach San José Purua except by automobile. The resort maintains daily limousine service for guests, leaving every morning at 9 A.M. from its Mexico City office at 146 Paseo de la Reforma.

INDEX

Aberdeen, N.C., 54
Acapulco, Mexico, 214–19
Acapulco Hilton (Acapulco, Mexico), 215
Adirondack Center and Colonial Garden (Elizabethtown, N.Y.), 111
Adirondacks (N.Y.), 106, 108–12
Aiken, S.C., 63
Air Force Academy (Colo.), 148
Alabama, xii, 100–5
Alberta, Canada, xiii, 129, 131–39
Alcazar Hotel (St. Augustine, Fla.), 83
Algonquin Hotel (Passamaquoddy Bay, Canada), 207–10
Animal Forest Park (York Beach, Me.), 26
Apache Trail (Ariz.), 194
Appalachian Mountains (Pa.), 121
Arch Rock (Mackinac Island, Mich.), 163
Arizona, xv, 186–202
Arizona Inn (Tucson, Ariz.), 198–200
Arizona-Sonora Desert Museum (Ariz.), 201
Arthur, Chester A., birthplace of (Vt.), 45
Ashburn Farm (Va.), 78

Balboa Park (San Diego, Calif.), 184–85
Ballast Point (Calif.), 181
Banff, Alberta, Canada, 136
Banff National Park (Alberta, Canada), 131, 135

Banff Springs Hotel (Alberta, Canada), xiii, 129, 131, 135–39
Bar Harbor (Mount Desert Island, Me.), 17
Bath County, Va., 2–10
Bay of Fundy (Canada), 207–10
Belleview-Biltmore Hotel (Clearwater, Fla.), xiii, xvii, 98–100
Bellingrath Gardens (Ala.), 104
Besh-Ba-Go-Wah (Ariz.), 194
Big Sur Road (Calif.), 180
Bishop's Lodge (Santa Fe, N.M.), 152–56
Blairsden, Calif., 149
Blue Mountain (Appalachians), 121
Boca Raton, Fla., xiv, 84, 85–90
Boca Raton Hotel (Boca Raton, Fla.), xiv, 84, 85–90
Bow River (Alberta, Canada), 135
Breakers (Palm Beach, Fla.), xiii, 84, 95–97
British Columbia, Canada, 171–75
Broadmoor Hotel (Colorado Springs, Colo.), xv, 129–30, 144–48
Brown's Camp (Me.). See Severance Lodge
Brown's gambling house (French Lick, Ind.), 167–68
Brunswick, Ga., 72, 74
Buck Hill Falls Inn (Pa.), 107, 116–21
Burlington, Vt., 45

Cabrillo National Monument (Point Loma, Calif.), 184

California, xiii, xvii, 130, 148–52, 172, 175–85, 186
Camelback Inn (Paradise Valley, Ariz.), 189–95
Camelback Mountain (Ariz.), 189–98
Campobello Island (Passamaquoddy Bay, Canada), 207–8
Canada, xiii, 129, 131–35, 171–75, 204–10
Canadian Rockies, 130–31, 132, 134, 135–36
Cannon Mountain Tramway (White Mountains, N.H.), 34, 36
Cape Cod (Mass.), 17
Cape Kennedy (Fla.), 97
Carmel, Calif., 176, 179–80
Carmel Bay (Calif.), 175, 176, 177, 179
Carmel Mission (Carmel, Calif.), 176, 179–80
Carmel-San Simeon Highway (Calif.), 180
Carolina Hotel (Pinehurst, N.C.), 26, 57, 59
Casa Grande National Monument (Ariz.), 188, 194
Cascades Inn (Healing Springs, Va.), 7, 9
Castillo de San Marcos National Monument (St. Augustine, Fla.), 93
Cathedral of St. Francis (Santa Fe, N.M.), 155
Challenger Inn (Sun Valley, Idaho), 140, 141
Chamcook Lake (New Brunswick, Canada), 209
Chandler, Ariz., 187–89
Chateau Lake Louise (Alberta, Canada), xiii, 129, 131–35
Chesapeake Bay (Va.), 77
Chesapeake Club. *See* Tides Inn
Cheyenne Mountain (Colo.), 146, 147
Cheyenne Mountain Museum and Zoological Society, 146
Chittenden, Vt., xv, 30, 37–42
Christ Church (St. Simons Island, Ga.), 72

Clarendon Gardens (Pinehurst, N.C.), 61
Clearwater, Fla., xiii, 84–85, 98–100
Cloister (Sea Island, Ga.), 65, 69–71
Cloister Inn (Boca Raton, Fla.), 86–87
Cocoa Inn (Hershey, Pa.), 124
Cog railway (Mount Washington, N.H.), 33
Colorado, xv, 143–48
Colorado Springs, Colo., xv, 144–48
Columbia Ice Fields (Alberta, Canada), 133
Conley's Lobster Pound (New Brunswick, Canada), 209
Coolidge, Calvin, birthplace of (Plymouth, Vt.), 41
Cooper Inn (Cooperstown, N.Y.), 114, 115
Cooperstown, N.Y., 106–7, 112–15
Coronado Peninsula (Calif.), 181–85
Craters of the Moon National Monument (Idaho), 142
Cripple Creek (Colo.), 144

Daytona Beach, Fla., 93, 109–10
Del Mar, Calif., 185
Del Monte Forest (Calif.), 176
Del Monte Lodge (Monterey, Calif.), xvii, 172, 175–80
Dollar Mountain (Idaho), 141
Duxbury, Mass., 17

El Camino Real (Fla.), 86–88
Elizabethtown, N.Y., 111
El Mirador Hotel (Acapulco, Mexico), 215
El Presidente Hotel (Acapulco, Mexico), 215
Emerald Lake (Alberta, Canada), 132
Epworth-by-the-Sea (St. Simons Island, Ga.), 72
Everglades National Park (Fla.), 97, 99

Falling Springs (Va.), 7
Farmers' Museum (Cooperstown, N.Y.), 113, 115

Feather River Inn (Calif.), 130, 148–52

Fenimore House (Cooperstown, N.Y.), 113, 115

Florida, 83–100, 109–10

Fort Constitution (Fort William and Mary) (Portsmouth, N.H.), 19, 20

Fort Frederica (St. Simons Island, Ga.), 67, 72

Fort Gaines, Ga., 104

Fortín de las Flores (Mexico), 219–21

Fort Mackinac (Mackinac Island, Mich.), 159, 163

Fort Michilimackinac (Mackinaw City, Mich.), 163

Fort Morgan (Ala.), 104

Fort Point Lighthouse (Portsmouth, N.H.), 19

Fort Ticonderoga (N.Y.), 41, 111–12

Fort William and Mary (*now* Fort Constitution) (Portsmouth, N.H.), 19, 20

Franconia Notch (White Mountains, N.H.), 33, 36

Fredericksburg, Va., 80–81

French Lick, Ind., xv, xvii, 165–70

French Lick Sheraton (French Lick, Ind.), xv, xvii, 158, 165–70

Garden of the Gods (Colo.), 148

Georgia, xii, xvii, 64–77

Glimmerglass Lake. *See* Otsego Lake

Globe, Ariz., 188, 194

Golden Islands. *See* Sea Islands

Grand Canyon (Ariz.), 195

Grand Central Hotel. *See* Greenbrier

Grand Hotel (Mackinac Island, Mich.), xiv, 157–65

Grand Hotel (Point Clear, Ala.), 100–5

Grand Hotel (Tampa, Fla.), 84–85

Grand View Hotel (Lake Placid, N.Y.), 109

Great Lakes, 157–65, 204

Great Stone Face (White Mountains, N.H.), 33–34

Greenbrier (White Sulphur Springs, W. Va.), xiii, xv, 4, 10–16

Greenbrier Valley (W. Va.), 3

Green Mountain National Forest (Vt.), 37

Green Mountains (Vt.), 37–45

Greenville, Me., 46, 48

Guadalajara, Mexico, 220

Guaymas, Mexico, 213

Hacienda Uxmal (Mexico), 213

Harrison Hotel (British Columbia, Canada), 172–75

Harrison Hot Springs, British Columbia, Canada, 173

Harrison Lake (British Columbia, Canada), 172–75

Healing Springs, Va., 7, 9

Hell's Gate Canyon (British Columbia, Canada), 174

Hershey, Milton, School (Hershey, Pa.), 124, 126

Hershey, Pa., xv, 107, 121–27

Hershey Museum (Hershey, Pa.), 126

High Sierras (Calif.), 129, 130, 148–52

Holly Inn (Pinehurst, N.C.), 55, 57, 59, 62

Homestead, The (Hot Springs, Va.), x, xiii, xvii, 3–10

Hotel Club de Pesca (Acapulco, Mexico), 215

Hotel Coleta (Acapulco, Mexico), 215

Hotel Del Coronado (San Diego Bay, Calif.), 172, 180–85

Hotel Hershey (Hershey, Pa.), xv, 107, 121–27

Hotel Prado-Americus (Acapulco, Mexico), 215

Hotel Ruiz Galindo (Fortín de las Flores, Mexico), 219–21

Hot Springs, Va., x, xiii, xvii, 3–10

Idaho, xiii, 139–43

Indiana, xv, xvii, 165–70

Indian Museum (Cooperstown, N.Y.), 113, 115

Inn at Buck Hill Falls (Pa.), 107, 116–
21

Jamestown, Va., 1
Jasper, Alberta, Canada, 133
Jefferson, N.H., 29–30, 34–36
Jekyll Island State Park (Ga.), xii, 65–
66, 72, 74–77
John Brown's Farm (Lake Placid,
N.Y.), 111
Johnsville, Calif., 151
Jones, John Paul, House (Portsmouth,
N.H.), 24

Kezar Lake (Me.), xv, 30, 48–52
Killington Peak (Vt.), 37

La Jolla, Calif., 185
Lake Agnes (Alberta, Canada), 133
Lake Champlain (N.Y.-Vt.), 41, 42,
44, 111
Lake Huron, 157–65
Lake Louise (Alberta, Canada), 131–
39
Lake Louise Village, Alberta, Canada,
134
Lake Michigan, 157–65
Lake Minnewanka (Alberta, Canada),
137–38
Lake Okeechobee (Fla.), 97
Lake Otsego (N.Y.), 106–7, 112–15
Lake Pátzcuaro (Mexico), 221
Lake Placid, N.Y., 106, 108–12
Lake Placid Club (Lake Placid, N.Y.),
109
Lake Superior, 164
Lake Texcoco (Mexico), 212
Lake Worth (Fla.), 95
Las Brisas (Acapulco, Mexico), 216–17
Las Vegas, Nev., 186
La Villa Real de la Santa Fé de San
Francisco. *See* Santa Fe
Lee, Robert E., birthplace of (Freder-
icksburg, Va.), 80–81
Les Cheneaux islands (Lake Huron),
163
Lincoln, Abraham, cabin (Ind.), 170

Little Warm Springs, Va., 3
Lodge at Smugglers' Notch (Vt.), 30,
42–45
Long Trail, Vt., 37, 40
Los Angeles, Calif., 175

Mackinac, Straits of (Mich.), 157, 158,
164
Mackinac Island (Mich.), xiv, 157–65
Mackinaw City, Mich., 161, 163
Maine, xv, 17, 19, 25–27, 30, 45–52
Manitou Mountain (Colo.), 145
Manoir Richelieu (Murray Bay, Can-
ada), 204–7
Marshall House (York Harbor, Me.),
19, 25–27
Marshmallow Hill (Ariz.), 193
Massachusetts, 17
Mazatlán, Mexico, 213
Mexico, 211–21
Mexico City, Mexico, 220
Miami, Fla., 84, 86
Michigan, xii, xiv, 157–65
Michilimackinac Island. *See* Mackinac
Island
Mid-Pines Club and Golfotel (near
Southern Pines, N.C.), 62
Mission Bay Park (Calif.), 184
Mission San Diego de Alcala (San Di-
ego, Calif.), 185
Mitchell, Ind., 169
Mobile, Ala., 104
Mobile Bay (Ala.), xii, 100–5
Mohawk Valley (N.Y.), 106
Monroe, James, birthplace of (Va.), 80
Monterey (Calif.), xvii, 175–80
Monterey Peninsula (Calif.), 172,
175–80
Montreal (Quebec, Canada), 204
Moosehead Lake (Me.), 46–47
Mooselookmeguntic Lake (Me.), 48
Mother Lode country (Calif.), 152
Mountain Top Inn (Chittenden, Vt.),
xv, 30, 37–42
Mountain View House (Whitefield,
N.H.), xv, 29, 31–34
Mount Baldy (Idaho), 141

Mount Desert Island (Me.), 17
Mount Kineo (Me.), 30, 45–48
Mount Kineo Hotel (Me.), 30, 45–48
Mount Lemmon (Ariz.), 201
Mount Mansfield (Vt.), 37, 42–45
Mount Marcy (N.Y.), 108
Mount Orizaba (Mexico), 219
Mount Palomar (Calif.), 185
Mount Palomar Observatory (Calif.), 185
Mount Rundle (Alberta, Canada), 136
Mount Victoria (Alberta, Canada), 132
Mount Washington (N.H.), 31, 33, 36
Mount Whiteface (N.Y.), 108, 109
Mount Whitehorn (Alberta, Canada), 134
Mummy Mountains (Ariz.), 190–95
Murray Bay (Canada), 204–7
Museum of New Mexico (Santa Fe, N.M.), 155

National Baseball Museum and Hall of Fame (Cooperstown, N.Y.), 113, 115
Natural Bridge (Va.), 15
Nevada, 186
New Brunswick, Canada, 207–10
New Castle, N.H., xv, 19–20, 23–24
New Hampshire, 19–25, 28–36
New Mexico, xiv, 130, 152–56
Newport, R.I., 17
New York, 106–7, 108–15
Nogales, Ariz., 201
Nogales-Sonora, Mexico, 201
North Carolina, xiv, xv, xvii, 26, 53–63

Old Man of the Mountain (White Mountains, N.H.), 33–34
Old Tucson Village (Ariz.), 201
Old White Hotel (White Sulphur Springs, W. Va.), 4, 11–12
Otesaga Hotel (Cooperstown, N.Y.), 106–7, 112–15
Otsego Lake (N.Y.), 106–7, 112–15

Pacific Grove, Calif., 179

Palm Beach, Fla., 83–84, 86, 94–97
Palm Springs, Calif., 186
Paoli, Ind., 169
Paradise Inn (Paradise Valley, Ariz.), xv, 195–98
Paradise Valley (Ariz.), xv, 189–95
Passamaquoddy Bay (Canada), 207–10
Pennsylvania, xv, 107, 116–27
Pennsylvania Dutch Country, 107, 121–27
Phoenix, Ariz., 186–98
Pierre Marques (Acapulco, Mexico), 217–19
Pikes Peak (Colo.), 143–48
Pinehurst, N.C., 26, 53–62
Pine Needles Lodge and Country Club (*near* Southern Pines, N.C.), 62–63
Plumas-Eureka State Park (Calif.), 151
Plymouth, Vt., 41
Pocahontas coal mine (Va.), 15
Poconos (Pa.), 107, 116–21
Point Clear, Ala., xii, 100–5
Point Loma (Calif.), 181, 184
Ponce de Leon Hotel (St. Augustine, Fla.), 83, 94
Ponte Vedra beach (Fla.), 91–93
Ponte Vedra Inn and Club (Fla.), 91–93
Portola, Calif., 149
Portsmouth, N.H., 19–24
Presidential Range (White Mountains, Me.-N.H.), 29, 31, 48
Presidio of Monterey (Monterey, Calif.), 179
Princess Issena Hotel (Daytona Beach, Fla.), 109–10
Puerto de Marquez Bay (Mexico), 217
Puerto Vallarta, Mexico, 213
Puget Sound (Wash.), 171

Quebec, Canada, 204

Rampart Range (Colo.), 148
Rancho Santa Fe (Calif.), 185
Retreat Plantation (St. Simons Island, Ga.), 68

Rhode Island, 17

Ringling Museum (Sarasota, Fla.), 99

Rockwood, Me., 47

Rocky Mountains, 128–32, 134, 139–48, 152

Roosevelt Dam (Ariz.), 189, 190, 194

Royal Poinciana (Palm Beach, Fla.), 83–84, 95, 96

Rutland, Vt., 39, 41

Saguaro National Monument (Ariz.), 201

St. Alice's Well (British Columbia, Canada), 173

St. Andrews-by-the-Sea, New Brunswick, Canada, 208, 209

St. Augustine, Fla., 83, 93, 94

St. Ignace, Mich., 161, 164

St. Meinrad's Abbey (Ind.), 170

St. Petersburg, Fla., 84

St. Simons Island (Ga.), 66–68, 72

Salt River Valley (Ariz.), 194

San Diego, Calif., 184–85

San Diego Bay (Calif.), 171, 172, 180–85

San Francisco, Calif., 175

San Francisco Bay (Calif.), 171

Sangre de Cristo Mountains (N.M.), 130, 152–56

San José Purua resort (Mexico), 214, 220–21

San Marcos Hotel and Country Club (Chandler, Ariz.), 187–89

San Miguel church (Santa Fe, N.M.), 155

San Simeon State Park (Calif.), 180

Santa Claus, Ind., 170

Santa Fe, N.M., xiv, 152–56

Santa Fe National Forest (N.M.), 155

Santa Fe Trail (N.M.), 152, 155

San Xavier del Bac mission (Ariz.), 199, 201

Sapelo Island (Ga.), 68

Saranac Lake (N.Y.), 109, 111

Sarasota, Fla., 99

Sault Sainte Marie, Mich., 164

Sawtooth National Forest (Idaho), 140

Scottsdale, Ariz., 189, 194, 195, 196

Scripps Institute of Oceanography (La Jolla, Calif.), 185

Sea Island (Ga.), xvii, 66–72

Sea Islands (Ga.), 66–77

Sebago Lake (Me.), 48

Seventeen Mile Drive (Calif.), 176

Severance Lodge (Kezar Lake, Me.), xv, 30, 48–52

Silver Strand (Calif.), 181

Skull Cave (Mackinac Island, Mich.), 163

Smugglers' Notch, Vt., 30, 42–45

Sonora Desert (Ariz.), 198–202

South Carolina, 63

Southern Pines, N.C., 62–63

Southwest Arboretum (Ariz.), 194

Southwestern Archaeological Center (Ariz.), 188

Spring Mill State Park (Ind.), 169

Spruce Peak (Green Mountains, Vt.), 43–44

Stanley Basin Recreational Area (Idaho), 142

Starr King Mountain (N.H.), 35

Sterling Game Farm (Lake Placid, N.Y.), 111

Sterling Mountain (Vt.), 42

Stowe, Vt., 30, 42–45

Straits of Mackinac (Mich.), 157, 158, 164

Strawberry Banke (Portsmouth, N.H.), 24

Stroudsburg, Pa., 116

Sugar Loaf (Mackinac Island, Mich.), 163

Sulphur Mountain (Alberta, Canada), 135–36

Summit House (Mount Mansfield, Vt.), 43

Sun Valley (Idaho), xiii, 139–43

Taliesin West (Paradise Valley, Ariz.), 194

Tampa, Fla., 84–85, 97, 99

Tampa, University of (Fla.), 97

Taos, N.M., 156

Tarascan Indian country (Mexico), 221

Tarpon Springs, Fla., 99

Thousand Islands (St. Lawrence River), 204–7

Ticonderoga, N.Y., 41, 111–12

Tides Inn, The (*near* Irvington, Va.), xv, xvii, 65, 78–82

Tijuana, Mexico, 185

Toluca, Mexico, 221

Tombstone, Ariz., 201

Tonto National Monument (Ariz.), 194

Trail Creek Cabin (Sun Valley, Idaho), 141

Tubac, Ariz., 201

Tucson, Ariz., 198–200

Tumacacori National Monument (Ariz.), 201

Uxmal, Mexico, 212

Vermont, xv, 30, 37–45

Victoria Glacier (Alberta, Canada), 132

Virginia, xv, xvii, 1–10, 15, 65, 78–82

Warm Springs, Va., xii, 3

Warm Springs Hotel (Va.), 3

Washington, George, birthplace of (Va.), 80

Waumbek (Jefferson, N.H.), 29–30, 34–36

Wentworth-by-the-Sea (*near* New Castle, N.H.), xv, 19–25

West Baden, Ind., 169

West Rutland, Vt., 41

West Virginia, xiii, xv, 2–4, 10–16

Wheeler Peak (N.M.), 152

Whiteface Inn (Lake Placid, N.Y.), 106, 108–12

Whiteface Mountain (N.Y.), 109, 111

Whitefield, N.H., 29, 31–34

White Mountains (Me.-N.H.), 28, 29, 31–36, 48

White Sulphur Springs, W. Va., 3, 4, 10–16

Williamsburg, Va., 81

Wilson Castle (West Rutland, Vt.), 41

Woodland Museum (Cooperstown, N.Y.), 114, 115

Woodstock, Vt., 41

Xochimilco, Mexico, 212

York, Me., 25

York Beach, Me., 26

York County (Me.), 25

York Harbor (Me.), 19, 25–27

Yorktown, Va., 81

York Village, Me., 26

Yucatán, Mexico, 212–13

Zitacuaro, Mexico, 220